Acclaim for
William Least Heat-Moon's
HERE, THERE, ELSEWHERE

"Hallelujah! William Least Heat-Moon is on the road again....
He slices down through layers of biography, history, folklore, and
geology to deliver a place in full."

—Bill Marvel, *Dallas Morning News*

"Heat-Moon's curiosity and adventurous nature have not
dimmed, making him a first-rate travel guide. He is an original,
memorable wordsmith."

—Steve Weinberg, *St. Louis Post-Dispatch*

"Heat-Moon wanders off in every direction in this scintillating
collection of short writings.... A master at conjuring place, Least
Heat-Moon intertwines primeval geology with modern social
mores, gorgeous scenery with tourist tackery, vast landscapes
with intricate psychologies.... There is a dazzling variety of
places, people, and curiosities, linked by a highway of funny,
perceptive, and generous prose."   —*Publishers Weekly*

"A captivating new collection of his short-form travel stories...
which are always greater than the sum of their parts. But the
most endearing tales are those closest to his home and heart."

—Kristin Baird Rattini, *American Way*

"Least Heat-Moon is truly one of this nation's best travel writers,
if not the best. He takes travel writing seriously as a literary
genre. An essential title; highly recommended."

—Lee Arnold, *Library Journal*

"Heat-Moon is at his finest when in often overlooked places.... *Here, There, Elsewhere* is worth the investment in time, a good dictionary, and open-mindedness."
— Katherine Hauswirth, *Christian Science Monitor*

"Heat-Moon unplugged!... An admirable combination of reportage and boots-on-the-ground observation.... Within this praise for America, no matter when it was penned and who did the final edit, you feel the lament of a man watching the homogenization of place and the diminishment of what it means to be curious about one's surroundings."
— Stephen J. Lyons, *Minneapolis Star Tribune*

"Because nearly a decade often passes between Heat-Moon servings, devotees of his books have necessarily learned to be epicures rather than gluttons. Such an unexpected feast thus provides longtime readers a rare opportunity to gorge.... *Here, There, Elsewhere* provided a sufficiently splendid meal."
— Cliff Froelich, *Columbia Tribune*

"William Least Heat-Moon's latest book is not a meandering travelogue, but a philosophical peregrination about the act of travel, its universal effects and personal consequences.... To William Least Heat-Moon, travel is a means of becoming, a way to realize your full self. It is a path to both journeying outside your current frame of reference and also to delving more deeply into your inner being. Heat-Moon loves to relate a good travel story, but he's not one to settle for the superficial overview. Whether in explicating geologic strata or the essence of the inner life, he digs deep and is ever the explorer."
— Lois Carr, *Wichita Eagle*

HERE, THERE, ELSEWHERE

HERE, THERE, ELSEWHERE

Stories from the Road

WILLIAM LEAST HEAT-MOON

BACK BAY BOOKS

Little, Brown and Company

New York   Boston   London

Back Bay Books / Little, Brown and Company
Hachette Book Group
1290 Avenue of the Americas New York, NY 10104
littlebrown.com

Originally published in hardcover by Little, Brown and Company, January 2013
First Back Bay paperback edition, October 2013

Back Bay Books is an imprint of Little, Brown and Company. The Back Bay Books name and logo are trademarks of Hachette Book Group, Inc.

The publisher is not responsible for websites (or their content) that are not owned by the publisher.

The Hachette Speakers Bureau provides a wide range of authors for speaking events. To find out more, go to hachettespeakersbureau.com or call (866) 376-6591.

Photographs on pages 74, 131, 167, 305, 314, 367 by Edgar Ailor III of
Ailor Fine Art Photography
Maps by the author

ISBN 978-0-316-11024-2 (hc) / 978-0-316-06753-9 (pb)
LCCN 2012953180

10 9 8 7 6 5 4 3 2

LSC-H

Printed in the United States of America

*To the good readers
who made these journeys possible*

The Mole Lady

I live downtown and I work uptown. Six days a week, back and forth, fifty-nine blocks, fifty-five of them underground on the subway. The Lex Line number four-five. That's my godforsaken life right now. But one of these days I'm going to get out of here and go to, I don't know, just call it elsewhere. Like, you know, somewhere, anywhere, because I want to see what goes on out there in all those wheres.

— Dolores, New York City waitress, 2001

Contents

HERE, THERE,
ELSEWHERE

THITHERWARD

About a decade ago, I overheard the epigraph to these pages and jotted it down. In what follows, the other key words—hither and thither—I heard in Ireland when I was about to return from a 1966 jaunt—"a larking around," in my father's terms. While asking a policeman directions to the ferry-slip in Belfast, I turned away from my two pieces of luggage. Nobody saw anything, not even the bobby, but my small grip vanished and with it camera, photographs, logbook, shaving kit, pint of mead, passport, and my Icelandic Airlines ticket home. I still had the dirty laundry.

When I phoned my father to explain a delayed departure, he said, "So now you're over there in a dither in one of your pet thithers." I've come to appreciate his accidental rhyming because it's proved useful for notions in the next few pages intended to launch your way a caboodle of thithers. Come to think about it, maybe I've also found a future epitaph:

> Here Lyeth
> William So-And-So
> Another Gone Thither.

The Here Within There

If you have a willingness to consider hypotheticals, then I have one concerning you: Were it not for a cuspidor, you just might not be reading this sentence. The spittoon belonged, in a way, to Ted Williams, the Boston Red Sox left fielder known as "the Splendid Splinter" because of his lanky frame, and the last major-leaguer to bat .400 for a full season.

In July of 1956, during a spell of feuding with Boston sportswriters over issues of reportage, he clocked his four hundredth home run, the only score in a one-to-zip victory over the team I followed, the Kansas City Athletics. As he crossed home plate, Williams lifted his head toward the men in the pressbox and expectorated an arcing shot in their direction, the first incident in a multi-game fit of temper that came to be called Great Expectorations.

I suppose in our time of even more coarse and nasty behaviors—a day when a yokel will send a wet aerial at a black congressman not for being black but for simply being a Democrat—my repugnance in 1956 might seem unworthy of notice. But to my sixteen-year-old mind, an honored player celebrating a record home run with sputum was deplorable and worse than taking a swing at an annoying reporter.

I was especially attentive to the event because in that golden era of magazine journalism, I wanted to become a photojournalist specializing in sports photography. Embracing the cause of my future fellow tradesmen, I wrote a letter to the *Kansas City*

Williams: No Sportsman!

TED WILLIAMS is surpassed by few as a hitter; he is surpassed by *many* as a sportsman. I sincerely hope that young ballplayers who have held Williams as their idol will find a new one. An idol survives on respect—who can respect a man who will spit at a crowd when it is cheering him?

America is known for its competitive spirit and sportsman-

LEFT FIELD
315

—From the Providence Sunday Journal.

ship. How long can this impression last if we acknowledge athletes so lacking in sportsmanship?

To be a fine athlete, it takes sportsmanship and ability. Williams definitely has the latter; definitely not the former. My question is this: "Does a player with such a lack of sportsmanship belong among the ranks of Ruth, Gehrig, Mack and the other Hall of Famers?"

WILLIAM TROGDON.
7403 Flora.

Star for its regular boxed-column "Speaking the Public Mind." To my surprise and delight, a few days later when the Red Sox were in town, the little dispatch appeared alongside five others, mine illustrated with a two-by-three-inch cartoon of the Splendid Spitter—as some had begun calling him—standing in left field, a cuspidor within salivary range.

Those 125 words were my first to be published. Neither I nor my family had any notion of how easy it is to get a letter accepted in a newspaper, and in our naivete we treated publication like an accomplishment, my mother referring to my "story" or "article," as if I'd written a real column. While I knew it was only a boy's letter, I could imagine something more, a dream made graphic and, as it proved, indelible in memory because of the illustration. I soon forgot my written words but not the cartoon image which I thought lent the piece gravitas. My mother had planted a seed that began germinating, only to wither, resprout, shrivel, revive once again to eventually produce seeds of its own, which is to say, my interests moved from photojournalism to literature to photojournalism to journalism and eventually on to what a chatty fellow waiting for a casino cashier in Las Vegas once said to me: "Oh, you're that other kind of bookmaker. Do *your* 'bets' pay off?"

Writing books is indeed a gambler's trade because it's one of hope against probability: the belief someone somewhere sometime might choose to spend money on your words rather than on a nice bottle of cabernet or on a couple of lottery tickets. What's more, perhaps vanity oversteps itself when writers gather their stories into *collections*, a thing so literary I offer it with considerable diffidence. Nevertheless, I remind myself of the old journalistic adage: No guts, no story. Besides, experience makes me confident it's unlikely you will have come upon more than, at the most, a couple of these pieces because many of them surely went to ignite barbecue briquettes or stuff parcels before you could see them. One advantage books have over a newspaper or magazine is that it's harder to wrap yesterday's fish with them.

So your being here now comes down to what life comes down to, and that's the inescapable linking of events, the perpetual outfall of circumstance and consequence: a left fielder with a cartoon cuspidor, a kid with a typewriter, a reader with a book.

These stories, each initially having a life span equivalent to a mayfly's, are not every journalistic piece I've ever written; in file folders are an equal number I'm leaving there because — to use a phrase employed by bookmakers of the pari-mutuel sort as well as by the other kind — I felt they were, so to speak, tales without legs: Even if they made it around the oval once, they are unlikely to do it again. But we readers have our own, different tracks — some for sprinters, some for mudders, others for beasts with great lungs. I hope the horses here will have a chance on your track and can at least finish in the money.

*　　*　　*

I initially assembled the contents in chronological order which did little more than suggest ways my writing may have changed (I'd like to say *developed*), but who would care besides me? Instead, I've arranged them intuitively, and that means you too can intuit an order to suit your experience. I believe there are continuing themes here, and finding them replicates the fundamental quest for connections forever necessary to make any sense of any *whatever*. Knowledge is a gathering for something greater: assemblage. One is collecting, the other constructing. The young absorb information at a prodigious rate, but interpretation and amplification, if they actually happen, develop slowly.

My mind functions like a kaleidoscope: bits and chips collect and, if things go well, arrange themselves over time into gestalts which once in a while transform into a concept of usefulness and, rather less than once in a while, of originality. My books in their greater freedoms, I trust, refract such a process as the words reflect a person, a place, an event, and the pieces adhere into a story; it's then that a writer turns to a reader's intelligence to take up the finishing stage and transform tale into personal meaning. That's the way writing—of a certain kind anyway—works if it is to work at all.

That notion raises another reason for bringing what's now before you back into light. Despite assertions to the contrary, exceptional is the magazine editor who truly trusts in the intelligence and creativity of his readership. How many times from an editorial desk have I heard, "Our audience won't understand this." "This" being an idea, a word, sentence construction, sentence length, literary allusion, historical reference, or a brief digression underpinning an idea. Too few editors grant American readers much capacity or willingness to think critically, just as they believe their audience will not tolerate a vocabulary beyond the basic five or six thousand words in common usage. If I formerly thought editors were wrong on those questions, now I believe my argument is weaker. Evidence of America getting "dumbed down" in self-fulfilling ways grows apace.

To look into the archives of almost any nineteenth-century newspaper or popular magazine is to see a level of expression that makes much contemporary journalism look like burbles from Simple Simon. The so-called plain style with its hallmark, the simple declaratve sentence free of subordinate clauses, reigns supreme and with it, too often, a decline of fluently sophisticated locutions and illuminating modifiers. I just now randomly took down an old book from my shelves: Edmund Flagg's 1838 *The Far West: or, A Tour Beyond the Mountains*. (The subtitle contains another twenty-one words, including two *et ceteras*.) Again with randomness, I opened it to page 187 and found the Ohioan's sentence about a night in Illinois:

> It was near nightfall when, wearied by the fatigue of riding and drenched with mist, I reached the log-cabin of an old pioneer from Virginia, beneath whose lowly roof-tree I am seated at this present writing; and though hardly the most sumptuous edifice of which it has been my lot to be an inmate, yet with no unenviable anticipations am I looking forward to hearty refreshment and to sound slumber upon the couch by my side.

Would I like to have written that sentence? No, but I like following its sinuousities and partaking of the richness. It's not thin gruel. Today, how disheartening to see our willingness to give up banquets and smorgasbords for drive-thrus, libraries for game rooms, bookshops for places selling bookish items (Thoreau T-shirts, Brontë note cards, Dickens coffee mugs, Dickinson throw pillows).

*   *   *

Setting these stories forth again has allowed me to restore elements one editor or another deemed too challenging for the audience he perceived. My mind is an ordinary organ and thereby useful to judge contemporary capacities; if I can follow along, then so can thousands of others, including those who, unlike me, don't repeatedly have to look up the meaning of *algorithm* or the spelling of *rabbit* and *sheriff* to see where the double consonants belong. What the hell. Largely because of his name, I incline to sixth-century philosopher Simplicius. I admit to knowing little about him other than his disposition to observe nature (he coined the phrase *ta panta rhei*, "all things flow") and his uneasiness about a rising Christianity encroaching on freedom of thought. The annual sales of dictionaries and atlases probably indicates the existence of readers who own and sometimes use them, people who believe the jolliest part of knowledge is its discovery.

To my surprise, I've liked doing the restitution of the pieces here as I've liked returning details and sentence structures I dared not even try with an editorial practitioner of the hack-and-hew school where contravention passes for editing. In a few places I've put back what one editor called my "questionable earthiness" so *you* can judge whether it's relevant and thematically appropriate. To be no longer constrained by editorial presumptions and whims and word counts has been a relief, despite the risk of trying a reader's willingness to accept an occasional challenge. In a few places, where time and experience have clarified my intention, I've slightly reworked or expanded ideas. What is here now is as I want it, and that means I own any defects of judgment. (Be all this as it may, some of these stories have been lifted by instances of editing excellence for which I deserve no credit.)

On a number of assignments I was hired because an editor thought my "voice" right for a particular story; yet when I read his version, I saw paragraphs revamped, restructured, restated, reworked, and reduced so that the hired voice, now homogenized by erasures, became pabulum. That very sentence serves to illustrate my point: For some editors it would be too long, the five *re* words redundant, *pabulum* too esoteric, and *homogenized by erasures* too quirky with a meaning not readily apparent. The term for what numerous editors wanted—a word they would blue-pencil—is *luculent*. (In case you've forgotten or a dictionary isn't at hand: "easily understood.")

Why then, you might ask, accept certain assignments? Because of the offers of grubstaked journeys to places I wanted to visit. The lure was never exposition but exploration, the pursuit not for discourse but for discovery. My introduction to such "work for hire," the first story here, happened at the peak of magazine journalism when I was flown to New York City, put up in a fine hotel, and invited to lunch with an august editor before being sent to the comptroller's office to work out my expenses for a trip into the backcountry of Japan. An account executive's opening question to me was "How much do you need up front?" Flummoxed by the possibilities, I had no answer, and she said, "Would ten thousand dollars get you started?" This for a fellow who began his writing career by scrivening in a small van with a bad water pump, sleeping in the back, living on peanut butter and cottage cheese. Ten grand was a nice embrocation to effect a temporary cure for the itch of wanderlust. (I hear an editor: "*Embrocation?* Can't you just say *liniment?* What is this, a damn think-piece?")

To me, a road map is the printed lyrics to a siren's song where highways and rivers are like stanzas, and the little circles indicating towns are notes—some flat, some sharp, a few off-key. To begin a journey is to hunt for its tune, its melody, its harmonics, and to follow along from stanza to stanza is to hum a route from, say, Waxahatchie to Marfa, Shamokin to Altoona. The

Sirens of classical mythology, each half-woman and half-bird, sang their enticements from a flowery island garden-meadow, surrounded there by moldering bones of wanderlusting men who heeded the lure of the bird-women's song only to die infatuated, turned to fools by deceiving temptresses knowledgeable of all that happens on earth.

Some of these archetypal elements—gardens, temptation, knowledge, death—may remind you of the Book of Genesis and the Omnipotent One's very first question to Adam hiding his naked belly full of forbidden fruit taken from the tree of knowledge of good and evil. Walking the garden in the cool of the day, the Voice asks, "Where art thou?" (One hopes the question, coming from a Grand Omniscience, is rhetorical.) The query, as I take it, is not about location but about condition, and it is the unspoken but implied existential response from the Voice that's important: "Now that thou hast chosen, where dost thou stand? Dost thou see thy way hence among the thorns and thistles beyond the garden?".

Nineteenth-century drawing of a siren

I can't recall any cosmic voices ever asking me where I stand and how I plan to proceed from there, but it's a question I do ask myself, considering that we all arise in a scarcely known uterine thither and inexplicably end up hither and faced with making sense of an initial journey we have no remembrance of. Every night in our dreams we find ourselves in some location, and never do we know how we arrived at that place: arrival without passage (the very thing you want when flying commercial air). Proof you're dreaming is the inability to explain how you arrived where you are: you're in a barn or basement or bubble chamber, yes, but just how the devil did you get there? Answer that. And then, alakazam! the barn or basement is a beach or a belfry, and you have no idea how you got there either. It's such universal passages between hithers and thithers that have made the journey the earliest and most common literary and spiritual motif on the planet; in some form in all cultures it exists.

Every journey begins with a here and lights out for a there; but to a traveler bent more on the *there* — on destination — a *here* often receives little exposition beyond a name; yet within every there and elsewhere and somewhere and anywhere hides a here. And so the question: Just how far is here from there? From one point of view, we can visit a there or elsewhere only in memory or imagination because every actual moment can occur solely in a here, just as a now never allows arrival in a then. Yet, it is the beyonds that validate and authenticate the heres we must perpetually travel in and can never depart. Hithers hold the light to thithers and reveal them for what they are and are not.

The more I travel and embrace geophilia, the less perceived distances can become so that the end of a good journey suggests the wholeness of things and the connections that erase an illusion of separation. "Contact! Contact!" cries Thoreau in *The Maine Woods*: "Who are we? Where are we?" thereby raising the question of links between who and where.

When Pascal writes, "All man's troubles come from not knowing how to sit still in one room," should we believe him? His are the words, of course, of a privileged man who had brought to him his sausages and bathwater. As for the rest of us, we must get up, go out, and set forth. God asks Satan, "Whence comest thou?" and Old Harry grumbles, "From going to and fro in the earth, and from walking up and down in it." Satanic or not, that reply gives an excellent means of finding one's path.

Elementary navigation relies on first establishing two other positions, so that by triangulating, a precise location—a fix, an *I am here*—can be determined. It's the situating of those first two that's the rub, and I have yet to discover any method other than by striking out from some here bound for some where; that's why the symbol of philosophy could be represented with greater accuracy not by a brass lamp but by a brass sextant. (How about a GPS you say? Not so graphic.) What is wisdom but perceiving how heres connect to theres, hithers to thithers, I to thee? Elsewheres are heres waiting to be uncovered and seen anew, and separations are veils hiding the wholeness of subject and object, now and then, truth and misperception, your belief and mine.

In one way or another, the stories in this book are theres and elsewheres I try to connect with heres, each of them chanced upon because I couldn't sit still in my room, although at this moment I am in there once again, pen in hand and sitting at my desk, with a hope this sanctum of a here somehow has become larger than when I first left it so long ago. If not, my duffel bag sits ready.

DOSOJIN

In 1983 I received an assignment for a special issue of Time magazine about the new Japan as the economic engine of Asia; my plan
was to wander off into the backcountry and find a story. I had traveled there some years earlier for the ostensible purpose of "studying"
(admiring) Zen art, but even more to rid myself of notions left over
from World War II, then only a couple of decades past.

For this second trip, Time put me up in Frank Lloyd Wright's
wonderfully peculiar Imperial Hotel, now demolished, and the
editor gave me a few days in Tokyo to get the feel of Japan. Then, I
and my interpreter, Tadashi Sato, headed up into the mountains of
Honshu. We were the same height, the same weight, and I think we
looked out onto things from about the same plane, and he seemed
to embody my Japanese pen pal whose 1946 letters I still hold. For
me to move beyond Pearl Harbor and for Tadashi to put Nagasaki
in the past were of much importance, and I think that's why the
mysterious, stone Dosojin figures spoke to me.

Let me add: An editor demanded I quote Tadashi in perfect
American English. Now, at last, he speaks as he actually did—
charm over perfection.

Up Among the Roadside Gods

We had come out of Tokyo, Tadashi and I, come out of the chaos of bodies and things; come out by the Bullet Train providing hundred-mile-an-hour passage through rice fields hard by small industries and then up through mountain valleys. We had left a city of rooftop birds — pigeons, crows, sparrows — and we hoped to see a different life in these mountains, among the greatest in Japan, the ones even the Japanese call "the Alps." Here was the Hida Range.

Now, instead of dingy city birds, in Nagano prefecture of central Japan, we saw turtledoves with feathers tipped gold like scales of the carp, and swallows dipping low, and skylarks singing from their hovers. "I know birds," Tadashi said. "There's big ones and small ones."

A city fellow all the way, after serving sixteen years in the national Self-Defense Forces, he took up work in Tokyo as a translator. Although raised in Fukuoka, he was born in 1942 in Nagasaki because his mother, following custom, returned to her natal city for his birth. Because of that, as well as to escape air raids near Fukuoka, she and Tadashi went back again to Nagasaki in August of 1945 for the birth of his brother.

He does not remember the explosion. But he does remember his anger when, a few years later, classmates began dying from radiation-induced leukemia. He has worked to put the bitter memory behind him. As a survivor of the nuclear fire, Tadashi receives free, lifetime medical care, and he reports twice annually for a physical examination. Perhaps because one of the high hills of Nagasaki stood between him and the epicenter, his health is good.

As for me, born in 1939, I too grew up on *the* war. The tales of my childhood were more often stories from the front than from the Brothers Grimm or Mother Goose. A disabled marine told me that the Japanese had green blood, and that's why they craved red American blood. And one time I sneaked a look at snapshots of POW-camp atrocities worked on Chinese women. For a while thereafter I did not doubt that blood came in different colors to match hearts.

We left the Bullet Train, on which we got to know each other, at Niigata and took an ordinary limited southwestward down along the blue Sea of Japan. At the coastal city of Itoigawa we boarded a primitive local that followed the Fossa Magna, a grand cleft dividing interior Japan, into the Hida Mountains. The train chugged up-country, passing through hot-spring villages with station names now no longer painted in both Japanese characters and Roman letters, passing the jade mines near Hotaka. The railroad paralleled the Hime Kawa, a river that seemed to flow granite, so gray and stony it was. The dark, snowy Hida peaks had gone into another weather, but in the valley the day was warm, and a butterfly wobbled through an open window of the slow coach, turned an unsteady circle, and, having effortlessly gained ten feet of elevation and a tenth of a mile of ground, flew on out the other side. Many things—insects, machines, workers—chugged along slowly up there.

At last the incline leveled to a high flatness split by the Azusa River and surrounded by mountains called "the Roof of Japan." Even at this elevation, rice sproutings lay in all directions. The planting was finished but for a paddy field here and about, and seedlings grew green, ready for the "plum rains" of June. At Misato, a farm village with no lane running straight, we left the railroad and walked up into the foothills where we took a room

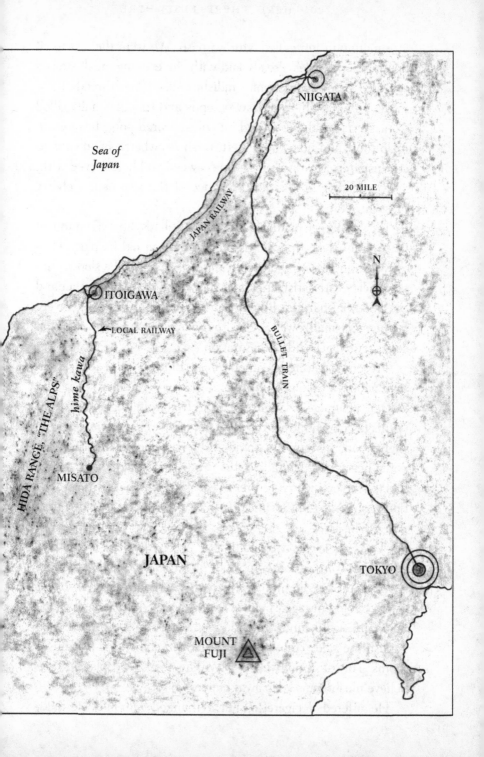

at a mountain inn called Muroyamaso. We were the last to sit down at long tables already laid with the evening meal: stewed seaweed with onions, white radishes sliced into threads ("For digestion," Tadashi said), raw octopus and tuna, a small grilled trout served cold, deep-fried bits of skewered pork, bean curd, miso soup, and rice. For dessert, fresh strawberries and *kanten,* a transparent gelatin made from seaweed and here served with, as if to apologize for the inelegance of the seaweed, a cherry blossom set in the center.

We drank beer, but the local farmers, still rosy after a communal bath, drank sake from bottles the size of an old fireplug. They drew the corks with their teeth and looked down the slopes onto their fields with satisfaction and speculations about weather and the potential harvest. Bound tightly around their temples were *hachimaki,* small towels to absorb the perspiration from their hot soaks, but also to aid concentration.

Present too were members of an Elders Club—each man matched to a woman—everyone wearing a starched, post-bath *yukata.* Their age having freed them from minding a field, from requisite concentration, the elders did not wear *hachimaki.* One slight man, his curving spine that of an old field-worker, sat down beside me. He talked, his words coming quickly. Tadashi had to stop eating to interpret the rush of sentences, his translations containing not a single definite article. The fellow's name was Michisada.

"I was in big war," he said to me. "Navy. All of us here fought. To live on was our fate—not our glory." He took my hand and shook it repeatedly and between shakes continued to hold it softly. "Guess my age." I chose to guess sixty. He cackled, shook my hand again, and stroked my face: "I'm sixty-seven!" To Tadashi he said, "You and our American come visit my mushrooms. I'm mushroom farmer. We are foolish people, and we believe mushrooms keep away cancer."

He offered a cigarette, but I thanked him no. He said,

"Tobacco not for you?" Leaning close, he inserted his thumb between two fingers. "For you, only sex?" He carefully shielded the gesture from the women, some of whom, listening to the radio, were humming along with "I Never Promised You a Rose Garden." Michisada-san laughed at his gesture, shook my hand, and whispered, "No tobacco, no sex—coffin still wait."

Pulling me to my feet, standing alongside, his arm linked with mine, he motioned to a friend who had been a naval officer of high rank but was now only wondrously long-headed and bearded like Jurojin, god of wisdom and longevity. "He takes picture," Michisada-san said, nodding. "This picture goes to you in America. A souvenir. Look for it one day."

From our room, Tadashi and I watched dusk come down the valley to conceal smoke from burning rice-straw of last year as the small bright fires became celestial in a bowl of night turned topsy-turvy.

On the tatami-covered floor we set out our quilts topped with pillows filled with buckwheat chaff. We lay listening, drowsiness slowing conversation. Then there started up in a grove of near pines an unearthly sound. Soon, from farther away, an answering call, and, from farther yet, another, until the slopes rang with the cries. I asked what night-bird it was, and Tadashi said, "Can it be a real bird? Wild monkeys also live in these mountains." We lay and listened to the darkness for some time, and the last thing I heard was "Who sleeps with such sounds going?"

Well into the night the invisible creatures struck their calls against the dark until toward dawn cuckoos joined in with their ceaseless two-notes, then a rooster, then small chirping birds— buntings and white-eyes—until the morning was a racketing to match the night.

Michisada-san joined us in the big, communal bath, a steamy pool of water reaching to my neck. We were all naked, and the genitalia of the old men hung thick and long from the warm water. He had been waiting for us. With a grower of mulberry leaves, we all sat and soaked, and through a half-misted window we looked down onto the fertile plain below. "Eat all your food this morning," Michisada-san said. "Especially egg. For sex energy in middle of man." He pointed to his middle parts.

I did as I was told and ate all of my breakfast: raw egg over rice, sliced yellow radish, fresh seaweed, fermented wheat, *konago* (dried fish smaller than matchsticks), bean soup. And then Tadashi and I went out.

Instead of the road, we followed a shortcut under large pines into the valley orchards and vineyards. The rocky soil was fertile where it got water, so, although too far above the river for paddy fields, it did produce fruit, melons, and chestnuts, all irrigated by timer-controlled sprinklers.

Toward the end of a dusty lane we came to the farm of people he knew and wanted me to meet. The Misawa family had lived in Nagano ("long field") for a thousand years, most of the millennium as rice growers. After the Second World War that took both of his brothers, Daimaru Misawa bought an inexpensive piece of land on the dry slope above the valley floor. He cleared off mountain pines and, with other villagers, put in a cooperative irrigation system. In the nineteen fifties, he built a small home, then a larger one in the seventies. His five-acre farm was about twice the average size here, and his grapes, apples, peaches, and melons did well. His eldest son, Isamu, had just set up vinyl tents, a promising new method for improving grape production.

Now, Daimaru, at seventy-two, had time to build a traditional Japanese garden with a small fishpond, and he was free to watch television documentaries and foreign movies late into the night. Through Tadashi, I asked him about the strange night-bird cries. "I know," he said. "Only come with darkness. Called Bird Nobody Knows. You have also in America?" I said, "Oh, many species of BNKs."

To welcome us, the women, Michiko and Fuyuko, served a lunch of barley tea, small buns stuffed with pigweed, slices of intensely cured pickles, strawberries from their patch, fresh grape juice from the vineyard. We sat beneath an old peach tree in the orchard, the grass full of the vernal blooms. I pulled off a couple leaves of a dandelion, held them up, and said some Americans eat the tender shoots in a spring salad. As Tadashi translated, the women's expressions changed from curiosity to surprise, before looking to me to see my nod that such was indeed true, and then the women giggled into their hands. Eating dandelions! Daimaru pulled one from my hand and said, "We eat everything, but this! This is *weed!*" I picked a leaf of a plantain and said it was also a good spring green, and to that the women were beside themselves with laughter. Then Daimaru, holding both dandelion and plantain leaves to appraise them, said, "Next spring, I try," and the women again put small hands over their laughter.

The family rose to continue stripping their fruit. From a branch holding six or seven olive-sized green peaches, the women would pluck all fruits but the largest so that it might grow to its maximum. That painstaking attention gave them a good living.

Tadashi and I hiked down lanes lined with mugwort smelling like sage, through a bamboo thicket, into a blossoming locust grove, on past rice fields beside small houses, many of them with ridgepoles carrying a golden ideograph symbolizing water, a kind of invocation not for rain but for protection against house fires. The oldest homes had thatched roofs caked with moss, and the newer places synthetic tiles and solar panels. "Japan," Tadashi said. "Always mixture."

Somewhere near each house was a small garden of leeks, bottle gourds, eggplants, cucumbers, cabbages, tomatoes. There was almost no open land not turned into a rice field, an orchard, a vineyard, a vegetable patch. Along the lanes were hedges of yew and slender irrigation troughs rushing swift, cold water, some of it carrying clover blossoms children had launched a mile away. Above, winged shadows of circling buzzards sent pigs squealing for cover, and in the afternoon a wind from a dark, mountain storm set scarecrows to flapping but dropped no rain.

Often, out of a paddy field, muddy prints from a worker's bare feet walked bodiless up the road to the next plot. Stepping along in the tracks gave me a sense of moving in another time, and I thought how, in 1945, such a trek here would have been unimaginable for an American. Occasionally, an unexpected flock of blurred, dark shapes of rice-field birds rose screeching into the air like so much winged mud flung upward. It was as if the damp earth itself thought to take flight.

Hiking that piece of remote Japan was an encountering of so many unknown things that my curiosity began to feel overloaded, and my perceptions seemed to be narrowing to the point of closing down, and that's when I became aware of having passed several carved-stone markers set along the waysides. They awakened me, and I began seeing again. There were dozens of them: at crossroads, above fields, next to boundaries, beside a brook. Each was of gray granite, each uniquely shaped and chiseled, but all of them showed a pair of figures cut into the face of naturally shaped or smoothed stones

Stone Dosojin figures in Nagano Prefecture

about three feet high. I asked Tadashi were they tombstones, and he said, "Shinto roadside gods. In Japanese, we call Dosojin. Very ancient."

Sojin means "ancestor deity," but *do*, a homonym of philosophic significance, with a slight change in the vowel sound can mean either "road" or "earth." The figures reminded me of the once-prevalent wayside shrines of crucifixes carved by peasant farmers in the Tyrolean Alps. The figures in Nagano conveyed not a Christus in agony but workers living sometimes in resignation and at other times in vibrant acceptance of difficulties. Across parts of Japan, Dosojin smile and scowl, dance and kiss, drink and sometimes copulate; along our route they were often a couple standing simply in quietude, holding hands, bodies scarcely distinguishable one from the other. Always it was man beside woman, because Dosojin are female and male, singular and plural, sweet and bitter, health and sickness, life and death, one and its other. They are a linking figure, an earth-ancestral deity to guide lives passing by.

They are not stripped-to-loincloth saviors long in dying; rather they are field hands garbed in wrinkled trousers or courtiers enwrapped in robes, whose sagging eyelid or curled lip or impudent chin thrust upward may express a countryman's untutored chisel responding to existence. Dosojin care not about sin and redemption; they belong to Shintoism where there's no necessity to exclude alternatives or opposites; if something is useful, then use it, and if not, ignore it. In their ordinariness and sublimity they are about nows moving in a long flux of befores and afters.

I began, so it seemed, hearing them. From one face staring brazenly: *Eat all your egg? Keep on trudging!* Another with half-closed eyes: *What's your hurry? The coffin will be waiting.* And one standing alertly: *Good luck, boys!* And then one who spoke not at all, smiling slyly as his hand groped for a smooth breast under his companion's kimono while she reached deftly toward his middle, she surely hoping he'd eaten all his egg.

Seventeenth-century stonecutters, freed from building forti-fications during ruinous civil wars, returned home to carve fig-ures that might promise peaceful days and protection against destructions; from them emerged godheads made in the image of peasant realities where the traveler sees not the human in the god but rather the power of realizing life—a capacity for deity—in the human.

The older Dosojin are sometimes in the form of massive stone phalluses but the genitalia is about regeneration and fertil-ity, not unlike some ancient American rock art. If these deities expose an organ of increase to passersby, it is not to flash an obscenity but to bless them with the prosperity of generation and to give affirmation of creative powers that lift a life beyond animal existence. That's why, at the New Year, the Nagano Dosojin festivals are children's celebrations where new life hon-ors the *continuance* of life. If, during the rest of the year, chil-dren throw mud at the stone figures, or whip them with sticks, or urinate on them, the long-suffering Dosojin will be cleansed by the festival-night fires and will reemerge again to offer a quickening and endurance to human souls.

Layers of meaning here are ancient and many and reveal an ambiguous fluidity requiring not literateness but simply a will-ingness to interpret a three-dimensional art. The invitation to the traveler is to abandon exclusive definitions and limitations created by presumed absolutes. Dosojin suggest reaching beyond bewilderments of contemporary life—where time is scarce to get one's bearings—and into an older realm where change was evolutionary and thereby unquestionably significant, and one knew what to pay attention to. They intimate that underneath rapid and bewildering turns, there is a more stable spiritual sub-structure for all who will seek it.

On our way back to the farm for the night, Tadashi and I became confused about our course. After a wrong path, we

Stone Dosojin figures at crossroads in Nagano Prefecture

happened upon a crossroads Dosojin carved with a kind of crude compass rose as if pointing out the ancient reminder that life itself is journeys crossing othernesses offering fellowship and unions. Pointing to the compass-like carving in the stone, Tadashi said, "Dosojin showing us which is way."

SECOND DRAFT

Traveling through England in 1966, I discovered the excellence of genuine ales, only to return home with a longing for an authentic pint. In the early eighties I read about nascent efforts to brew, once again, good beer in America, and I thought a story about why such a movement was rising and what it promised might further the cause of independent brewers boldly taking up against the crushing power of certain corporations. I wanted to help underdogs snap at the heels if not bite into brewery magnates, and, to be sure, I hoped to make it — at last — easier on my travels in America to close a day with a good ale or lager, a fine pilsner or porter, maybe even a barley wine.

Of all the stories I've written, "A Glass of Handmade" has had the widest circulation and impact, and even a quarter-century later, I continue to hear responses to it. If only other casus belli I've tried to champion in short pieces and in books could have been so quickly and happily concluded! But their time also will come.

For this piece, I have let stand references to dates as they originally were in 1985 so that now the story is partly a history of a movement. To bring a couple of details forward: Redhook Brewing got bought up by giant Anheuser-Busch which later got bought up by an international corporation even bigger, and the day of my being able to sit down over a pint with a brewing pioneer has passed. Instead, my town now has a pair of brewpubs, two of nearly two thousand now across America, the most since the 1880s. A local grocery carries some two hundred kinds of malt beverages made by independent American brewers: ales, porters, pilsners, stouts, Oktoberfests, lagers, and wheats, some made from or flavored with cherries, peaches, vanilla, chilies, agave, cocoa nibs, hemp seeds, sorghum, and, for all I know, kohlrabi and turnips.

One last detail: In 1986, a small company making home-brewing equipment sent me a kit as thanks for the reportage, a gift I forwarded to the Venerable Tashmoo who spent his last years concocting a variety of (usually) toothsome suds we often shared at his home in the foothills of the Bear River Mountains in northern Utah. Our final conversation was mellowed by a wedge of sharp cheddar and a glass of his Tashmoo Titillator.

My curiosity about beer began in 1949 (I was nine years old) near the shore of Pelican Lake in central Minnesota. One morning, as I was picking blueberries from a thicket, I found an empty cone-top beer can; although it was a near-relic even then, that wasn't why I picked it up: I liked a brand name that sounded like a gulp.

A Glass of Handmade

Jack Kerouac often went in search of the perfect American bar, a quest I have furthered for different reasons and with results steadily diminishing, mostly because of the continuing absorption of American breweries into larger corporations. Today [1985], only ten companies brew 95 percent of American beer, with Anheuser-Busch and Miller controlling more than half of that output. By 1990, I read, they will have two-thirds of domestic brewage. Now, if you consider Lite a beer rather than a mere beverage, or if Budweiser satisfies, then you have no need for concern. On the other hand, if you desire beers regional and traditional, even idiosyncratic, in those statistics you may see alarm. After all, how can a perfect bar exist without genuine brews? Drinking Lite in an estimable bar is like watching donkey ball at Wrigley Field.

A longtime friend who appears in my work here and there as a handy foil and commentator, a journalism professor and a Canadian expatriate of Scotch and Ojibway ancestry, had recently heard that an authentic, traditional brew was available in Albany, New York, once an Erie Canal city known for good ales. He (I call him the Venerable Tashmoo) and I set out for the capital in quest of a glass of genuine handmade. In an industrial-district warehouse not far from the Hudson River, we found the tiny operation William Newman opened in 1981 after learning the craft in England. Standing in the brewhouse, he explained how he made his Amber, Winter, and pale ales in the traditional way, using nothing more than barley, water, hops, and yeast. Because his annual production was fewer than ten thousand barrels (a barrel holds thirty-one gallons), Newman's operation is a boutique, or micro-, brewery. Last year he handmade some 4,600 barrels of ale, about what Anheuser-Busch pumps out faster than I can, on a hot day, finish a bottle of it.

One September afternoon, the Venerable and I watched Newman brew, and we tasted grains of his various malted barleys, and helped him stir the mash; we sampled the sweet wort (pronounced "wert"), the hopped wort, the green beer, and the finished ale fresh from the maturing tank. Young Newman (to be a microbrewer is to be under forty) wanted to give his city a choice of flavors and fill a vacuum industrial breweries have left as they bought up makers of regional beers. He wanted something distinctively local and good, worth a customer's effort to find his products, and he planned to make it all himself rather than resorting to contract brewing whereby a larger company turns out a beer according to a recipe provided by a would-be brewer. New Amsterdam of New York City and Samuel Adams of Boston are contract breweries, not micros. But now that demand for Newman's ales has grown, he uses the Schmidt Brewery in Pennsylvania to make his bottled lager, although he is in attendance.

From Bill's old warehouse, Tashmoo and I broadened our search for good beer—beer of another time, we believed—to Rochester, New York, at the other end of the Erie Canal. There the California Brew House (a tavern, not a brewery) offered 178 different labels. We refreshed memories of domestic brews we hadn't poured in years—like Yuengling's Porter and Ballantine India Pale Ale—and imports we'd never poured, from Norwegian Aass to Polish Zywiec. "When I was about thirty," Venerable said over an Old Peculier of peculiar orthography, "I ordered a corned-beef sandwich and a beer. The waitress said, 'What flavor?' That was a time when a brand meant a distinctive taste."

In October, we learned of a bar in the basement of an old Washington, DC, apartment building where the Brickskeller offered nearly five hundred bottled beers. Before the winter was out, we'd visited twice. Late on the second trip, dedicated to foreign beers, we shared Pfungstadter, Stingo, Gorilla, Leopard, Bombardier, Double Dragon, Damm, Zipfer. As Tashmoo finished half of a Samuel Smith's Taddy Porter from England and I a Smith's Nut Brown Ale, I noticed inside our glasses the drying foam created strata called Irish lace. Looking across the table at the other empty glasses still splendidly layered, I pointed out the stratifications, the archaeology of an evening. Tashmoo, raising his glass as if hunting a small shard, said, "Try to get that with a mug of insipid American brewage."

At the next table, a man raised his Thousand Oaks Cable Car and said, "You gents need to try a West Coast beer. Meet the future of American brewing." That was the sentence that offered what was to become a kind of salvation, a knowledge forever bringing either joy or sorrow—the first when you have it, the other when you don't.

Still, our quest might have turned out differently had I not misjudged the climate of southeast Alaska and overloaded my backpack with unneeded cold-weather gear. On my way north to write a story about fishing and logging among the Tlingit and Haida Indians, I stopped over in Seattle for an interview. Later, walking down Madison Street toward the Alaska State Ferry slip, and wanting to get from beneath my pack of miscalculations, I happened on the Mark Tobey pub. It was what they call well-appointed, right to the blackboard menu: Scotch eggs, smoked salmon, mushroom canapés, brandied bread pudding. The tap handles gleamed with local names I'd never heard of: Redhook, Pyramid, Bridgeport, Hale's Pale, Grant's Russian. Because I liked the name, I ordered a Redhook and lifted the pint for a gargantuan gulp, dimly aware of a fellow watching me. The ale rolled and jumped in my mouth, in my head. It made me drink with palate, tongue, cheeks, nose, throat, and—according to my observer—with my eyes. "Well?" Brian Milbrath asked, and I mumbled it couldn't be an American who brewed anything like that.

"Yep, right here in Seattle," he said. Milbrath understood my need to taste, to fight guzzling, to keep silent for the concentration. "I see you're not a Wet Air or a Green Death man." Wet Air is the insanely popular American light beer with the orthographic cuteness which, he believed, was its single claim to distinction. Green Death is a local term for the large-selling green-labeled beer named after the grand Seattle volcano.

Milbrath told me he was a keg specialist, one who installs and maintains beer-tap systems. While I sampled my way down the draft line, he listed the microbreweries of the Northwest: Redhook, Thomas Kemper, Yakima, Hart, Hale's, and Kufnerbrau, all of Washington. In Oregon there were Bridgeport, Hillsdale, and Widmer. In California, Sierra Nevada, Palo Alto, Stanislaus, Thousand Oaks.

Along the entire West Coast, more were appearing. Throughout the region were also brewery pubs, and in San Francisco was the microbrewery that outgrew the term but retained the quality, Anchor. Seattle is a wellhead for people who honor taste buds as much as appetites: Cooper's Alehouse had twenty-two taps, eighteen of them microbrews; Jake O'Shaughnessy's restaurant had a backbar of more than a hundred-fifty

bourbons and fifty single-malt Scotches; even a Safeway not far distant sold thirteen roasts of coffee beyond the cans of Maxwell House and Folgers. Seattle, Milbrath was saying, had become *the* city in America for serious beer explorations because the citizens prefer to taste what they pay for. Maybe it was the frequent vapors of the Northwest coast: Even they had more color, flavor, and aroma than Wet Air. Light beers did not sell here as they do in, say, Phoenix or Cincinnati or Atlanta. In Seattle, it was becoming more difficult to peddle a beer with a lone attribute: chilled wetness.

The conversation drew a circle around us as if we were rolling dice. Everybody, including one brewing chemist, had a charge to make against the big beer companies. The group hooted down a couple of patently loony claims, but on three there was consensus: (1) Industrial brewers are turning more and more to "heavy" or high-gravity brewing whereby beer is made with strong alcoholic content only to be watered down before bottling. (2) The "beechwood" aging proclaimed by Anheuser does not mean beer stored in wooden casks; rather, it refers to thin strips of wood thrown into the steel maturing tanks. (3) Miller Lite contains propylene glycol alginate, a seaweed extract supposed to leave a residue on the tongue to hold a bit longer what little flavor there is. That charge, the chemist said, could be checked in *Chemical Additives in Booze,* a booklet published by the Center for Science in the Public Interest. Before I got under my pack again to leave for Alaska, I wrote a postcard to Tashmoo: *The quest—Next stop, Puget Sound.*

Home again, I bought the booklet and found these compounds listed for Miller Lite: propylene glycol alginate, corn syrup, chemically modified hop extracts, amyloglucosidase, papain enzyme, liquid sugar, potassium metabisulfite. I phoned the company and got spokesman Bob Bertini, who said, "We have no additives in our beers." I read the list to him. He answered with what sounded like a dismissive snort: "I won't get into the items one by one, but there's no way that list is factual. Other than corn syrup, yeasts, hop extracts, and water, we don't discuss our recipes—for competitive reasons." Wasn't that rather convenient? "Look, we're advertising purity now because we saw a growing concern regarding any product with preservatives or additives. We haven't changed our beers—we just changed our labels."

Tashmoo and I arrived in Seattle on an English spring day— dim and damp—just the kind of weather for a small tap house in the late afternoon with an occasional seagull flapping down the street. Cooper's, although not in Kerouac's perfect-bar category, nevertheless had the feel of a neighborhood place, a corner tavern, but this one was a tabernacle of handmade brews and side-order food. Despite the loudly testosteronerated, meathook softball teams which meet there to swill plastic pitchers of Green Death, other customers, although young, generally knew what should and should not be in a glass of real beer. Zymurgy was a serious topic.

We had just sat down when, as if choreographed for us, over the television came a loud *Boom-diddy-boom-boom...Made the American Way!...No preservatives!...No additives!...Purity you can see and trust!* To the beer commercial, a young chap called out a common term for male bovine scat. Pleased by my smile, he said, "Clarity ain't purity! You gonna trust a company that manipulates its beer so it can put it in *clear* bottles?"

While the city dripped, the Venerable and I sat snug and judged Northwest handmade. He considered Bridgeport the best, we both deemed Pyramid Ale with its high hoppiness a splendid thing, but I chose the whole line from Redhook Brewing Company: Redhook, Blackhook, Winterhook, Ballard Bitter. I liked moving from one to another. It kept the taste buds alert.

A man trying to save money—microbeers are about half-again higher—ordered a Bud Light. The Venerable said to him,

"If you want to save money, order a seltzer with lemon." Soon after, Tashmoo, becoming bold as a zymurgical evangelist, lectured a young woman dithering about her thighs and the calories in a Bud Light. "Miss," he said, "that beer has only a third fewer calories than a regular Budweiser. The same ratio between Miller and Miller Lite. Fifty calories less, that's it. You know what fifty calories is? A half-cup of soybean sprouts. Light beers are jokes as beer and hoaxes as dietetics."

That's when I reminded him of what we'd seen at lunch in a place downtown: A man—fifties, blue blazer, penny loafers, *Wall Street Journal* under his arm—ordered a Hale's Pale Ale, took a single sip, handed it back to the bartender to dump, and ordered a Heineken. The Cooper's bartender, who'd begun listening in, said, "The beer a guy drinks at twenty-five is the one he drinks at fifty-five." Considering it, Tashmoo, just beyond the half-century mark himself, said, "Then I should still be drinking Old Wooden Shoe of Minster, Ohio."

Over the course of the evening this notion emerged: The microbrewers confront a generation of World War II servicemen who learned beer from the 3.2 percent stuff in olive-drab cans, men who came to believe that taste in beer, like taste in water, was to be avoided. With a younger generation, small brewers must face those brain-stunned by television advertising that has made them unwittingly want to drink only what corporations want to sell. Tashmoo, ever the commentator: "Shape the audience to your product—that's where you make money."

The small brewers of traditional lagers and real ales must address customers who will consider a lo-cal lunch to be a diet soda with a side of fries. Yet, in Seattle, Portland, San Francisco, Denver, and even Dallas of all places, microbrewers, if not nipping at the heels of the industrials, were at least growling low in the corner. The next day, the Venerable and I went off to a growler.

*   *   *

The Redhook brewery was in a former transmission-repair shop in Ballard, Washington, near the waterfront of Seattle. Although the lower area was still a kind of seagoing place, now it also had galvanizing companies and genetic-engineering labs. Ballard stood with one leg in the past, one in the future—about the same position as Redhook Brewing.

Paul Shipman, president of the company, grew up in Philadelphia, was graduated from Bucknell in English literature, received an MBA from the University of Virginia, learned wine-making in Lancaster County, Pennsylvania, and, in the seventies, sold wine door to door as if it were encyclopedias. When he moved to Seattle, he worked first for a winery even though he had long been passionate about beers of full flavor. He never gave any thought to improving wine, but he knew that beer in the United States was another territory. Travel in England had confirmed how far Americans have strayed from their earlier tradition, but, he told us, "I just couldn't see any kind of a business in beer." Then, in 1981, his friend Gordon Bowker, chairman of Starbucks Coffee and Tea Company, gave him "a pitch" about opening a boutique brewery.

Shipman said, "The brewing industry showed signs of being ripe for a small entrepreneur." The megabrewers, growing huge by absorbing regional breweries, had such a lust for profit they moved all of their beers toward the middle of a public taste they could create and control. Their lager-style beers became ever less flavorful as they proved Americans would *buy* slightly alcoholic carbonated water, a solution one small brewer calls "lawn-mower beer—what you drink mowing the yard." The brewing process changed as zymurgical chemistry developed and per-barrel cost dropped. Industrial chemists found ways to control the highly erratic nature of beer fermentation, methods requiring chemical inducements. "The bigger the scale of operation," Shipman said, "the safer a corporation wants to be. It moves toward the middle to avoid risk, and chemically manipulated brewing helps reduce risks."

With the repeal of the Volstead Act, in 1933, of the some fifteen hundred American breweries in 1918, only about 750 resumed operation. By 1980, of those remaining 750, only forty had survived. But even these numbers deceive: Virtually all of the few regional breweries hanging on today imitate the industrials by turning out chemistry-set beer. The result? Corporations like Anheuser, Miller, and Heileman have been able to wipe them up like so many wet spots on a bar.

In the pogrom, the behemoths, as if using the science-fiction novel *The Space Merchants* as a guide, took on the public taste primarily through commercials and made it serve their ends. But for at least one megabrewer, Schlitz, cost-cutting through abbreviated brewing in the mid-seventies caused sales to drop by half in five years before the Stroh Brewing Company swallowed up Schlitz.

By 1980 retailers began to notice increasing requests for imported beer, never mind that an import is rarely the same here as in its native land. People, their tastes awakened and maybe even informed by various new American wines of California, looked unsuccessfully for something genuine in domestic beers while buying imports to strike back at corporations controlling choices. Import profits soared.

Shipman and Bowker noticed all this and in August of 1982 brewed their first batch of Redhook. Emphasizing his qualifying words, Shipman said, "We wanted an individually crafted, top-fermented brew, a *real ale* made from only the traditional four ingredients — malted barley, hops, yeast, and water. We started with Redhook to create a bold statement, an ale people would not confuse with something already available. If our brew had to be more expensive, then we had to give a customer a reason to change. Well, we got that with Redhook. Today it's the most radical beer in America."

Excluding some explosive accident a home brewer brings forth in his basement, Redhook for now is indeed the most extreme brew in the country. Even Joseph Owades, the renowned American brewing chemist and inventor of Lite beer, agrees. Drinkers who love Redhook ("It's why I drink beer") and those who hate it ("Right out of the cowshed") agree. "With Redhook," Bowker said, "we polarized the market. Our success began with that." When the men, both still in their thirties, introduced the ale to Seattle in the fall of 1982, the mayor publicly, grandly, tasted a glass, looked about, his eyes staggered, and said, "This is no quiche-eater's beer."

No eater of quiche is Rod Mason, six-foot-four, two-hundred-fifty pounds, a former trooper in the Royal Horse Guards Household Cavalry Regiment. In that first Redhook autumn, Mason, retired from the Queen's Guard and settled in Seattle, owned the Guardsman Tavern just north of the Redhook brewery. He was a critic of Redhook ale; that is, his English palate considered it one of the few brews in America worth criticism. His grandfather, owner of a small pub in Gloucestershire, was a dedicated cellarman who knew how to care for beer: how to store it, how to tap a barrel and pull it through the hand pumps into a glass. He taught Mason that special knowledge, and the boy learned, he said, "from the cellar up."

A brewer can make the finest beer in the land, but if the publican is careless, the customer might as well buy some slumgullion. In the Guardsman, Mason saw that Americans were ready: "I knew the number of people who were happy with their beer was small, but they didn't know where to turn. Then came Redhook. It was alarmingly inconsistent in those days of working out the crinkles." The brewery hired Mason as a kind of ambassador of its new world of old-style beers. He said, "The ales here are finally perfected. They're what we want them to be. If we get a bad batch now, we sewer the whole lot."

Inconsistency is both bane and boon to the microbrewer; Americans want, he thinks, strict consistency in a beer, while Englishmen realize that small variations are proof of handcrafting, something more valuable than assembly-line sameness. Shipman said, "Redhook is going to be a slightly different taste every time you drink it. It doesn't pretend to be consistent. By that I mean, precisely the same. That's the real nature of an ale brewed in the traditional way."

Americans once drank top-fermented, English-style ales, rich of color, full in flavor, heady with aroma, and delightfully variable. In the years following the 1812 war with England, the newly arriving middle Europeans—Anheuser, Busch, Heileman, Mueller, Pabst, Schaefer, Schlitz, Stroh, and more—brought along German-style lagering, a technique lending itself to mass production because lagers are cheaper to brew, easier to transport and store than are top-fermented ales. As a result, older American brewing methods disappeared for the usual big corporation reasons.

Today, microbrewers find themselves educating Americans to what another century knew. "Six years ago this country didn't have any reference point for tasting a real ale," Mason said, "and even today Americans are still edgy about the very word *ale*. Even the color of some ales intimidates. Few people realize that the so-called ales produced by the large companies are not truly ales at all. The word has been terribly abused in this country." The Venerable, in an Orwellian pronouncement, said, "Control the language and you control the people."

I asked Shipman, if an eighteenth-century brewer like

George Washington were in Seattle today, which beer would he recognize? "I'd guess Redhook. It's traditional—almost a barley wine which Washington would know." So is the past the future here? "I believe we're going to leave the lager age. It's had its time or at least its dominance. What we'll see is both industrial beers *and* postindustrial beers. Redhook will be here with Budweiser, but I don't believe Anheuser-Busch will begin making anything resembling a true ale. The economics are against it. Ale is expensive to brew, and the demand is still limited. But what you see with us is one more sign that smokestack America is dying. We're brand-new, four years old, and already we're brewing five-thousand barrels a year. In 1985 we grew by fifty percent. Five years from now we can be up to twenty-five-thousand barrels. Anchor Brewing was an inspiration to us, and we can grow the way it has. We can get as big as our ability to stand the stress."

The stress lies in the touchy nature of ale brewing. When top-fermenting yeasts go to work on hopped wort, when they begin to shape the character of the brew, it all happens quickly—within an hour or so. The critical time for a bottom-fermented lager may last a day. The ale master must decide fast what to do with the fermentation, and on his decision company profits ride. The success of Redhook comes from good decisions in several places, none more critical than in the brewhouse; after all, a barrel of Winterhook is not a washing machine that can be sent back up the assembly line to have a gear replaced. It's more like a jump shot in basketball: Once the ball is off the fingertips, the character of its flight has been decided. If there is excellence, it's already in the shot.

It took nine thousand dollars and thirty-two days to clean the Redhook brewhouse of its transmission-shop crud, but that once-oily floor became the point of departure for brews that helped change the way people perceive and drink beer in Seattle. To the freshened building, the partners brought from Germany a stacked, copper brew kettle so fine it's almost high-end sculpture, and the cost was commensurate: something more than a half-million dollars.

Of the seven traditional steps in brewing—malting, milling, mashing, boiling, fermenting, maturing, racking—Redhook does each but the first. Its entirely American malts—no extracts like some micros that start with step four—come from an independent maltster. Redhook adheres to the sixteenth-century *Rheinheitsgebot*, the Bavarian purity law still exercised in Germany, that requires a brewer to use only barley, water, and hops (the action of yeast was then unknown). No adjuncts of corn grits, flakes, or starch; no rice, sorghum, milo, or syrups; and no additives, no chemical compounds. In the United States it is legal for a brewery, as at least one major company has been alleged to do, to introduce forty-eight additives and four adjuncts and still call its beer "pure" in prime-time commercials. Several of the additives—foaming agents, head stabilizers, taste enhancers, colorings, antioxidants, emulsions—are a reason for industrial brewers to print on their labels incomplete lists of ingredients.

During our yeasty, malty investigative imbibing over the last months, the Venerable and I had noticed an absence of hangovers, although on a couple of evenings we edged, in the interest of complete reporting, toward immoderation. Rick Buchanan, the Redhook brewhouse foreman, said, "True ales tend to be less, let's say, toxic than industrial lagers. Alcohol poisoning comes from fusel oil, and brewing at higher temperatures the way industrial breweries do, increases fusels." Maybe low fusel oil explains how Queen Elizabeth's handmaidens

in the sixteenth century withstood a sixteen-pint daily ale allowance.

When we went from the brewhouse into the conference room, Rod Mason drew glasses of Winterhook for us. We appraised, sniffed, sipped, and even tapped on the firm head composed of almost microscopic bubbles. The composition and durability of the froth are such useful indicators of quality that a German patent on a beer tap has one legal-sized-page description of a proper head: It should be persistent from first sip to last; bubbles should linger from the initial tilt of the glass to the last; and they should be uniform, without randomness, and "possessed of minuteness."

At noon we drove to the Pacific Inn, a small eatery serving good grill-food, to see what can happen between a racked keg and a tapped beer. "Most taverns," Mason said, "even in Seattle, set their refrigeration for Miller or Rainier because that stuff won't pour warm. It turns to foam. At an industrial-based temperature, you won't be able to taste a good ale, and your extra brewing cost is wasted."

(I remembered a Georgia gas station where a man came in wanting a bottle of beer—this in the days of primitive refrigeration—and the proprietor asked what kind. The customer said, "That bottle that's froze to the coils.")

Shipman said, "We've found that drinkers abuse what they can't taste. To compensate, they drink too much."

"Our ales lend themselves to moderation because they're flavorful," Mason added. "We gain customers by improving our beers. A big brewer can't do that without raising costs and that means losing customers. Factory beer gets locked into mediocrity."

The Venerable: "I don't suppose corporate greed could have anything to do with it."

By the individual character of its beers, a good micro can take sales from industrial brewers, but it struggles with distribution. Since bottling is expensive and retail shelf space can be hard to get, most small brewers initially produce only draft beer. Redhook waited four years before beginning to bottle a small percentage of its beer for sale only at the brewery, a change Shipman hopes will be a first step toward reaching customers beyond Seattle. From that point, he sees three courses open: "We can remain small and sell only locally. We can serve our beers only here at the brewery by piping it directly from the maturation tank to the tap—the brewpub method. Or, we can grow into a middle-size regional as Anchor has."

Tashmoo: "Or you could get bought up," and to that the Redhook crew smiled.

In San Francisco, the Anchor brewery, near Franklin Square, looks onto worn warehouses—one on its way to becoming a mall—and onto tennis courts and the hind ends of half-century-old houses. As in Ballard, the past is jowl by rosy cheek with the future. The Anchor building, a Depression-era structure, was once a Chase and Sanborn instant coffee and pudding factory. When Fritz Maytag, whose grandfather founded the Iowa washing-machine manufactory, bought the historic but foundering Anchor Brewing Company in 1965 and later moved it to these larger quarters, he had to sandblast the interior to get out the smell of roasted coffee. Now the brewhouse—with fine German-made kettles looking like great coppery onions, the brass fittings and chromium knobs gleaming, the air full of hops and ferment—may be the most handsome in the country.

Maytag is a former student of literature—an interest he shares with a number of other new brewers—and a devoted reader of Thoreau. Now president and brewmaster, Maytag walked us through the brewhouse. He said, "Making steam beer is a *what-the-hell-is-this?* business." Unique to San Francisco, steam brewing is a cross between English and German methods: a lager yeast fermented at higher ale temperatures. The "steam" appears when the pressurized maturation tanks are opened and carbon dioxide hisses out. When Maytag bought the company, it brewed only draft beer, and that poorly. He started with improving the quality by using top-grade ingredients, by taking greater care, and by reviving traditional ways. Only then did he begin bottling. Later yet he added an ale from a recipe he himself wrote; then he added a porter, an annual Christmas brew, and recently a wheat beer and a barley wine. Eighty percent of the annual production of 38,000 barrels is Steam Beer, with Liberty Ale and the porter making up almost all of the other 20 percent.

He brews tiny quantities of the three newest types for several reasons, all of which come down to his love of beer. He said, "A Christmas ale is a brewer's midwinter tradition. It's also a present to the people who support us, and it's a way of reconnecting with the roots of a holiday custom. This year, all the barley in our seasonal beer comes from one farm near Tule Lake, California. Our employees went up there for the harvest to see the source of what we make and to see our connections with nature—and the risks in nature. As for barley wine, I make it because I believe in it. I came to love it when I studied brewing in England. Our Old Foghorn costs twice as much for half as much yield, and it's a damned nuisance to bottle, and it's expensive for the customer. But barley wine is one of the most interesting malt drinks on earth, although it's poorly understood and not much appreciated. It's something to sip by the hearth. A contemplative drink. It'll never have wide popularity, but I own the place so I can do what I like. A brewery should have a hallmark—a drink of absolute distinction. Old Foghorn will become ours. Wheat beer? I've said for years that it could have a big

audience, and ours will. In a way, it's the opposite of Old Fog-horn—it's a hot-day, light beverage. It's our lawn-mower beer."

When we were there, only 10 percent of Anchor production was sold on draft, all of it Steam Beer available only locally. But, in bottles, Steam and Liberty Ale are making their way across the country. Maytag said, "If micro means production under ten-thousand barrels a year, then we were a micro for a decade. But we've grown because what we make is true, traditional, honest, and good. We celebrate the materials for what they are." By that he meant at least 80 percent two-row barley. He believes the cheaper six-row barley used by the industrials produces a coarser beer. Maytag adds three hoppings of whole flowers—no hop pellets—and is always ready to dump any batch that goes awry. For Liberty Ale there's a dry hopping—a second addition of hops that gives superb aroma and splendid taste. Nowhere an adjunct or additive; Anchor Brewing observes the *Rheinheitsgebot.*

Maytag's change to quality gave his beers recognition, and the move to bottling gave a wider audience to make Anchor for a while the fastest growing old-name brewery in America, but he told us the growth would stop at fifty-thousand barrels. "I won't swear I'll stop there, but one should have guidelines, a control-ling principle. I like business that's small enough for the employees to see our interdependency."

"Against the corporate tide," said the Venerable.

Production Manager Mark Carpenter, his white overalls turned to camouflage by yeast stains and penciled-down brew-ing times, said, "One of my fears is that Anheuser-Busch will start making a real ale. I'm afraid our growth will catch their eye. Maybe keeping customers was easier when people laughed at something called 'steam beer.'" His anxiety is whimsical. Makers of traditional brews know that the market for Wet Air will remain huge. After all, popular tastes in America rarely have been noted for discrimination.

After we came out of the Anchor brewhouse and headed toward the tasting room, to our amazement, we came upon the Arch Satan himself, the Dark One incarnate, the father of Wet Air: the biochemist Joseph Owades, inventor of Lite beer. The Venerable now alleges that upon seeing him, I began fumbling about my belt as if reaching for a sidearm.

Within a handshake of me stood one of the very men who had done in American beer. I asked him why he did it. Owades — suited and vested without flaw, a trim man, clipped mustache — had just finished teaching his seminar "All About Beer." The biochemist earned the first doctorate in the country in brewing science and wrote his dissertation on cholesterol before going to work for Fleischmann's Yeast Company where he began studying the microbial action of yeasts. Later, he joined Rheingold Brewing in New York City and started working to remove "calories beer doesn't need." He believed people resisted drinking malt beverages for two reasons — the taste and their fear of weight gain. After much research, he wrote a recipe that reduced calories and "lightened" even further the mild taste of lager. He said, "Lowering carbohydrates — calories — also lowers the mouth feel. The analogy's not exact, but a regular beer stays on the tongue like ice cream. A light beer slides off like a sherbet, and that changes taste perception."

Rheingold produced the recipe under the name of Gablinger, but after tobacco behemoth Philip Morris took over Miller Brewing, the corporation bought the rights to the name Lite from Meister Bräu Brewing Company. With parts of three breweries assembled into one, Philip Morris set loose the advertising, and American beer hasn't been the same since.

I asked Owades what beer he drinks. "Since I live in San Francisco now, I usually drink Anchor Steam."

Tashmoo, under his breath: "He's standing in its brewery."

Had the inventor's discovery made him wealthy? "All I received was my usual monthly salary."

Murmuring Tashmoo: "Ask about CEO-style bonuses."

Not to atone for Lite but because he was hired to create them, Owades wrote the generally respected recipes for several East Coast contract brews from New Amsterdam and Samuel Adams.

"Tell me," the Venerable said, "can you tell the difference between, let's say, a Budweiser and a Coors?"

"All major American beers are structurally very similar. No, after two beers I won't be able to tell the difference between a Budweiser and a Coors, but with an Anchor Steam and a Redhook, I could distinguish them after a half-dozen. It's true that microbrewers are broadening the spectrum, but you'll see a lot of them fail because brewing's hard work and what they produce just isn't good. But the best ones, a metropolitan area will support."

Microbrewery failures so far have come more from undercapitalization than a poor product. New Albion Brewing of Sonoma, California, the first true American micro, went under because it began bottling before it was financially stable. When it comes to distribution, Jonah must face the leviathans. An industrial brewer can make (sometimes through illegal means) distribution difficult for a small company, particularly by demanding extensive shelf space from retailers. One solution for a micro is to eliminate shelf space and distribution

altogether by running beer from the maturation tank directly to the customer's glass, or, as the Venerable said, "Put the cat under the milk cow. From teat to tongue." In this country, brewpubs are still scarce, but in colonial America, a traveler could find tavern after tavern serving its own beer, some of it, assuredly, swill.

The brewpub also provides the owner with complete control over his ales and lagers, an important aspect when excellence is the aim. No other alcoholic beverage is so sensitive, so perishable as beer. It can be changed by towel lint in the glass, a refrigerator three degrees off, a poured beer sitting on a waiter's tray in a warm room an extra few minutes, on and on. Virtually everything that is not beer is its enemy.

In Hayward, California, on the lower east side of San Francisco Bay, Tashmoo and I found Buffalo Bill's Brewpub where founder Bill Owens, an affable and articulate man, told us, "The wave is the brewpub, and I'm on the crest, dudes." In 1976 he won a Guggenheim for an influential book of photographs entitled *Suburbia.* Then he published *Our Kind of People,* and after that *Working: I Do It for the Money.* The collections of photographs earned him little more than respect for his artistry. As for his newspaper job with the Livermore *Independent,* he clearly wasn't doing it for the money. "Look," he said, "photojournalism has peaked. I got in on the dying days, the back end. Now I'm in on the front end of something. Now I can write checks that don't bounce. In ten years there'll be a hundred brewpubs in the United States, and you'll see me in *Fortune.* Instead of shooting assignments on colored popcorn for them, I'll be the subject. That's the difference between back ends and front ends."

Owens began brewing a few gallons at home in the early seventies. At his fortieth birthday party in 1978, a friend said, "Let's open a brewery," so they looked at a couple of micros and decided a bottling line was too expensive and too complex. They abandoned the idea. Then, a year later, they heard about brewpubs opening all across England. In 1983, when the brewpub became legal in California, Owens set up a limited partnership, sold twenty-seven shares, and raised $110,000. "A good idea," he said, "sells much easier and for more money than a good photograph." He rented an old downtown building, once a camera store, gutted it, and built a tiny brewhouse in the back with a picture window so customers could sit, sip, and see their suds made. Owens scrounged equipment from a candy company, a food manufacturer, and a dairy, and with the help of an investor who worked on nuclear bombs, they tore up the floor and from the tanks to the bar they laid sixty-two feet of pipe—his entire distribution system. As much as anything else, those pipes, running the distance from a pitching rubber to home plate, allow him to compete with the industrials.

In September of 1983, Owens opened the third brewpub in the United States, and the very first tank of Buffalo Bill he brewed went on sale. Four years later he doubted he'd ever dumped a batch, even if he should have. A customer told us, "That early stuff was out of the buffalo's posterior. It had hoofs and horns in it. But now, he's about perfected it. I'm a fixture here. My throat is part of the pipeline."

Owens brewed six barrels every Monday, about three-hundred barrels a year. "For a hundred-thirty-dollars' worth of ingredients, I can make a profit of twenty-five-hundred dollars. My cost to make a glass of lager—and that's all I brew now—that lager costs seven cents. I sell it for a dollar and a half. My profit on a bottle of commercial suds is forty cents." Last year, half of his $200,000 income

came from Buffalo Bill and the other half from sandwiches—and factory slosh.

He wrote a book, *How to Build a Small Brewery*, which he sells over the bar and by mail, and he bought up two home-brewing magazines and consolidated them into a quarterly, *Amateur Brewer.* "Publishing doesn't bring in money so much as it puts me on the map as a pioneer. It keeps me in touch with people in the industry."

He'd begun work on a second location and wanted to trade-mark the term *brewpub* in California with the idea of opening up a half-dozen of them, some in malls with the brewhouse in a front window to lure in strollers. He wanted to franchise. "My fun is promoting. If the television camera is here, I get out my big paddle and stir the mash. It's not necessary to stir it. It's just something graphic. Hey dudes, remember, I was a photojournalist."

He demonstrated how he performed his "photo-ops," and as he did he said, "Look, everybody wants to be an entrepreneur now. I'm on the edge of the revolution—the making-money-and-enjoying-it revolution. A lot of microbrewers are purists. Ale is their holy grail. I'm not interested in that. You find chemists and chefs—I'm a chef. I think my truth is best. I do it the easy way—boil for an hour because my brewhouse timer only runs for an hour. I use pellet hops, but not malt extracts, and I don't filter. My water is snowmelt from the mountains just like Anchor's. But I don't care if Americans have no idea what ale is. I don't care if they're afraid of it. I know that light rum outsells dark rum three to one, and I know that Americans want their beer cold, clarified, and carbonated, so I don't make ale. I can't waste time educating Americans about ale. Not my job. I'm interested in making my own kind of beer. This isn't Burger King—you can't have it your way here. You get it my way. I work by one rule: Don't get complicated. Don't build a Rolls-Royce factory to make a go-cart. And there's one other rule: Take the profit off the top."

The Venerable, always ready to advocate for the Devil, asked, "Would you say you emphasize style of dispensing over the product?"

"The style," Owens said, "brings a customer in, but it's the beer that has to bring him back."

South of Sacramento, near Interstate 5, we stopped in a bar over-hung with ferns, clogged with stained glass and olde-tyme signs. We went in not looking for the perfect bar but for a working tele-phone. We knew that men who discuss the size of bubbles in a head of beer and who read patterns of Irish lace in an emptied beer glass, we knew those men do not come in bars like that one. Yet, we had a small hope for some bottle of an untried odd-ity tucked away. The offerings, of course, were Hobson's choice. Maybe the wish to put a touchstone to those last days of golden glasses urged us, I don't know, but we ordered our Hobson's, our industrials. The Venerable scowled, hoisted his mug, took a hearty swallow, and set the glass down. He turned to me blankly and said, "Did I miss my mouth?"

PUTTING LEGS
BACK ON A STORY

"A Little Tour" is the only chapter here I might call a memoir, although I hope it reaches well beyond me. Even before I wrote it, the assignment editor insisted I avoid most names and some events and many details, a curtailing that crippled the tale. The material remaining was so insufficient I nearly withdrew the piece, and maybe I should have. But now, years later, the restoration at last gives the story I'd hoped to tell about a journey taken two decades earlier. To hear those Mississippians talk again is strange and wonderful, something I didn't imagine as I listened to them in 1961, and today it's even better to imagine their voices speaking once more to some readers not yet present on earth when first the Oxfordians spoke.

The copy of William Faulkner's Three Famous Short Novels you will soon learn of, I can happily report, is still in my friend's possession. Only recently, after a half-century, I was allowed to hold it again before having a second time to return it. But now I know it's valued.

A Little Tour in
Yoknapatawpha County

About a year before the United States Navy exacted its term of service from me in the early nineteen sixties, I had some days that belonged only to me, a time good for looking into a part of America I knew largely from books. So, age twenty-one, I persuaded a friend to take off with me from Missouri down into a place my literature professors believed didn't truly exist: Yoknapatawpha County, Mississippi, the mythical corner where William Faulkner set the action of his finest novels. He even drew maps of it complete with hamlets, homesteads, roads, rail lines, and rivers all neatly delineated and with labels like *Old Frenchman Place which Flem Snopes unloaded on Henry Armstid and Suratt, and where Popeye killed Tommy.* He enumerated the inhabitants (*Whites, 6298; Negroes, 9313*), and he signed the drawing *William Faulkner, Sole Owner and Proprietor.* I believed if there was a map, then there was a place to match it in some way or other, and in my imagination I carried my own rendering of Faulkner's fictional—and perhaps fictitious—county in north Mississippi. I believed it existed as I believed its author existed although I'd never seen either one.

So Ollie (as I'll call him) and I, in my Ford coupe, lit out for Faulkner's county town of Jefferson—labeled on my filling-station map as Oxford, the seat of actual Lafayette County and about fifty miles south of the Tennessee line. Even though I could say Yoknapatawpha correctly (Yahk-na-pa-*taw*-pha), I'd soon be corrected by a shopkeeper on pronouncing *Lafayette*: "Little Yankee fella, we say 'Lah-*fay*-et.'"

I'd just finished my final examinations and had a week before commencement in June of 1961; graduation in something called agricultural journalism was yet a year away for Ollie. He was slender, inclined toward the unstudious, amiable, and often on the hunt for adventure. His interest in Faulkner was matched by the number of the author's books he'd read—zero—but I persuaded him to join me if not for the promise of pilgrimage then at least for the promise of discovery. After all, it would be easier than our earlier plan to bicycle to Cape Horn. I intended to meet the master, learn what kind of man he was, see his country; maybe I'd write something about how books arise from actuality and, in that peculiar turning almost miraculous, show how a different reality can proceed from fiction. Around and around it all goes, pulling us always deeper into the middle of things where lies the heart of existence and meaning.

Ollie and I passed through Memphis and on southward into the Mississippi pines and hills to Oxford—Jefferson in my mind. At the center of town were the square and its courthouse burned by Union general "Whiskey" Smith and rebuilt ten years later. On the south side rose the slim, stone column of 1907 and atop it a Confederate soldier holding his rifle before him, muzzle skyward, the monument Faulkner's character, mentally deficient Benjy, always circles three times in *The Sound and the Fury*. Standing on the square, I felt I'd actually seen it all before, and that confirmation of authorial description feeding imagination added an enriching element to books—*good* books—which remains with me still.

The next morning, in search of characters and settings, we went out to get the feel of the square and its voices, and we walked the alley Joe Christmas runs down when he breaks loose from the law. Just south of the courthouse we came upon a café in a small building not from the time when the stone soldier was flesh and blood but the place looking as if it could have been. It was called The Mansion, the very title of Faulkner's most recent novel. Did Faulkner eat there? Had he taken his title off the breakfast menu? Ollie and I went in. Here's the gist of an entangled conversation over eggs and grits: Indeed, said the waitress, a jolly, blue-haired lady whose shape was something like a muffin, Mister Faulkner on occasion stopped by, but who could truly say where an odd duck of an artist came up with his titles? Why didn't we go ask at his house? Did we dare?

Rowan Oak, the name Faulkner gave to the antebellum home he restored at the edge of town (as it was then), looked like inspiration for the dust jacket of *The Mansion*. What's more, in the gloom under the big cedars he had planted and in the damp from the surrounding woods, the place gave off the aura of that novel. Our little tour was moving along as my innocence assumed it would. Any minute the door would open, the master would listen to our wish, would invite us onto the veranda for a glass of whiskey, and (seeing our passion) would listen with keen interest to our questions.

We knocked on the front door. We waited nervously. I reviewed my introduction. There came no answer. Thoughtless of any violation of privacy, we went around to a side entry and knocked again, louder. Ollie called out, "Anyone home?"

His interest already slackening, he suggested we come back later, so we headed out of town on a rusty-dust road into Lafayette County, past wooden barns and hardscrabble farms with tenant shacks propped up by poles like aged men leaning on canes. It was a land where an old way of living, like the buildings, was about to topple; the next year, the first Negro (as the term then was) would at last be admitted to the University of Mississippi lying just west of Faulkner's home place. By burning barns and cabins such as those, exploited sharecroppers had put the torch to the final days of a plantation system, and soon federal legislation would help do the same for an iniquitous class-system. If Faulkner's books depicted such arson, they ignored desegregation coming from the outside.

From those thinned and scattered woods—no longer forests—men, white and black, had exterminated bears and most of the indigenous peoples to leave a desolation only a desperate someone or an artist might productively use. That whole day, the filling-station map be damned, we traveled within Yoknapatawpha County, the place that didn't really exist.

In the evening we returned for fried chicken and corn bread at The Mansion, where we reported on our tour to a young waitress, Doris. She had heard of our quest from the breakfast lady and was amused that two boys would come so far just to see a writer. I think she liked our naive notion that we could "just waltz in and meet America's most famous author." Ollie suggested maybe we could hang out in the café until the master happened by. "Well," she said, "I guess I'm the one to disappoint y'all. Mister W. isn't here. He's in Charlottesville, Virginia, where he's teaching for a spell." Such a possibility had never crossed my mind. She added, tellingly dropping the second-person plural to singular as she looked only at Ollie, "I see you're real let down." She paused, then, "I'll tell you what, honey. You come around in the mornin. Bring him along if you want."

We went off to our quarters just down the hill and talked about my fatuous assumption. I tried to ease my disappointment by saying maybe Faulkner—the man—was in Virginia, but in many ways the writer was visible as all get-out right here in Mississippi—at least for someone who has *read* his books.

The next morning we returned to The Mansion and found Doris. When we'd finished breakfast she came over, sitting down beside me but again looking only at Ollie. Here I must reveal that under certain conditions he had a slight stammer which could become almost theatrical upon his meeting an attractive female, and then the breaks and following plosives got ratcheted up to deadly effect. Surely enough, it worked magically on Doris. After he mentioned we'd be heading back to Missouri, she nodded and went over to the counter and rummaged beneath for something and returned with a pocket-size paperback book. It was *Three Famous Short Novels*, a recent collection of Faulkner tales, including "The Bear," a tale I deeply esteemed, a story that made me want to be a writer. "You came so far," Doris said to Ollie, "and for what? Well, honey, here's a lil ol compensation." She handed him the book.

In disbelief I watched him flip it open to the title page. He read aloud the pinched handwriting, stammering only once or twice for her: "'To Doris Vance, William Faulkner, 23 March 1960.'" During all this, she never once looked at me. She said, "Mister W gave it to me one day as a tip. He watched his money. I'm bad, I suppose, but I haven't read it, and I guess I'm not likely to. If you ever meet him, don't tell on me." I was almost crazed to hold the book. Just touch it. Doris said to Ollie, "It's yours, honey. Take it along with you so you have something to show for your effort." Effort! *His* effort?

My interior voice was screaming: What's with this Ollie thing? He doesn't know William Faulkner from Wee Willie Winkie! He thinks "The Bear" is an animal! Hasn't read a word Faulkner wrote! I had to talk him into coming down here! I'm the one! I'm the one who reads Faulkner! Ollie doesn't care about that book! It'll be in tatters or lost before the year's out! I'm the one with the library! This is rank injustice! Doris! Can't you see?

What I actually said was only to ask him to let me look at it. Doris got up, patted him on the hand, *the one holding the book,* and said, "Honey, you keep yourself out of trouble, now." And that was it.

*　　*　　*

To Dani Vance
from William Faulkner
23 March, 1961

Three Famous
Short Novels

by

WILLIAM FAULKNER

William Faulkner

SPOTTED HORSES

OLD MAN

THE BEAR

MODERN LIBRARY
PAPERBACKS

PUBLISHED BY RANDOM HOUSE NEW YORK

We returned to our room to pack up, and already I was thinking how a college boy could easily disappear in these piney woods. There were a thousand places to hide a cadaver. The master knew how to get rid of a body. Hell, in one novel, he stuffed a corpse into the hollow of a dead tree. Ha! How about a stump for a college boy holding something not rightfully his?

Before we got our gear together the next morning, there was a knock on the door. Outside stood a small man, trim, dressed for a woods conceived by Abercrombie & Fitch. Almost dashingly, he leaned on a splendid walking stick of twists and gnarls.

"I'm Malcolm Franklin," he said. "Pappy's boy." Who? "Faulkner's stepson." Ollie had come up to look over my shoulder, but I skillfully blocked him from getting past me—just in case. Franklin said, "I hear you're wanting to see the real county." Whose real county? I thought. "If you have a car, we can take a look."

Franklin was thirty-six years old and, like his stepfather, of slight but wiry build. The family called him Mac. The next morning he took the wheel of my car, and we went off into wooded slopes that have, in Mississippi anyway, just enough rise to be called hills. The elevation of Carter Mountain, seven miles from Oxford, is 454 feet, the distance of a major-league home run. He said, "Pappy, of course, could tell you more than I can, but he wouldn't do it. He'd find your visit less than cordial. Even on a good day, he's indifferent to readers of his books. That's just not what he cares about. You'd be an annoyance." After a couple of warm and dusty miles, he added, "I've got less to tell, but I'll tell you all of it."

We drove the county up and down, Franklin pointing out locations linked with Faulkner's stories and sometimes giving his own relation to a place. Struggling to keep up, I took notes and snapshots where I could. He drove to the edge of the territory where "The Bear" is set, a holy land to me, although most of it now lay at the bottom of the dammed Tallahatchie River.

He introduced us to family—aunts, uncles, cousins of his stepfather—and in each of them I looked closely for any sign of William. Mostly they were amused and not surprised by Franklin's unannounced dropping in with a pair of callow, college boys, one of whom asked a few too many questions, but only an academic acquaintance of the master considered us dusty intruders and gave us short shrift. Possessed of the Southern capacity for stories, Franklin spoke of his stepfather honestly but without warmth. I surmised a friction, a pulling between them.

In the afternoon he turned down a wooded road and without explanation stopped my car. "Get out," he said. His jaw was set tight. As we opened the doors a bit uncertainly, I heard Ollie murmur, "I don't like this." Franklin motioned toward an old, broken trunk about nine feet high, hollow, but with a narrow opening. "Go squeeze into that stump," he said. Ideal, I thought. Hadn't I foreseen this? I tried to push Ollie forward, but he didn't budge. "Go ahead!" Franklin ordered. "One of you chickenhearts get in it!" So *I* had to. My shoulders scraped the interior, and the center of the doomed oak was cool and thick with dry decay, like an old root cellar. Franklin called into the hollow: "How is it? Just right for a dead man?" I asked why I was in there, and he said, "You asked about it. You wanted to see the real county. Pappy showed me this tree one night and told me he jammed a corpse in here years ago."

Ollie said, "Faulkner s-s-stuffed a corpse in there?" I said I thought I had the feel of it inside pretty well absorbed. When we were again in the car, I told Ollie about *The Hamlet*, where a murdered man gets hidden in a tree. "You got it," Franklin said. "I just played the role of Mink Snopes and you were the dead man, Jack Houston." Dead man? I thought. Perfect—unless he hands over that book.

We rolled on through the pines and rusted soil, past washed-out cotton fields and eroded hill farms, Franklin's commentary flowing almost without pause. Once the afternoon heat came on good, he wound us into a copse to a worn cabin, its paint sun-bleached here, peeled to bare wood there. In a metal lawn chair sat a man, grandly bellied, in bib overalls; he was about seventy years old. Franklin said to us, "Come meet Walter Miller. We call him Uncle Buddy."

Uncle Buddy? The one in several of Faulkner's stories? *That Uncle Buddy?* Miller said, "I don't know whether I'm him. Maybe I must be. I don't much take up with books, but Bill and the others, I know we all sure went out on enough coon hunts."

I felt I was standing in front of Huck Finn or Natty Bumppo.

Before us was a fellow who had gone into the night woods with his friends, one of whom was a young Bill Falkner before he changed the spelling of his name. Here was a man who had told stories while the fire sparked and dogs howled and the hunters raised tin cups of shine or, when a little more money was available, bootleg. Out of him and the others—farmers, merchants, a lawyer or two, ne'er-do-wells—from them had come tales that got turned into some of the grandest work in American literature. I was sitting at the feet of a source. For the first time, I heard within a phrase that to me would become a travel refrain: *It is for this I came.*

My questions poured out, and Uncle Buddy didn't resent my eagerness or curiosity. *Did Faulkner ever take notes around the campfire?* Wouldn't have dared. *Did he himself tell stories?* Once or twice. *He was a listener?* Mostly he was, yes. *Did he drink out there in the big woods?* The first time he did, he drank himself sick, and he later pledged he'd not do it again—on a hunt anyways—and he kept his word. Then Uncle Buddy added, "You won't find a gooder hunter or woodsman out here. I never had to go in after him."

I could see it: the jug going around, a small, sober man sitting and taking in the stories right with the baying of the hounds. From those hunters, some virtually illiterate, he filled himself with the land and its history and a hostility toward any parvenu Johnny-come-lately who arrived to dispossess the woods of almost all it held that was natural and genuine and good; he was standing ready to absorb the myth of the big woods to tell the story to the world, to turn the land into his real subject and make his protagonist what the land had been.

Uncle Buddy went into his cabin and returned with a couple of tin cups. "Afore ye go on," he said and nodded toward a rocky crevice in his hill from which a small spring seeped out to flow on down to Toby Tubby Creek. From that cleft Faulkner and the night hunters had pulled a thousand drafts, so we too dipped into the cool, kindly water, and Franklin drew a flask from his pocket and ameliorated our cups with a finger of bourbon, and Ollie—this time stammering in genuine emotion, "Boy, this is m-m-m-memorable!"

Before dusk, we drove back to Rowan Oak to see Faulkner's favorite—if skittish—horse. The animal trotted up, shook and snorted, and rolled its eyes and reared when I reached to stroke it, and it kicked at me, a hoof nicking my hand. "Beautiful trouble," Franklin said. A year later, a new horse equally fractious would throw Faulkner, and from that fall he would never recover.

Might we see the master's writing room? I'd heard he'd scrawled across a wall an outline for a chapter of a novel. "We better not," Franklin said. "It wouldn't be right, you know. He's not here. You can understand." It was the only request Malcolm declined.

At supper he explained about how he'd made his walking stick from an old huckleberry, giving details on the craft, then we returned to our room, and he came in for a nightcap, staying long, sipping his whiskey, talking, talking until Ollie fell asleep and I began nodding. Sometime around two in the morning I woke and found him gone. We didn't see him again.

A year later, before I went to sea, *Life* magazine reported on Faulkner's funeral, and in a photograph taken at the grave site there was Malcolm in a seersucker suit, his face more serene than I'd known it, comforting his mother, the master's wife. At first I thought my sorrow was for Faulkner, but then I realized it was something else: The chance to meet him face to face was now forever gone. How could we have come so close and missed?

In the years since, I've come not to count it a miss. We had been privileged to travel Yoknapatawpha County with a man who called the master Pappy, a fellow who also saw the land deeply entwined with stories and myth as did he who was never

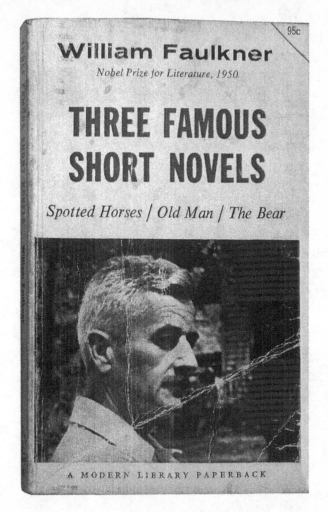

present to reveal to a young adulator flaws any man can be heir to. My perception was safe in imagination, my image pristine and unsullied by reality, a legend I could hold the rest of my life.

On our last evening together, I had become comfortable enough with Mac to ask what it was like to be William Faulkner's boy. After a long quiet and without further explanation he said only, almost inaudibly, "He's ruined me."

A CONDUCER

When the first editor of this story referred to it as a "memoir," I asked her to look at it more closely and choose another descriptive term, because a memoir so often lies centered inescapably on self. For several reasons, I have little interest in autobiography. The best memoirs, to my mind, are those reaching far enough beyond an author's life that they leave the genre altogether; like an innocent prisoner, they succeed when they escape confinement.

In my writing, as the narrator, I'm useful only as eyes and ears for the reader. I'm a mere conductor—not in the orchestral sense but rather in the electrical: a transmitter of sound, heat, light, and latent energy residing in people, places, events. Perhaps a better word is conducer, and what we have, when it works, is conduction.

Oysters and American Union

I have a penchant for trying to discover initiating causes, and although I believe beginnings are as infinite as their results, I nevertheless like to look for where and when something got started. Usually I trace a thing backward from effect to possible source. These last several days I've been hunting origins of my interest in roadways and connections, and yesterday it was as if I was again in Murphy's drugstore in Kansas City, Missouri, circa 1951, before me a chocolate ice-cream soda. Take away those basic ingredients—soda fountain, vanilla ice cream, chocolate syrup, and pressurized carbonated water—and I could readily have ended up nowhere near where or who I am now. Ruling out any endeavor requiring higher mathematical skills or daunting physical size, I might have found my way into almost any other location and another life: a clerk in Poughkeepsie, a teacher in Pocatello, a carpenter in El Paso.

My preferred seat at Murphy's soda fountain was nearest the large plate-glass window giving a wide view onto the intersection of Seventy-fifth Street and Troost Avenue. With a filled, footed soda-glass before me, I could take in events passing outside: my brother getting cuffed for a flirtation too forward, a distraught mother who had just dropped a glass jug of bleach and splattered her small and screaming son, the cocksure preacher failing to yield the right-of-way to the detriment of the grille of his Hudson.

One 1951 October afternoon, the streets empty as they rarely are now, I stared vacantly at the pavement of Troost Avenue which at that location was also U.S. Highway 71, the route from Rainy Lake on the Minnesota-Canadian border to the swamps of southern Louisiana. In a week, I was to leave with my parents on my first long road trip, a southbound one with me as navigator; having learned to read maps soon after I learned to read words, I considered myself qualified although innocent of actual over-the-road pilotage. In the midst of imagining our destination at New Orleans, I suddenly realized those concrete slabs of Troost were like a frozen river: They extended in a continuous if unmoving flow from where I sat all the way to the ferry landing on the Mississippi River at Baton Rouge about an hour northwest of New Orleans.

For a twelve-year-old unexpectedly to comprehend that Murphy's soda fountain belonged to a distant world of alligators—unseen but nevertheless there, like a character in a book I'd heard about but not read—was to reformulate my perception of American geography. Education and maturity, civilization and creation itself, depend on making connections. Eureka: Alligators lay outside that drugstore window just as did my bedroom, never mind the distance.

In those days it wasn't so easy to see a Louisiana alligator, and my lone disappointment of our journey was, disallowing those at the alligator farm, I didn't spot a single one in nature. But I did discover another ancient creature of Southern waters: a fresh oyster, shucked before my eyes and set out on the counter at a French Quarter oyster house. With boldness fortified by ketchup and horseradish, I nipped into one and was no longer just a kid from Kansas City—now I was on my way to becoming a citizen of America, for it was then and there I began a lifetime of conjoining places and people, accents and aromas, ice-cream sodas and seafood. Murphy's window, edged with gold letters promising SUNDRIES and PRESCRIPTIONS, was an opening to a nation linked by a federal highway where a wayfarer could find oysters and shrimp at one end and walleyes and pike at the other.

A year earlier, on Pelican Lake not far off U.S. 71 in upper Minnesota, my father and I pulled in one of each. Traveling the thousand miles between walleyes and oysters put in me a love of the American open road and its landscapes that eventually turned me from a traveler into a writer of travels.

A year ago I retraced a fair portion of another highway that passed near my boyhood home. The Old National Road ran from Atlantic City to St. Louis, and from there, under the newer name of U.S. 40, through Kansas City and on two thousand miles farther westward to San Francisco: the Boardwalk at one end and Golden Gate at the other and our kitchen table in the middle. Our house on Flora Avenue was at the center of a radiating web of exotic places: Longitudinally, latitudinally, diagonally, the links ran from moose to horned frogs, from longleaf pines to bristlecones. That simple discovery with its accompanying sense of belonging has held me in thrall ever since, and from it came a wish to memorize the face of America by visiting every American county, all three thousand and some of them, and to get within at least fifteen or twenty miles of everywhere, both slowly evolving quests that required fifty years to complete. (Well, I'm still working on that second phase.)

It's difficult to be an American today and be unaware of the significance of the Lewis and Clark Expedition that Thomas Jefferson dispatched to facilitate bringing much of the western half of the United States into a variegated union with the East — politically, strategically, culturally. But another Jeffersonian action to further union is less widely known than the name of Jefferson's second-term vice president. The earliest published account by a participant in the Lewis and Clark Expedition was still three years away when Jefferson's secretary of the treasury sent a report to Congress. Addressing the national necessity for good roads, Albert Gallatin in 1808 wrote, "No other single operation, within the power of the Government, can more effectively tend to strengthen and perpetuate that Union which secures external independence, domestic peace, and internal liberty."

I poked along the National Road and eventually reached its halfway point at Zanesville, Ohio, where once stood the National Hotel, a name presumably taken from the route at its front door. In 1831 the road had just been completed to that point when the proprietor, Colonel Henry Orndorff, saw an opportunity. Up till then, common fare in eastern roadhouses included pickled oysters eaten with buttered bread or crackers and sometimes accompanied by a side of pickled pigs' feet. Pickling, of course, was a substitute for refrigeration. The new highway, the colonel reasoned, could make it possible for Chesapeake oysters right from the bay — and unpickled — to reach Ohio. Orndorff rounded up enough wagons to haul the critters from Baltimore to Zanesville — and later on to towns farther west — in such abundance that his transport company became known as the Oyster Line.

Few things — perhaps no other — have served more to unite Americans than roads which allow us, whether we're aware of it

Highway 50 in central Nevada

or not, to feel that eating oysters in Zanesville helps us share a piece of national destiny with tongers on the Chesapeake. Perhaps I'm thinking this because soon after visiting Zanesville I stopped for gasoline along Route 40 in Somerset County, Pennsylvania, not far from Shanksville on the tenth of September 2001. A few miles distant from the National Road lay the grassy field where the fourth hijacked airplane in the September aerial attacks, the flight that didn't reach its target, came down. In a way televised pictures or printed words never could, my physical passage through that landscape allowed me the next day to imagine with clarity an aspect of those dark final moments.

The pavement of our highways is more than just concrete—it is also the cement of our national culture. Without the topographical communications that allow and encourage us to meet each other directly and indirectly, whether on my territory or yours, the Constitution would be little more than a theoretical document of a lost history. We have a commonweal and a shared destiny because we can *reach* each other; we can meet face to face: the Texans (*Pass the pepper sauce, please*) sitting across the table from the Oregonian introducing them to Yaquina Bay oysters; the Arizonan (*May I stand you another round?*) explaining to Michiganders why the bed of the Salt River is dry. When such interchanges occur, we continue our perpetual forging of nationhood. Through transport we transform political theory and national history—a meal into a memory, a conversation into a concept—and we become Americans linked into union not just gustatorily but also intellectually, emotionally, spiritually.

It's a commonplace to say that no one can interpret America without understanding our use of automobiles, but I think what we really mean is that one doesn't comprehend the United States without taking into account our *mobility,* and preeminently that means roadways, perhaps the most American of symbols, one even more functionally representative than the Statue of Liberty or Mount Rushmore. We are a widely dispersed and numerous people bound together by three million miles of painted stripes atop concrete and asphalt. The ancient Egyptians didn't invent the pyramid although it's the emblem of their desert kingdom; and we invented neither the highway nor the automobile, yet within living recall of our eldest citizens, those paired pieces of engineering—for better and for worse—have put their mark on us because they remade us as soon as we made them and began to use them to find our way onto our land, into our own selves, and unto each other. After all, beyond everyone's street, somewhere between the oysters in Chesapeake Bay and those in Yaquina Bay, on three-hundred-million little shores and intersections reside fellow citizens.

YUCATÁN

A few months after my trip into the backcountry of Japan, I went into a remoteness in the Yucatán Peninsula. Accompanied by a Maya named Berto who in several ways reminded me of my Japanese interpreter, Tadashi Sato, I again found friendship that entered the story. Both Berto and Tadashi, small men agile in mind and body, interpreted far more than just words: Their presence shaped each narrative in ways past ready explanation.

For a reason I can't recall, I did something in "The Nose of Chaac" I now avoid unless there is a compelling rationale: I set the story in the present tense which, in a travel account, I've come to consider a mark of amateurism, perhaps because the first draft of Blue Highways *was eight hundred typed pages of present tense before I dumped it in the third version. Well, I've dumped it again, appropriately, I believe, since the events here happened almost thirty years ago.*

The Nose of Chaac

It was mid-March, and the place was Santa Elena on the Mexican peninsula of Yucatán, nine miles southeast from the grand Mayan temples at Uxmal. My Mayan friend and guide, Ahau-Kin-May-Dzul, called Berto, and I were standing on a rocky road in a village of only a half-dozen lanes, none paved. A domesticated turkey, still sporting wild featherage, had just chased an iguana up a lemon tree and was gobbling either in frustration or exultation. Other animals—roosters, chickens, pigs, a donkey—were sounding out the notes of the national anthem of the third world. A villager burned leaves, the smoke carrying a tinge of banana oil. The family gardens there grew bananas, papayas, lemons, limes, and bitter oranges. An hour earlier, watching a man climb a papaya tree to chop out leaves for his pig snorting below as it shook them from its back to eat, I had trouble believing that Brownsville, Texas, lay only six-hundred air miles distant.

We were in Santa Elena, an important place in the Mayan uprising of the past century, because my wish to see something genuine of Mayan life had been almost extinguished a day earlier at Uxmal. I'd overlooked the detritus of tourism: film wrappers, beverage cans, fouled diapers, and human excrement in the temple rooms. But, after dark, the famed sound-and-light show with its overripe voices of canned drama about Indian stereotypes and its overwrought choral music overwhelmed any classic Mayan traditions to leave me with only what I already had: secondhand knowledge of those small people who built so large and lastingly.

I hadn't really come in search of monuments or a pre-Columbian populace but rather for expressions of both that were yet alive. I asked Berto whether any such presence remained. "Tomorrow," he said, "we go to a village where Mayas live and still are coming to *templos*—no—temples for real ceremonies when tourist people are away. If you see my people there, maybe you see different."

So, that morning I was seeing Mayas who happen to be Mexicans only by historical chance. Like those almost pure-blood villagers, Berto had a marvelously classic nose that seemed to start at midbrow and curve down like a palm frond to near his upper lip. I'd thought profiles such as his existed only in the Mayan codices where the faces are so different from the fierce and grimacing visages of the ancient Aztecs to the west. A compact, nimble man, Berto was forty-two and unmarried. Yesterday he said cryptically, "I am a wind." When he named things, he gave me first the Yucatec Mayan word, then the Spanish, then the English, only occasionally hunting the right term.

Santa Elena, in low jungle growth, sat at the foot of a hill surmounted by a cathedral. From the dusty plaza, steps cut into a living rock ledge led to the church, a worn limestone building of the eighteenth century. Growing in the step crevices were cardo santo plants with roots, when pulverized, that make a purge for stomach ailments, a remedy passed down from the ancient people. Here also grew Santa Maria, an herb to treat fevers. Beside the church, formerly also a small fortress, once stood a monastery, but only crumbling walls remained. Berto pointed to the cathedral: "Many stones come from a Mayan temple that was long ago on this hill." He regretted the destruction, yet to him, the broken stones imparted an additional dimension to the church because ancient Mayas usually did not destroy an earlier structure, instead building over it to layer meaning and power. Some archaeologists believe Mayas were motivated by superstition,

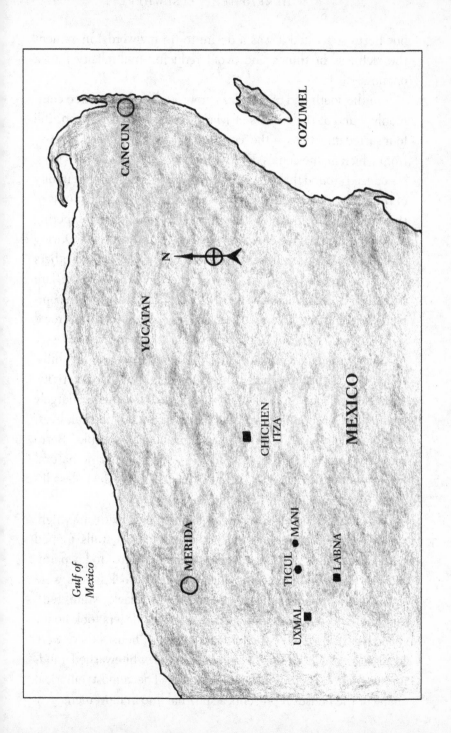

but Berto suggested it was a desire to (in my words) increment the richness of things and avoid reducing multiplicity into a oneness.

On the south end of the plaza grew a tall ceiba, the tree commonly found at the corners of Mayan village plazas to honor the four sacred directions—the "cosmical points" Berto called them—from which all life comes. Every third week in January, the villagers danced around that ceiba in a ceremony to ensure the fecundity of the fields and people. I couldn't comment on the fruitfulness of the land, but to judge by the number of children scampering about, the old rites were working well on the human side. During the dance, several men carry pig heads on trays while four others circle the tree as they pluck live turkeys; when the birds are defeathered, the dancers wring the necks. If a man fails to complete the plucking before the ceremony ends, a scornful crowd will beat him on the head with the bald if still-living turkey.

Later, villagers will go off into the *monte bajo*, the low hills, to make offerings to Chaac, the deity of rain and productivity. Because the Yucatán is virtually riverless, and rainfall is largely seasonal, Chaac moves at the heart of their spiritual lives. "Without right mentality, it is easy to misjudge my people," Berto said. "We are not worshipping idols—we are honoring natural force—energy." Indeed, it seemed villagers took Chaac less literally than they did painted saints in churches.

We walked down the rocky lanes lined with hip-high, stacked-stone fences—clearly not the defensive walls topped with broken glass of Mexican cities, but enclosures to keep animals in rather than anything out. Behind the rock fences were family plots of corn, squash, melons, beans (black, white, red), and fruit and nut trees, and from the hills, villagers took honey made from blossoms of the tajonal tree. Most houses there were in classic Mayan design: small ellipses of whitewashed mud-and-wattle walls, roofs of palm thatch. The almost elliptical shape of the houses represents a spiritual line in movement:

The figure is an old notion that reminds Mayas of the turning of seasons and of life itself. Even the famous Temple of the Sorcerer at Uxmal, one of the purest examples of the regional Puuc style, is an architecturally rare, nearly elliptic pyramid. But Santa Elena now had several newer, square houses of concrete blocks. One old man earlier said to me, "In them there is no power." Explaining, his fingers circumscribed an ellipse in the air.

Each house, with floors of concrete or packed and swept earth, contained but a single room about eight-by-twelve feet; typically, several houses clustered around an open-sided cooking hut. The only furniture was a table, a few straight chairs, and hammocks — if hammocks are furniture; no one had a mattress-spring bed. Most homes had a television, many an electric sewing machine, some a stereo, a few automatic washers. I saw no refrigerators, electric ranges, or telephones. Scarcely anyone owned an automobile. Looking past electrical lines running into the houses, I was in a Mayan village the conquistadors might have encountered.

Like the ancient pyramids in Yucatán, Santa Elena was more overlaid than assimilated, and Hispanic culture there seemed only to be pausing because villagers accepted Western ways selectively and somewhat superficially: electricity, a church, and, to a degree, a language. They had not forgotten their old tongue, deities, or dances. Beneath the layers, the Mayan presence waited, a fertile garden under a long winter.

The spring day warmed, and the people took to the dim cool of their huts to sway silently in hammocks and so move the air, but for us, we walked to the Tienda de la Esperanza, the Shop of Hope, for a cool drink. We passed only a girl bearing on her head a bag of cornmeal from which her mother would make *keyen*, a kind of fermented mush. The girl's blue eyes were striking against her dark skin. Berto pointed upward. "Kukulcan, the first Mayan god, he came from another place. His blue eyes he left among a few of us. Maybe a reminder. Yesterday leaves reminders, don't you think so?"

The uncultivated portions around the houses were gravel and dirt and sometimes glinted with twenty-centavo pieces, coins so worthless even children did not gather them. Villagers commonly laid down a threshold of bright ceramic tiles, but at one house the entry step was of worn and rounded stones which Berto pointed to: "These ones are from a lost *templo*. Do you see the design? It is nose of Chaac." He drew in the dust the rain god's long and upwardly curving proboscis that's more akin to an elephant trunk than a human nose. That Mayan design, like the old houses and the temple at Uxmal, describes a virtual ellipse.

But wasn't a step made from a deity's face a desecration? "If the face is pieces," Berto said, "then it is only rock again. We honor the energy, the circling power inside." I bent to touch the broken nose smoothed by bare feet of our time but quarried by hands centuries gone. "You like Chaac," Berto said. "Maybe you are a worshipper of secrets in stones."

The Shop of Hope was shut down as was its promise of a cold beverage. Berto recommended going on to the town of Ticul to get a café meal before returning at sunset to keep his appointment with a *h'men* — that is, loosely translated, a medicine man who would try to ease pain in Berto's shoulder.

A sign along the road forbade leaving rocks on the pavement. That stony region of Yucatán was the Puuc ("hills") where the soil showed a deep orange. Although the route to Ticul cut mostly through low jungle, we saw occasional fields of sisal, once the crop of the region but now largely done in by plastic fiber.

Miles distant from their villages, men pedaled bicycles along, their backs slung with fagots of firewood or sugarcane or a rifle to hunt deer, turkeys, robins, and iguanas. Exposing themselves for a sunning, the big lizards made an easy target. One even sat boldly on the crossbar of a telephone pole, and Berto said, "His time will be short." I asked what a hunter did with a dead iguana, and Berto smiled. "Good for to eat." Abruptly, from the middle of the warm pavement, an oil stain rose, got legs, and walked to the shoulder. I stared in disbelief. "Tarantula," he said. "We don't eat him."

In Ticul we stopped at Café Los Almendros and went out back to wash off the dust from our arms and faces, then took a table by the air conditioner. To the machine Berto whispered, "*Gracias*, Ik." Ik is the god of winds. "First beer for thirst," Berto said, "second for digestion." The meal was *botanas*, small plates and bowls of various things. As we emptied one dish, the waiter brought another of something else: venison strips marinated in radish and coriander, spiced boiled eggs, black-bean soup seasoned with bitter orange, all of it accompanied by olives, spiced cucumbers, tortillas, and a salsa smelling like a blossom and tasting like hot smoke from a pistol barrel. With the last plate empty, Berto called for an iced pitcher of *horchata*: pounded rice, sugar, and cinnamon in water. I asked if *botana* didn't refer to a plug to stopper something, and Berto nodded: "The empty stomach, it must be plugged, and then it stops making noise."

The *h'men* we returned to see was a field-worker who also conducted rain and planting ceremonies. *H'men* literally means "doer-undoer," as in doing what needs doing and undoing what needs undoing. Berto's ache needed undoing. To me, the treatment sounded like sorcery, and to that he answered, "I am always trying to know things—not believe things. But with a *h'men*, it works better believing than knowing."

In the dusky streets of Santa Elena, from around a stone wall, a cluster of blue specters suddenly loomed before us, and we both recoiled. Four girls, faces painted deep azure for a purification rite, were on their way to a fiesta. Berto was happy because their presence created a good aura for the *h'men*, whose dark hut happened to stand just behind the little specters. After disappearing inside, Berto came back out to invite me to watch—*if* I would keep silent about what would occur. So the *h'men* had requested. "I have luck today," Berto said. "First, the blue girls, and now Tuesday—it's good for, in your word, sorcery."

In the early afternoon two days later we drove to Labna, a small Mayan ruin relatively few travelers visited. On the road, we saw only one other car, an old smoking Dodge so full of people that the last two passengers huddled in the opened trunk. Once arrived, we followed a trail into a thick growth, past the hut of a family earning a few pesos from overseeing the Labna temples and from expertly carving cedar bas-relief images taken from the Mayan pantheon. Through a wood of bitter-orange trees and pitya cacti that yielded a good fruit, we wound our way in until the path turned from under the shade of large elephant's-ear trees (so named for the pods) into an opening of hot sun, and there Berto said, "Here is many wonderful things." Labna was a place of collapse with no colossal pyramids, no high temples, no reconstructions, nothing but desolate, stone ruins, many of them still suggesting an image of what they once had been.

Travelers in the Yucatán, if they persist, may come upon a monument to fulfill a particular historical imagination. From the side of a caved-in cistern grew a ramon tree, its twisted trunk greater than my outspread arms. Berto surmised that ramon

Frederick Catherwood's 1841 illustration of Labna

seeds once were stored in the cool cistern where somehow a sprout found a home in a cranny. On the north side of Labna lay long, low rows of small and windowless stone vaults, the unmortared joints precisely fitted, the facades incised with suns and moons and lattices of "cosmical points," every corner hung with long Chaac noses cut and carved from limestone fresh from the quarry before the exposure to air hardened it. Some of the buildings had collapsed into undifferentiated heaps, and others were so far gone they were just scrubby mounds protected from the elements by brushy leaves whose roots had found a way into crevices, undoing the preservation.

In the mid-nineteenth century, the American traveler and father of Mayan archaeology, John L. Stephens, with artist-draftsman Frederick Catherwood explored deeply into the overgrown peninsula and brought to light places unknown to all but the Mayas themselves. His *Incidents of Travel in Yucatan* describes an arrival that could have been exactly ours a century-and-a-half later:

We took another road and, emerging suddenly from the woods, to my astonishment we came at once upon a large open field strewed with mounds of ruins, and vast buildings on terraces.

At the top of one vault, an iguana lay warming itself and pumping its head and swallowing but roused itself from a half-doze to keep watch on the intruders. The sun was strong in heat and light, yet a clearing flashed full of winged motion — butter-flies, swallows, and a motmot, the bird whose froglike cry can lead a Maya to find a source of water. We stepped into a dank and dusky corbeled vault to sit and cool down as Berto lamented lacking both water and the toughness of an iguana.

Reviving before I did, he stood and walked across the clearing silenced by the heat. From the far trees came a high and wavering whistle, a pause, then again the thirteen notes in the pentatonic scale of the Indians of the Americas, a haunting minor-key melody. Unexpectedly, improbably, a breeze rose and rattled the dry pods on the elephant's-ear trees, and pushed into the vault a draft that circled as if to embrace me. Another thirteen notes, and once more the air moved. I had read about sha-mans in many lands who can whistle up a wind, but never before had I witnessed it, yet there it was.

When I joined Berto under the trees I asked had he made the melody, and he whistled the eerily bewitching run of notes, and again came a puff of wind. I thought he must have some capacity to sense an approaching breeze, and he said, "Do you think this is sorcery too?" I asked him to do it again, but he said only, "Very old Mayan song. *Muy antigua.* The words say, 'Come, Ik, come. Come, wind, come.'" In the hot dust he traced a pair of figures I'd seen many times in the past few days:

"*Vientos,*" he said. "Wind symbols. Labna is a place of winds." He pointed to a broken tower atop a high mound: "Wind observatory for the ancients." How does one, I asked, observe wind? And why? "Priests were climbing the tower for to feel wind with their faces," he said. "The wind tells the rains is coming and the direction they have."

West of the observatory stood the monumental arch of Labna inset with ornamentations. In its walls, more than ten centuries old, were depictions in relief of the huts like those at Santa Elena because *Labna* likely means "old houses." Nearby, Berto pointed to where once a pair of limestone figures had sat, both now stolen. "That is change that does us no good."

On the way back to the road, we passed a small line of rock cylinders rising from the red soil. One, a thirty-inch phallus, was remarkably like ancient fertility sculptures I'd seen in the backcountry of Japan, but the carvings here belonged to Chaac because he too is a force of fertility. Berto, perhaps thinking of his comment about the missing pair at the gate, said, "To disappear can also mean to be ready to be born one more time."

That night the birds of the *monte bajo* threw their weird cries into the dark like sharpened blades until the dawn came on more melodiously but with no less volume. We rose and followed a long and rough road through a jungle hung with the drooping conical nests of the yuya bird, and kept on course by asking directions at every crossroad. Often we stopped the car to roll rocks out of the way or into a hole to aid passage. Berto's shoulder pain had eased, and he happily reminded me that a Tuesday was usually good for sorcery, especially when it's blessed by children painted blue.

By early afternoon we arrived in Mani, a village settled a thousand years ago, before the fall of Uxmal and Chichén Itzá. At Labna, Berto had said as he waved toward the ruins, "For these I'm very proud for my people." But in living Mani, a quiet came over him, almost a sorrow. *Mani* likely means either "without a nose," perhaps a reference to a desecrated Chaac, or "it is finished." The village appears Hispanic in layout and only lightly touched by the Mayan past even though Berto assured me the ancient life was there yet. "Of course," he said, "many things are lost because the Spanish, *los conquistadores,* tried to change our mentality." Holy missionary fathers came and tortured and hanged Mayan priests, and Father Diego de Landa burned more than men here: He also destroyed artifacts and twenty-seven Mayan hieroglyphic rolls, historical resources of immeasurable significance. Then, as if to atone, he wrote a rich account about Mayan life, *Report of the Things of Yucatan,* and today the people revile him for what he destroyed and praise him for what he preserved, whatever its bias.

His presence remained beyond mere memory, Berto believed. I asked where, and he led me toward the large seventeenth-century cathedral, a stucco-covered limestone building made distinctive by nearly two dozen colonial arches along its front with many more inside. To reach the church portal we had to walk through a children's baseball game on the worn lawn where straying animals made it appear the second baseman was a pig and the left fielder a turkey.

Near the great wooden sanctuary doors, a schoolgirl sat carving a Mayan deity from soft stone with her barrette. I turned down her offer to sell the unfinished idol but asked would she draw a long-nosed Chaac in my notebook for the same price. She paused, perhaps to consider whether she was stealing, then went to work with much concentration. She signed her drawing: *graciana queme tún.*

graciana queme tún

Connected to the big sanctuary was a building of old frescoes faded nearly to nothing and a courtyard protecting a large, stone turtle with the head of a jaguar. "Everything is not yet all passing away," Berto said. "This *tortuga*—no—this turtle is my people still remembering this ancient figure for water." Upstairs, in a vaulted dormitory dusted with decayed stucco, Father Landa had lived. Across one corner, beside an arched portal, were two wooden wall pegs weathered to fragility; from them the missionary had hung his hammock for a year, and in those bare pegs his presence was starkly present.

The sanctuary contained a large, blockish Jesus with feet made broad by much working and walking, like those of a barefooted Maya. That stone Christo was a Mayan fieldhand with an Amerind curve to his eyes and a sparse, almost Asian, beard; he was a worker who understood toil and dance more than suffering and godliness.

Outside, three young women who had been mopping dust from the sanctuary tiles called out a Spanish flirtation to Berto: "Look at us, little *señor!*" His answer in Mayan surprised them to momentary silence, then they responded in timid Yucatec. He asked what they knew of Fray Landa, and one said *"¡Malo!"* and another, *"Sí, muy malo,"* and the third, the youngest, chanting, *"¡Malo, malo, malo!"* The eldest, a coin tucked into the top of her blouse, said almost reluctantly she once saw him when others were afraid to look. Those were the nights he came to the big ceiba tree by the cenote. His clothes were white, and his hair untied and it blew, and he never said even a word, and everybody ran from him, the men faster than the women. Berto suggested the holy father was seeking forgiveness. She shrugged and went silent. Loose talk could bring misfortune.

As we went on, the young women again called out taunting coquetries. Berto whistled the thirteen-note wind-song in hopes Ik would lift the girls' white cotton dresses. "They would like that," he said, "because then it is not their doing." We stopped to watch. The air remained still, and Berto tried again, and nothing happened but another come-hither from the girls. "Ik, he knows naughty sorcery." We moved on and passed a boy trying to run aloft a newspaper kite the size of my hand. Berto whistled the melody—twice—and up the kite went only to take a sharp nosedive just like the Mayan gods when they came from the skies to earth headfirst, plunging into this our existence. "For Christians," he said, "gods descend like down a stair, but our ancient ones, they fall into us."

We stopped under Father Landa's immense ceiba that appeared to grow directly from a massive rock plate. A spirit might well select that tree because ceibas are sacred and that one grew above an equally sacred cenote, a deep limestone spring at the heart of the village. Its curving, natural tunnel was mossy, damp, and the downward stone path slick from a thousand years of bare feet; down it went, remarkably down, to the water. At the cool bottom, the spring flowed clear, but around it, beneath the hanging bats, lay old shards of earthen pots. Berto thought they were not litter but gifts from the people who built Uxmal. "That's the reason they stay here."

Five days earlier, when we stood on the steep and gusty top of the Pyramid of the Sorcerer at Uxmal, Berto said for him the pyramid was a "receiver of energy" like other receptors: a threshold made from the curving nose of Chaac, the shape of a house, a stone gateway, a subterranean pool of ancient offerings. In rocks plain and carved, broken and entire, lay energy from what had long been Mayan, what will be Mayan, all of it attached to the earth and its fragments—some visible, much invisible, but none of it gone.

BEYOND CROSS-
PURPOSES

It may be presumptuous and even—to certain natives on both sides of the state line—offensive for a Missourian to write about Kansas, especially to interpret and, in a way, commemorate it. After all, the states began their entwined history with bloodshed now often considered the first drawn in the Civil War. For that reason, among others, I think an interstate sharing of interpolations is beneficial and conducive to improved understanding, and I hope a good-hearted Kansan someday will reciprocate for those of us living just east of that once internecine border.

Crossing Kansas

The memory of my first witnessing the Great Kansas Passage has, like an old sock, a hole or two in it now, but the shape and texture are still recognizable. That initial occurrence happened in late July of 1947, a warm early evening of cicadas chirring out their sharp-edged presence in the vaulted branching of the elms along the street. At that time, the Second World War had not been over long enough for people to cease speaking of it, especially on evenings like that one when the steady and pleasing rhythms of the neighborhood seemed to remind men of what, for almost half the decade, they had relinquished. When the husbands and fathers and uncles stood in the glow of their cigarettes near the corner streetlamp while they talked and watched the living-room lights come on up and down the block like signals from one station to another, I think they were taking the compass of what they believed—or hoped—they'd fought for. The children sat curbside and waited for the dusk to yield to a good cover of dark before beginning a game of kick-the-can. On such an evening, I saw the Great Kansas Passage begin in a next-door driveway.

The neighbors stood in the laughter and completions of their good-byes to friends from Scranton, Pennsylvania; the visitors were reciting their route, trying to foresee vexations and detours, readying themselves to press on into the last leg of their journey, that final segment from Kansas City, Missouri, to Colorado Springs. After arriving stiff in the knees and weary in the eyes the night before, they had rested most of the day. Now, from the street corner, the children and men observed the Easterners prepare their Pontiac for the westward traversing. At the passenger-side window hung a newfangled tubular device with a concave opening on the front end that made the machine look like a small jet engine. But the contraption did not produce thrust or heat; rather, in the days before refrigerant air conditioners, it supposedly created cool air. The thing worked by drawing in wind over wet filters and throwing a damp breeze into the car. We had heard that, on the desert, the coolers helped, but in humid summers of the middle latitudes, the machine turned a car interior into a place suitable for growing ferns and mosses.

That evening, the Pennsylvanian driver poured water into the cooler, then moved to the front of the car, where he hung twin canvas waterbags from the heavy chrome bumper (those were the days, of course, when items *could* be hung not only from bumpers but from door handles, grilles, trunk latches, hood ornaments; the traveler never lacked a protuberance to tie down a loose line or affix a wet swimsuit). Every now and then, the waterbags oozed a drip, thereby cooling themselves on the same principle as the evaporative unit at the window. The Easterner had already mounted a large sun visor above the windshield. We watched the last of the loading: two Thermos bottles of water and a metal cooler—the kind that left a square of rust over whatever it sat on—printed in the Scotch plaid of the Stuart clan. Clearly, he thought the family ready to *cross Kansas.*

The travelers had waited out the sun and now, with the last of the dusk, they were fixed to take off, to drive—appropriately—through the old Oregon and Santa Fe Trails' jumping-off place called Westport, to pass over the Missouri line, and then, already sogging in the damp air, the waterbags oozing, the speedometer locked down (as best one could on two-lane roads) at seventy or eighty, the darkness protecting them, their cache of sandwiches secured in the backseat, and, finally, they would begin to *cross Kansas*.

"Are you set, Marie?" the man asked his wife. He spoke in the tone Magellan may have used when he was ready to hoist sail in Seville to begin his great circumnavigation. She nodded grimly, her mouth pinched closed. They climbed aboard. She knew they were about to leave the elm-lined streets of Kansas City; she understood between them and the cool and forested altitudes of Colorado lay that great historic rectangle of discomfiture, a mythic expanse of national character-testing, a place that had done in pioneers by the thousands, a treeless, flattened, featureless, godforsaken, overheated, numbing 82,264 square miles called Kansas. After all, Marie had seen the Westerns and had heard the stories. She worked her Dentyne with a D-Day ferocity. She knew the time had come at last for her to *cross Kansas*.

They disappeared into the night as they headed toward U.S. Highway 40: Topeka, Junction City, Salina, Hays, Wakeeney, Oakley, and, if all went well, the blessed western state line. There would also be Tonganoxie, Terra Cotta, Black Wolf, Yocemento, Hog Back, and Voda, but they knew that—at least for outsiders— Kansas was a place only to pass through, a place to keep moving in and thereby lessen the chances of a mechanical or a spiritual breakdown. Whatever Zeandale, Moonlight, Hyacinth, Vesper, Smolan, Munjor, or Milberger might offer them, they would never discover. In Kansas you didn't monkey around: You just drove and drove and drove ever farther, and you drove fast, and you drove at night, and you understood during all those long hours your sole purpose in life was to escape, to get out alive.

The Pennsylvanians didn't mind driving hard or being driven hard by fears and preconceptions. After all, everybody crossed Kansas that way because everybody "knew" the least which could happen was getting trapped in monumental dullness. And wasn't it a tidy and sanity-saving fact of topography that if crossers left Kansas City at sundown and held to seventy-some miles an hour and kept bladder relief to a minimum, they could reach the Rocky Mountains in time to turn around and look out the rear window to see the sun begin its own zillionth half-hour-long crossing of Kansas? The travelers would learn the only thing, ignoring numbness, to temper the joy and relief at having crossed was knowing home now lay in the opposite direction, back on the other side of the state, and the return trip loomed like an appointment for a root canal.

We people of the Missouri border became accustomed to these passages and the elaborate mental and mechanical preparations they brought forth. I don't remember any of us ever telling Easterners—or Californians, for that matter—that we ourselves crossed Kansas in the summer with only the windows rolled down and a stop now and then for a cold bottle of Grapette. They would never have believed we made the journey armed with only common sense based on experience; rather, they'd have thought us self-mortifiers like pilgrims who follow the Stations of the Cross up the hill on their knees, where the goal is not travel but penance.

We state-liners also grew used to the reports outstate travelers gave after their Kansas crossing, accounts describing a grim land tediously flat. None of us challenged the notion of coastal people who concluded Kansas has all the depth and fascination of a highway center line. Because we were Missourians, we had no obligation to defend our neighbor (historically, the two states have gotten along like the Hatfields and the McCoys, Popeye and Bluto); but even in our silence before purblind Bostonians or New Yorkers or San Franciscans, we understood that they knew nothing about Kansas except the driving time.

I should qualify such a generalization: A Virginian once asked me, "When I go through Kansas next month, will I be near Dorothy's house?" I asked who Dorothy was. "The one in the

tornado. The one with the Wizard. The little gal on her way to
Oz." In another time, such as that often passed for outstate
knowledge of Kansas. But recently I got corrected: I mentioned
to a man (one widely termed here "an old boy") that I'd heard
Dorothy's house existed beyond the imaginary, and he said,
"Oh, hell yes. Somebody went and done it. Built her a place."
America: Where overnight fantasy becomes fact.

Today, so many years after my first witnessing the Annual Summer Crossing Event, I see those passages differently. The preparations of the Pennsylvanians, although mostly needless, weren't
as purely ludicrous as I once thought. Whether they knew it or
not, the piling of equipment and gumption and determination
was part of the very purpose of their vacation. What they wanted
almost as much as the Colorado mountains was that dreaded
Kansas planogram itself. They subconsciously wished for a genuine American pioneer experience, a trial to approximate the
grand nineteenth-century migrations that shaped the country, a
piece of history that has come almost to define America. What
the couple from Scranton desired was westering. Within their
easy comforts and switched-on atmosphere, they wanted participation in the danger and mystery of crossing a portion of what
was once known as the Great American Desert. Those people
wanted, within a huge margin of safety, to enter a history which
here happens to be in Kansas. They hoped for immersion in a
historical reality, and they longed to touch something elemental
if for no other reason than to give counterpoint to the picture-
postcard realm of the Front Range of the Colorado Rockies.
Entrepreneurial developers would, by the next decade, recognize that urge and build theme parks: Six Flags over Polyvinyl
Historyland. Instead of snickering at the vacationers, I should
have perceived their authentic longing to turn four hundred
miles of Kansas pavement into the Santa Fe Trail.

But an Easterner's nervous anticipations and preparations were nearly pointless because crossing Kansas in 1947 just wasn't that difficult any longer. Yes, one might encounter a surly pump attendant, a sour waitress, or a sheriff's deputy looking for his quota; but with a full tank, good tires, and a strong bladder, one need scarcely set a foot down *into* Kansas. And, unless the crossing was at night, it truly was difficult even to imagine the region as a grand plain beset with hostile and horsed red men; to do so required the specter of darkness when anything could be lurking beyond the narrow reach of the sealed-beam headlights. Then, with fields of corn and wheat, courthouse towers and church steeples, chicken houses and privies obscured in the conquered land, an outstater could envision—from behind the tinted Saf-T-Glas—dried-up water holes, Comanches, bison skulls, the yellow gleam of prairie-wolf eyes, and death—or its promise—everywhere.

It was those night crossings that eventually turned Kansas from a region curious and well formed into a conquered land more presupposed than perceived; to the nation beyond, Kansas became a preconception and thereby a misconception. Passages in darkness put a lie on the face of a historic land of hills, trees, prairies, streams, weird stone outcroppings, and hundreds of villages promising (and often delivering) good fried chicken and milk shakes. The mythic Kansas of our time became a distortion even more removed from reality than the Kansas of nineteenth-century myths. When the vacationers returned to our street at sunrise two weeks after their first crossing, they had become "authorities" on the country between the Rockies and the great eastern bend of the Missouri River. They would say, "Nothing out there." (At better than a mile a minute, a rider on a moonless night truly can approximate an encounter with nothingness.) They would grumble, "It's so flat." (A dark highway has no hills.) "So boring," they would crab. "Thank heavens for the Burma-Shave signs!" (Travelers see what they're educated to see.)

*   *   *

I've heard that some natives actually encouraged nocturnal passages in order to keep the state hidden from a coastal America that has long been packing people in tighter and tighter, but Kansans saw no cause for worry since it has always taken a bold person to give up the comforting confines of a city for the unnerving openness of the Great Plains. The kindest remark about the region I ever heard from a New Yorker was "There sure is a lot of air out there." Indeed, it's a fact of history that the massiveness of air, sky, and horizon also disturbed the first settlers who quickly found themselves longing for the protective enclosures of forest.

A few years ago, a Kansas friend, Fred Miller, picked up two college boys from East Orange, New Jersey, who were thumbing their way to San Francisco. Between Topeka and Paxico the conversation became spirited, so much so that one of the hitchhikers made a predictable comment about Kansas topography. Fred, who rarely sneers or hurries a rebuttal, asked, "Do you have a couple hours to waste on Kansas?" He turned off the four-lane

Chase County, Kansas

highway and headed transverse to the usual route of outstaters; he showed them Kansas longitudinally instead of latitudinally, and he presented them the country in the clean light of an early autumn morning. He has yet to divulge that route to me, but when the tour was almost over, one of the thumbers said, echoing Dorothy's now-classic comment when she and her canine arrive on the other side of the rainbow, "Toto, I don't think we're in Kansas anymore." But the New Jersey lads were indeed in Kansas and had been the whole time. When they got out and thanked Fred—as penitents, he claims—he answered that the best way to thank him was never to mention the truth of the land they had just seen and to keep spreading the word that Kansas is the billiard table of the gods.

Fred now says he's sorry he let his chauvinism get the better of his judgment, and he wishes he'd kept a few cats in the bag, but his response, historically viewed, is quite that of the ancient Quiviran Indians who did nothing so well as to convince Coronado that golden cities lay on beyond the horizon—maybe on over there by East Orange—and thereby earn themselves another couple of hundred years' reprieve from the horrific onslaught of culture from the Old World. Fred, by the way, denies in the face of evidence of some substance that he once wrote the Kansas legislature to suggest a new state motto—just don't hide it in Latin: *Colorado is thataway.*

Not every Kansan, I assume, agrees with Fred's Quiviran concept of improving the territory. Even though I confess a sympathy with the view, as a writer I must try to speak the truth of a place. So, what is the truth of Kansas? Let me begin with what everyone "knows": Kansas is flat, flat, flat. No, no, no. While one might describe with accuracy the horizon in the Kansas west of the hundredth meridian as smooth and unbroken, regular and apparently level, in truth, Kansas is marvelously tilted; that's how the Colorado Rockies can make their slow way, granule by eroded granule, eastward to end up in the Gulf of Mexico. A billiard table, perhaps, but if (on the western border) you were to whack a cue ball—sized to the state—on the western border, over the ball's four-hundred-mile roll eastward it would drop about three thousand feet (more than three Empire State Buildings) and crash into Missouri (an appealing thought to some Kansans). The ball would, of course, depending on its path, have to get over the Blue Hills, the Red Hills, the Chippewa Hills, the Smokey Hills, the Flint Hills, the Chautauqua Hills, and around any number of stony and upright natural obstructions like Castle Rock, the Chalk Pyramids, Mushroom Rocks, and Rock City (bumper pool would be a more apt metaphor), not to mention arroyos, creeks, rivers, and the eastern woodlands. Nevertheless, air travelers who think they have seen all of Kansas in one glance from 38,000 feet, and "know for a fact" it is indeed flat, may want to disabuse themselves by pedaling a bicycle from, say, Westport on the Missouri line to Kanorado on the other state line; along the way, let the cyclists tell their legs, "It's flat, it's flat."

What else is the truth about Kansas? It is, as the license plates once said, MIDWAY USA. If you cut out a cardboard map of the forty-eight contiguous states and stick a tack through the center of Kansas to pin to a wall, the map will hang nicely parallel with the floor. Knowing, then, that Kansas is the topographical heart of contiguous America, it seems reasonable to assume the state is a place of middle distance, a compromise: neither too far west, east, north, or south. It would appear as a balance point, the spot at the center holding comparatively steady in the revolutions of the "outer" nation. California is drifting north, New York may be on its way to sinking into the Atlantic, but dear old Kansas holds staunch. It has come to seem a place of equipoise, a still life, a region where movements end rather than begin, a land where the tumult settles down to the mere business of getting on with real things—basic things like bread and beef. (My Kansan grandfather used to say, "Kansas means *eat* as meat and wheat.") But, apparently, all this suggests to an outstater is that Kansas is only, at best, something to be unconsciously thankful for, like air. Rarely has it been a place to seek out.

If Kansas appears a wholesome middle ground without the fascination of extremes, does it then have to follow that middleness and goodness equal dullness? Certainly in the early days of Anglo Kansas—the mid-nineteenth century—as the Territory was being cut away from the Rockies and shaped into a state, things were hardly in a condition of equipoise, and, most unquestionably, they were not dull unless mayhem is dull. No state came into the Union more violently (hence the epithet Bloody Kansas or, more touchingly, Bleeding Kansas). By then the European descendants, as elsewhere around the world, had successfully bilked the native peoples out of their land and had settled into cutting up and shooting down each other over real estate schemes and the slavery question. Kansas did not begin as—nor is it now except in outstate preconceptions—a land of placidity and insipidity.

Consider some names: William Quantrill, John Brown, Bat Masterson, the Dalton Gang, Wyatt Earp, Wild Bill Hickok, the Bloody Benders, the Clutter family of *In Cold Blood*. Even the less sanguine history gives off an aura of discombobulations: Carry Nation; vigorous support of nation-changing reforms of the Progressive Era; *Brown v. Topeka Board of Education*; John Brinkley's goat-gland, male-rejuvenation xeno-transplants. The truth is that Kansas history is a tumbling of lawsuits, fists, guns, torches, hatchets, and absurdities. It's a tale often cutting to the bone, and its sharp edge is not reviled or denied by the citizens: The traveler today can find a monument or museum commemorating or at least mentioning all those names.

*   *   *

So, what is the reality of Kansas? Kansas is a complexity of moving points, a land of tilts and shifts, a region full of lives and ideas going this way and that and not infrequently colliding. It is the heartland reflecting an America whose own history begins with something close to genocide and carries on through deadly conflicts internecine and otherwise, with no generation not knowing war. Kansas beats at our center because it too moves in fitfulness, turbulence, and, somehow between times, in beauty. Its motto could be the nation's: *Ad Astra per Aspera,* "to the stars through difficulties." Kansas, as well as any other state, and far better than most, embodies the archetypal issues of this country, the movements—both splendid and evil—that formed Americans into something distinct from our Eastern Hemisphere ancestors: Indian dispossession, the westering movement, slavery, cowboys, exterminations of a natural world, women's rights. It is a spacious land of wheat, beef, and petroleum—American translation: hamburgers and automobiles.

On another scale of things American, it is the birthplace of the dial telephone, Mentholatum ("the Little Nurse for Little Ills"), and the Oh Henry! candy bar. It's the state that elected the first woman mayor (Susanna Salter), turned out the first woman dentist (Lucy Taylor), the first black woman to win an Academy Award (Hattie McDaniel). It was the first state to ratify the Fifteenth Amendment (black voting rights), and what is perhaps the most significant social movement of the sixties, constitutional change to end school segregation, formally started in Topeka. If Kansas is without the athletic idleness of ski slopes and surf—lacking mountains and oceans—it holds a more productive energy for national change. To be sure, some school board will embarrass Kansas by denying the teaching of evolution, and some politicians will confound science by refusing to address global climate change, yet Kansas remains a crucible of energy in its *informed* citizens.

*　　*　　*

I submit this notion: To see Kansas accurately is to find much that belongs at the heart of the United States. Like the nation, it is a land to be seen in the light of its days and in the shadows of its history. It is not a country to race across enfolded in the obscurities of speed and darkness only to arrive at the foot of the mountains at dawn as though one had slept through it all.

ALL KNOWLEDGE
HUMAN AND
COSMIC

To write about Pittsburgh or Kansas City or Albuquerque, or perhaps even Boston, is usually to discover resident readers both curious and often appreciative of such attention. But to take on New York City or its environs is to lay one's text out for flagellation by the esteemed cognoscenti living in celebrated parochialism, the flagellum being the attitude "What the hell does he know?"

I can't argue the point because whatever ground I write about, I never know enough, and that includes Nameless, Tennessee; and Cottonwood Falls, Kansas; and Cathlamet, Washington; and Starrucca, Pennsylvania; and a near infinitude of others. In my next life, I promise here—and you can then hold me to it—to silence my pen until I'm possessed of all knowledge human and cosmic.

Out East on the North Fork

If ever natural topography accurately and prophetically mir-
rored a place — at least in its earliest days — that spot might
be the glacier-chiseled surface of Long Island, New York. By
the time European explorers began actually setting foot on it in
the early seventeenth century, their rudimentary sea charts were
beginning to change from showing it as leviathan-like to a shape
more like a fish. The image of the island I'm looking at now, a
black-and-white satellite photograph, could almost be a depic-
tion of a coelacanth, a creature of deep seas, a fish so primitive
that paleontologists thought it extinct until a trawler in 1938
accidentally brought a specimen to the surface in the South
Atlantic. If your imagination has a contemporary turn of mind,
you might see Long Island instead as a huge bluefish, one of the
most sapient creatures still swimming the nearly twelve hundred miles of the Long Island coast.

From the western end — where the piscine mouth at Graves-
end Bay seems ready to eat Perth Amboy — to the point 124
miles eastward, where things conclude in a bifurcated tail (also
called the flukes, although that term describes whales, not fish),
this largest island of the U.S. Atlantic Seaboard owes its early
economy to the fruits of the ocean, preeminently fish but also
oysters, crabs, whales, and even seaweed.

In the autumn of 1679 the Dutchman Jasper Danckaerts
wrote from the western end about a dinner served up by a cente-
narian grandmother who set before him a meal of striped bass:

"It was salted a little and then smoked, and although it was now a year old, it was still perfectly good, and in flavor not inferior to smoked salmon." But his next repast pleased him even more. He sampled hot from roasting over an oak-and-hickory fire "a pail-full of [Gowanus] oysters, which are the best in the country. They are fully as good as those of England. I had to try some of them raw. They are large and full, some of them not less than a foot long." Upstate New Yorker eateries offer twelve-inch hot dogs, yes, but an oyster the length of a man's shoe?

Upon hearing Danckaerts's description, a friend of mine who grew up in Brooklyn only a couple of miles from Gowanus Bay said, in her inimitable Long-guy-land accent, "Foot-long oysters? And edible? If you fished up something from that bay now it would be a telephone booth or some goombah in cement foot-wear sent to swim with the fishes."

Walt Whitman found the name Long Island too prosaic for his native ground and preferred calling it by one Indians used — Paumanok, "place of tribute" — a description good enough were the American version not so accurate; Paumanok would indeed be better if only it meant what Walt wished: "fish-shaped." The distinctive outline is mostly an expression of waters: rain, sea, and ice, but especially ice. Glaciers, coming from hundreds of miles north to peter out here, cut, shoved, scoured, depressed as well as uplifted the terrain, only to retreat and leave behind sand, gravel, and boulders; the last are wonderfully evident along the North Shore, the Sound side, where a mariner sails past miles of glacially transported stones the size of armchairs to a few others that, were they hollowed out, could serve as cabanas. By charting the nearly due north–south abrasions over the face of the rocks, geologists can delineate the route those granites took from their sources in the mountains of New England.

But the South Shore, the Atlantic side, is comparatively free of such bouldery depositions; even more, the southerly latitudinal tilt of Long Island gives that coast such a low profile — its eastern tip near Montauk excepted—a careless sailor may run aground before distinguishing waves from beaches that can have a breadth of almost an eighth of a mile. On the north, though, a sand beach may be only a hundred feet from surf to terra more firma. Geology here, as almost everywhere, determines the kind of life humans live atop it. The North Shore at the western end is the "Gold Coast," with venerable forty-room mansions belonging to a realm Scott Fitzgerald called East and West Egg, a reach of small inlets creating peninsulas Islanders speak of as *necks*. (The description Little Neck clams refers to a location, not a presumed bivalve cervically revamped.) The Sound side is good for marine views, yachts, and privacy but poor for urban masses hunting tall breakers and long beaches. The Gold Coast has no barrier island to protect it, unless you share the view of a fellow who pointed north from Oyster Bay and told me, "That's our barrier island." I asked if that wasn't Connecticut. "Bullshit," he explained. "That's the ever-lovin continent."

My quest on Long Island, however, wasn't for swimming beaches or golden coasts but rather for what remains of an older island, one that has, at least for another few years, escaped the sprawl not just of New York City but of the urbed and suburbed human juggernaut now running almost unbroken from Boston into New Jersey and headed hugger-mugger toward northern Virginia. I set out for the east end with a few old recollections and a map that colored the fish-of-an-island in jaundiced yellow from mouth to well past the belly. But beyond there, near the end of the expressway west of the Peconic River, the map turned white, the customary—and ever more rare—cartographic color for openness.

From the Throgs Neck Bridge linking the island to the Bronx, I moved along the North Shore. When I crossed the Peconic seventy miles from Times Square, I began to sense an island within an island. In truth, the North Fork is a rather level, often treeless peninsula extending from the river easterly some thirty miles to its end at Orient Point, a name my Middle Western background finds peculiarly jolly, since a Missourian believes one goes *west* to reach the Orient — any orient. Indeed, people of the North Fork view geography differently from us continentals: To them Brooklyn lies "back west" and they live "out east." When one sees — and feels — how truly long this island is and how far it thrusts *out* into the Atlantic and then notices how protected the *back*waters are near Brooklyn, the reversal of customary prepositions makes sense. I knew I'd come well away from the boroughs of New York when, east of the Nassau-Suffolk county line, my ears made it evident that out here a canine isn't a *duog* but a *dog,* and the hard *g* in Long Island starts to slip. The native speech at this end is more Connecticut than Queens.

The North Fork tapers from a slender four miles across in the west to nothing at Orient Point which, by the way, actually happens to *point* at Northern Europe, and that might partly explain why Revolutionary War history out on this end is full of characters with Tory sympathies.

For some islanders, the North Fork is most important simply for not being like the fork south of Peconic Bay — at least not yet. Here a traveler sees little to suggest the Hamptons and all that attends such a privileged world of manifest plutocratic excess. The north is a quietly plainer place, still rather more rural if no longer rustic. Instead of designer-done estates, it greets the visitor with what may be the largest fowl on earth, a critter twenty-feet tall and thirty long, six tons of concrete painted white to look like a Pekin duck and once possessed of blinking Model-T taillights for eyes. The thing is so excellently outrageous that similar goofball roadside structures — elephants, coffeepots, derby hats, diplodocuses — have become known as duck architecture, or, to some people here, Art Ducko.

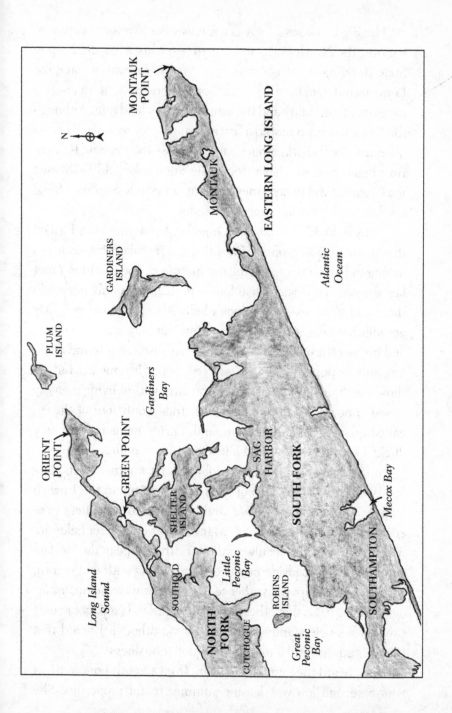

The Big Duck serves not as a gateway but as a sentinel watching over the North Fork, and it is to residents what the Empire State Building—both built in 1931—is to Manhattan. That the Long Island Duck still stands—more precisely, it sits—is a measure of durability and the esteem natives hold it in. Although the Duck has been moved a few miles and now technically nests upon the South Fork, it once sat just across the Peconic River in Riverhead, next to what is today the Snowflake Old Fashioned Ice Cream stand (where they serve up a Peconic Swamp Thing, raspberry with double chocolate sauce).

"Why a duck?" Chico asks Groucho. Inside the bird, I asked that of an amiable woman, Babs Bixby, a moniker that seems to belong in lights on a 1920s theater marquee. The morning I met her she was dispensing local lore—probably the only person in the world to do so from a duck's belly—and she told me, "My grandfather once said there was a time out here when every nut and his brother owned a duck farm." Because Long Island duckling was popular—not just on New York City menus but on those over much of the nation—one farm within living memory raised annually a half-million ducks. Today, only four of the so-called quacker ranches remain, and, during my jaunt, the only ducks I saw were a few wild idlers on village ponds.

In the past, Long Island was famous for another food: pickles. Babs Bixby said, "Two of the funniest words in the English language are *duck* and *pickle,* and both of those products were economically important here." Many former cucumber fields are now in flowers, especially sunflowers that appear during late summer at the roadside produce stands along with white corn, squash, and fruit pies; in other seasons one finds mesclun, asparagus, rhubarb. Of that other famous Long Island crop, potatoes, I saw but a single stand advertising them, although I heard that island spuds are still a multimillion-dollar business.

I also heard the immediate future from a South Fork waitress whose second job was leasing summer rental properties. She said, "These days out here we're all about the three Rs — restaurants, retail, and realty." There's no room in that abecedary for ducks, pickles, or potatoes, and that means a new Long Island has arrived and with it certain consumeristic attitudes reshaping the place. I think it wasn't coincidence that several blocks down the street from her East Hampton restaurant I came upon a shop with a stack of pillows in the window. Stitched elegantly on them were apothegms; next to *You Are Leaving Sunday Aren't You?* was *Screw the Kids — a Dollar Saved Is a Dollar Wasted.* Perhaps I read too much into small artifacts, but the difference between those pillows may indeed express something about the differences between the twin forks, about differences between pillows and potatoes, between seeing ducks along a creek and serving them on a porcelain plate.

In the seventies, when I first saw Greenport, the quintessential North Fork village, it was unmistakably a fisherman's harbor showing as much tumbledown-ness as quaintness and redolent of the day's catch rather than perfumed tourists. Its most famous store was S. T. Preston's, a marine hardware store with oiled wooden floorboards and shelves of stacked nautical gear primarily for trawlers and lobstermen. Today, with its maritime-themed doormats and highball glasses, Preston's is more gallery than chandlery. Where once I smelled diesel oil and sun-bleached fish scales, I now breathed vanilla and bayberry from candles delicately perfect for the table of that special vacation home. I heard a woman, looking at a lamp shaped into a plastic lighthouse, say to her little son tugging her arm, "Careful! Watch Mommy's manicure!" Old seafaring Greenport, like the rest of us, has changed, and, as far as I could tell on my return, the changes have not been to the detriment of the economy. The place hums in the summer, when strollers have to dodge the fleets of SUVs navigating the narrow streets. Then, a curmudgeonly traveler whose recollections face off against joviality can wish for the company of an ancient mariner who, as they say here, is a "bit long in the mouth" and whose glittering eye might so constrain a fellow that he cannot choose but hear a genuine tale of a genuine ocean.

I had recently read a *New York Times* article quoting a local real estate broker: "We see the North Fork as the next area of development. People are going there because it's quiet." And another agent claimed, "Nothing has happened here that hasn't been happening here for a long time. As long as we have agriculture, the sea, and second-home owners, we'll be okay." His logic escaped me; it was like a Mississippian saying, "As long as we have the farmland, cotton, and the boll weevil, we'll be okay."

Who can doubt the sea will remain? Who can doubt the influx of more urbanites hunting second-home plots? But just how many second homes can quiet agriculture accommodate? Can faux-colonial farmhouses alternating with faux-French country estates coexist with genuine farms? Confronting such pressure, various land-preservation plans, including one created by Suffolk County itself, have come about to help fields and farms remain in a use similar to the patches Corchaug Indians cultivated around Peconic Bay for at least six hundred years before Europeans arrived.

Facing a burgeoning American population and its demand for sprawl-malls, what's the future of east-end potato fields? The best ally of open land could prove to be the grape. Nothing to me was more surprising on my return than to discover acres of vineyards occupying plots I'd last seen growing potatoes. On the western stretch of State Route 25, the "Main Road" of the North Fork, I noticed a small sign: WELCOME TO LONG ISLAND WINE COUNTRY, and some thirty miles east in Greenport, I came upon another, this one hand-painted: LAST WINERY BEFORE FRANCE.

Between the signs is Cutchogue, an agreeable village with the cut of its jib clearly suggesting Connecticut to which it once belonged. It has a genuine trolley-style diner and a house built in 1649 along with homes, only somewhat newer, shaded by big sugar maples. It's also the epicenter of Long Island wineries. Recalling a pair of recommendations from a day earlier given by a South Fork sommelier and a wine merchant, I went out to Pellegrini Vineyards. A rather new tasting room beside a courtyard lay at the edge of thirty acres of grapes, both red and white, just then beginning to come into color above a slope not long ago given to tubers. It's such changes that have led to a Long Island winery or two being dismissed as Château Potato.

Perhaps because I've blown out my taste buds with too many New Mexican chiles (as a friend wishes to believe), I like deep and robust flavors — India pale ale, espresso, and, yes, green chiles — and I consider white and pale red wines beverages for palates more delicately inclined. Remembering remarkably undistinguished wines of yesteryear from Upstate New York, I ordered a glass of Pellegrini "table wine," and what I got was a deeply red robusto that would match up with more pretentious offerings from California. For me, the jokes about Appellation Spud vanished. It was clear that Pellegrini, along with several of the other thirty-five wineries on the east end, had found a splendid combination: glaciated ground with well-drained, sandy soil ideal for vinifera grapes. The best winemakers, realizing the limitations of space on a narrow peninsula, have consequently chosen to work for vintage over gallonage.

Ben Couts, a serious, crew-cut young employee at the winery and a native of nearby Southold, came out to sit with me. Too modestly he said, "Our notion is that if you have a good year in a good vineyard, your wine's made for you." He spoke about climatic differences between the North and South forks where, in a strange reversal, the upper side is milder and retains warmth longer than the southern only a few miles across the small bay.

Although the North Fork wineries are but a couple of decades old, they have quickly earned respect, and the federal government early recognized Long Island as an American Viticultural Area, a special designation similar to the French *appellation*.

It's a pleasant moment to drink a good wine and know with each sip one is helping to establish a promising tradition that can preserve open space. I mentioned a nearby sign:

SAVE THE FARMLAND
LET'S WORK TOGETHER

Couts said, "A lot of locals are thankful this is a vineyard and not a mall." So there I was that afternoon, a breeze off the Sound bringing in a scent of ripeness from the vineyard, doing my part with each lift of the glass.

Someday hence, if future historians go looking for an emblem of the eastern half of Long Island, they might find it in the Atlantic white cedar that once flourished here but is now rare. Or they could see it in the old Montauk Lighthouse, formerly three-hundred feet from the waves but today less than seventy and still standing only because of much human intervention. The emblem might even be the golden nematode that turned potato fields on western Long Island—in an area once called Island Trees—into dusty, dead patches that after the Second World War became the seventeen-thousand stamped-out-box-house development called Levittown. Maybe, however, a better emblem has emerged: a cluster of ripened grapes.

In another time, New England cleric and educator Timothy Dwight made a journey down the Eastern Seaboard and kept a rich account of his trip. While visiting the western end of Long Island, he commented:

The oyster beds at this place were not long since supposed to be inexhaustible; and supplied, not only the inhabitants of Long-Island, but the inhabitants of New-York, the county of Westchester, and the south shore of New-England, with immense quantities of this valuable fish. Now they have become lean, watery, and sickly, and have declined still more in their numbers than in their quality. Formerly they were large and well flavored, now they are scarcely eatable; and, what is worse, there is reason to fear, that they will soon become extinct.

The Reverend Dwight wrote that passage in 1804, a hundred twenty-five years after Jasper Danckaerts sampled oysters the size of platters.

Sitting with a glass of good red in hand at the edge of a vineyard younger than, say, just about any rock star you can name, it was good to think about a coelacanth-shaped place and to consider how it had continued an harmonious existence three-hundred-million years before the first human walked Long Island. Coelacanths, according to one ichthyologist, are "machines for reading the past backward," but it seems to me they might also serve to read in the opposite direction. If we discover their secrets, then maybe we can try practicing a few of their ways of continuance.

A DUST BALL
UNDER THE BED

On occasion, staying within a mile or two of my writing desk, I go out into my home territory and try to travel it as if a stranger so that I can see familiarities in a different light and from a new angle, commonplaces viewed freshly and examined closely. The point is as much discovery as rediscovery. Surprise can be an intellectually and spiritually salubrious event useful as a monthly or seasonal regimen for helping keep oneself awake to the wonderments lying all about us in familiar if unspied places: that mystery shrub down the lane, a house spider in the corner, a dust ball under the bed, a neighbor's turn of phrase. Anything that might lead to new awareness. "I have traveled a good deal in Concord," wrote Thoreau and thereby daily made himself into who he was.

Of Time and a River

ON THE STONE SEA. When I first moved to an old tobacco farm in the hills of southwest Boone County, Missouri, I sowed grasses into the tilled field, planted seedling trees, and cleaned out trash pits, all the while working to the frequent, distant train whistles and rumbles from the tracks of two railways, one on each side of the Missouri River. The Missouri Pacific Railroad (or MoPac, as it was then) lay on the far south bank, and on the north was the Missouri, Kansas, and Texas line (the Katy), this closer track about a mile from the house I was building. A carpenter working on a second-floor deck paused one morning to listen to the Katy pass, and he said, "I know why you want this here porch. It's so's you can hear them trains." Eighteen years later, another carpenter lifted his head to take in the sound of what had become a single and reorganized line, the Union Pacific, and in nearly the same words he too registered the lure of the mellowed voice from distant trains.

From my place I can't see the engines working their way between St. Louis and Kansas City, between East and West. Their presence is purely aural because the route here lies under steep and wooded bluffs the Missouri has cut through the limestone hills to create a landscape with the subdued beauty common to the lower Middle West, but their whistles are a call to quit work and wander off.

So, when the weather and seasons get themselves up into something pleasant or interesting, I like to leave my writing desk where I'm fogged in by words, and take a walking stick as my third leg, climb the old fescue-riddled hill pasture, its margins lined with sweet williams in the spring, slip under the barbed wire, cross the schoolhouse road, go on through Mister Poe's gate, on farther, past his tobacco patch, all the way heading west toward the Missouri River, 175 water miles above its junction with the Mississippi north of St. Louis.

The field narrows, a deer snorts and hoists its flag and disappears like a phantom of the old life. Just where the woods edge in are twin earthen Indian mounds, matched but smallish like young breasts. In years past, pot hunters dug into both only to find what turns to dust, something they couldn't pocket off, yet their craters remain. Beyond is a third mound, larger and also vandalized, and there the woods close: oak, hickory, ash, but mostly sugar maples. For the past half-century the maples have had their sap to themselves, but not far north, a big and rusting iron kettle sits tilted among the trees, a kind of forgotten tombstone to the old sugarmen.

Then a fourth mound, its contours perfect and unviolated. Whatever the Woodland people placed in it a thousand years ago lies, if not quite as they left it, at least undesecrated: perhaps a skeleton facing west and wearing a shell necklace; maybe a platform pipe alongside a broken pot, and charred elk-bones from a funeral feast there too. Only steps farther, the land gives way abruptly to air and drops a hundred feet down a limestone bluff to resume as the overgrown floodplain of the Missouri. In the days of the first white travelers here, the river lay directly below this precipice, so close that someone, mind or spirit gone, could have leaped into the mad currents. When President Jefferson's Corps of Discovery, on the fifth of June, 1804, poled their keelboat past this point, an Osage woman might have tossed a bouquet of sweet williams down onto William Clark's head.

Through the middle of the state, the Missouri River has cut a grand avenue two miles wide between calcareous cliffs that are, in truth, an old seabed solidified, a fossilated ocean of stone guiding newer waters. In our time, the channel, a quarter-mile broad, now lies across the valley and mostly obscured by willow, cottonwood, and sycamore. Were John James Audubon once again to pass here aboard the steamboat *Omega* in quest of beasts for his *Quadrupeds of North America* or were superb watercolorist Karl Bodmer to reappear aboard the *Yellow Stone* in search of Plains Indians, they'd find the shores more populated by bobcats than natives; but one day, when the Corps of Engineers and its infernal channelings and dammings have vanished—as they will—the river will return periodically to this east side, for the natural action of the Missouri is like a spouting firehose let loose in a street to thrash from curb to curb.

These upraised, rock seas can give a sense of standing on the edge of a beyond: Here is a jumping-off place, a depot for departures, a spot where a traveler can enter another realm, and that, I suspect, is one reason these headlands hold so many Indian burial mounds. When I sit here alone and put down my binoculars, I see no certain evidence—except my own skin and shoes—that white settlement ever arrived, and I can idle on this petrified sea, before me the river that proved, in the end, to be not much of a route to Cathay and the Indies. In this corridor to other times, it seems I'm carried atop the flow coming down from the western mountains, slipping silently and steadily toward elsewheres. It's as if the *place,* powered by gravity, moves, and I sit and travel on no vessel other than the Earth itself.

AN AMERICAN FLOWING. Two hikers, one walking from near Atlantic City to San Diego, the other from Seattle to Savannah, would cross paths at about where I'm standing now along the lower Missouri River, 2,300 miles from its source, half that distance from its conclusion via the Mississippi in the Gulf of Mexico. These waters are carrying away in apparent effortlessness the eastern slopes of the Rocky Mountains and a few outliers like the Big Snowy Mountains and the Crazy Mountains in Montana—bit by quartzy bit—at an easy, early autumn speed of three miles an hour.

Tomorrow, if the afternoon is warm, when the bluff tops have set themselves up in the colors of the lower end of the spectrum—yellows, oranges, carmines—I'll take my canoe and sleeping bag and paddle down Perche Creek (the old residents say "*Purr*-chee Crick") and onto the river and upstream to Plow Boy Bend, named for a sternwheeler that sank there; abandoned by the river that took it, *Plow Boy* likely rests broken under a bottomland cornfield. I'll pull up to a broad and level sandbar swept free of vegetation, its highest point a mere fourteen inches above the autumnal river. I don't fish the Missouri. I go there just to watch things and be reminded that, after the rock bluffs born of the ancient inland sea this place once was, the river is the oldest thing around; to sit beside its currents and eddies and boils is to rest in a seeming perpetual moment and rub up against the primeval.

Soon after dusk I'll doze off just beyond the reach of the dark current on sand once mountains now intermixed with eroded plains and prairies once Jurassic gulfs and saurian coastal swamps roamed by brontosaurs, tyrannosaurs, stegosaurs. Those crumbled mountains and dissolved-stone seabeds, and granulated reptiles shaped into something different by the river, so hold the afternoon warmth that sandbars make a fine place to drowse, to snooze atop the outfall of eons, time itself, to wake when a night barge rumbles by and plays its beam-from-hell on me till I rise and wave I'm not a corpse yet.

In those moments of half-sleep, I can imagine among the bankside willows and cottonwoods the Missouria tribe—now gone elsewhere, mostly into the near oblivion of genetic absorptions—and I'll listen for those who preceded them, the ones who a thousand years ago stacked the bluff tops with small mounds and who painted cliff faces fronting the river with ocher figures and geometric designs. Nearly a century ago, the Missouri, Kansas, and Texas Railroad blasted away most of the pictographs, and now its tracks too are gone. But above a large spring that pours almost directly into the Missouri, a few images the color of rust remain. One of them is of an upturned crescent moon holding a small, elliptical disk like an upside-down fermata symbol ‿•⁀. It's a configuration that appears in special locations around the world, and it may represent, as if a picture postcard sent from another millennium, an exploding supernova that appeared in A.D. 1054. Standing under the star-and-moon is a stickman, now nearly vanished, who has watched travelers on river and rails pass, all of them also vanished, leaving him to oversee an engineered and largely unpopulated river bearing a perpetual charge of earthen lees and dregs from a time when human predecessors were tiny rodents dodging massive reptilian footsteps.

Under the iron-oxide totem depicting a crescent moon and dying star passed people faceless and some famous: Lewis and

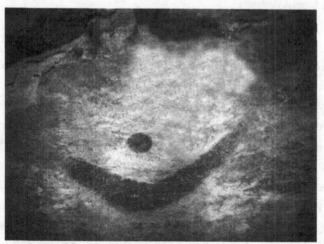

The pictograph above the Missouri River in Boone County, Missouri

Clark and crew searching a newly bought quarter-of-a-nation for a water road to the Orient that they would find does indeed exist—if a boat is no larger than a bucket. Prince Maximilian and Karl Bodmer out to make the finest record ever of the vanishing ways of the Plains tribes; and George Catlin, if less skillfully, also painting the end of an era. Mark Twain bound for the Far West, which he would describe in *Roughing It;* Francis Parkman on his way to the Oregon Trail, and Stephen Long and John Charles Frémont exploring the western lands in order to seize them and open them like ripe melons.

I've found two-dozen written accounts that only hint at the thousands of river travelers who left no record but who went past this very place to change the land and make it for better and worse into America, a country—no matter how you see it— impossible for the people who drew the rusty moon-cradled sun when the language of this sentence didn't yet exist.

At night, the sandbar becomes another vessel to travel not the river itself but the *times* of a river full of passages up and down its long American flowing of rock and mud, flotsam and men, shadows and murmurs, all through the night coming and leaving.

WALKING THE KATY LINE. One afternoon, wearied of planting trees, I followed a whistle down to the Katy tracks, passing the ghost village of Providence where all that remained were a couple of fishing shacks, a few rock walls, and the yet-standing stone chimney of the old steamboaters' hotel. The place was once the river landing for Columbia twelve miles north. I headed up the tracks toward Rocheport, another early nineteenth-century village, this one larger than Providence and still clinging to an existence. The nineteenth-century brick homes and worn shop fronts had been declining ever since the Missouri shifted its course about a century earlier and left the village a mile or so from the river. Some time later, when passenger service ceased and the Katy trains quit stopping at the little depot, Rocheport, like a dozen other former steamboat or railroad villages nearby, had the scarcest of reasons to continue.

For a couple of thousand years or more, passage up and down the nearly three-hundred-mile-long Missouri River channel between St. Louis and Kansas City had been by a vessel of some sort until the railroads appeared and provided stumble-inducing tracks with their maddening spacing that I tried to match to my strides before dodging a locomotive suddenly coming around a blind bend. A hike over those sleepers was full of easy thrills, and in former days occasionally fatal to a weary or intoxicated hobo. To take the alternate route across and up and down the wooded and poison ivy–laced bluffs, while not impossible — in theory anyway — would be intolerably irksome and done in total trespass. Both rail routes, MoPac and the Katy, lay so close to the bluffs in many places a passenger in an open-windowed dining car could toss a peach pit right into the swirling river, and ripping thunderstorms brought down rocks like hail onto passing boxcars and cabooses.

One month after my first track-hike, news came that the Katy was soon to cease its river route across Missouri and was about to sell the line: rails, ties, bridges, the track bed itself. No more Katy Flyer. Even before the company began pulling up the steel and wood, a struggle for the vacated right-of-way broke out. Abutting landowners, the most vehement of them a neighbor of mine, took guidance from a so-called property-rights group and erected barriers across the narrow rail bed, and extremists among them promised to shoot any "trespassers" hiking "their" land.

Others of us saw the change differently and gathered ten thousand signatures on a petition, and the mayor of Columbia, who had grown up on a hill above the Katy spur running into downtown, urged the state to buy the land for a long, linear parkway. The opposition argued that hikers and bicyclists would trash the route, frighten and maim livestock (of which there was virtually none near the line), and city-born "thugs with their watermelon" (in the racist code) would use the route to rob remote farmhouses.

Things became unpleasant, often bordering on the vicious, and the future of what had been the Katy hung undecided. Then, one morning I saw in the paper that Edward Jones, of brokerage-houses fame, had donated two-hundred-thousand dollars to a private foundation to buy the property from the owners of the Missouri, Kansas, and Texas Railroad. Opponents

Former railroad tunnel on the present Katy Trail in Boone County, Missouri

filed suit to force the issue into a federal court where, at last, a judge affirmed the constitutionality of an amendment to the National Trails System Act that allows abandoned rail corridors to be set aside voluntarily for use as trails until a day when they might be needed once more for train transport. There was an appeal to this "rail banking," but a second federal judge concurred with the original decision. A third appeal died when the United States Supreme Court decided in favor of a similar rail conversion in Vermont, and the Katy line was saved to find a new life.

But the project required more than mere possession of the corridor. Just before his death, Edward Jones gave the foundation an additional gift—two million dollars—to help build a two-hundred-mile trail from near St. Charles, Missouri, to Sedalia, with the possibility of continuing it one day into Kansas City. The handful of property-righters had to take down their illegal barriers and put away their promised shotguns, and the Katy Trail became the longest rail trail in the United States. The Missouri Department of Natural Resources laid atop the former track bed a crushed-stone surface good for wheels or shoes, and planked over the ties of seventy-year-old steel bridges.

And did the trespassers and vandals come, and did the cattle get mutilated and the path get littered with liquor bottles and watermelon rinds? Not at all.

What *did* happen along the route was the birth of a new economy: Without losing its quietude and quaintness, Rocheport, to pick a village, was remade. An old church, a bank, a drugstore got turned into antique shops, wooden-floor cafés, and exposed-brick-wall bistros serving Brie cheese drizzled with raspberry vinaigrette, panko-crusted sea bass, gooey butter cake, and clarets from the winery up on the hill. If it was another world from paddlewheeler roustabouts swearing and fighting, and Negro stevedores singing and loading bales of tobacco and hemp, and Katy gandy dancers staggering up Main Street, the villages were just as alive as before.

Former train stations became visitor centers; closed-up groceries and garages and schools transformed into bicycle-rental shops, bed-and-breakfast inns; a micro-publisher even opened a locally oriented press. In the words of a shop owner down the line from Rocheport, "People on the trail leave behind far more cash than trash, and they don't steal—they buy a meal."

The great westering river of canoes and pirogues, mackinaws and keelboats, steamboats and towboats, of bankside steam locomotives and diesel engines, all of them transmuted into a route of bicycle wheels and waffle-soled boots. I quote a woman, of some historical bent, who had just finished a three-hour pedal on the Katy Trail running alongside the Missouri: "If Ol Man River could talk, if he saw me pumping along, he'd have said, 'What in the hell! I've seen it all now.'" Well, the Ol Man hasn't seen everything—just everything along his shores for the last several thousand years.

TO EXPLAIN
DELIGHT

Among the great questions—those inquiries having answers so difficult they can be considered all but impossible of real solutions ("Why am I here?" or "Is this the life I truly want?" or "Am I bound for eternal glory or the simplicity of oblivion?")—there's one less asked than others. To put it plainly: "Why do I like what I like?" Or its negative.

My experience with that question often produces discernments too generic to yield much insight, but that doesn't mean the effort to determine something is bootless or unyielding of interesting things found along the way to an apparent dead end. After all, aren't answers, no matter how serviceable, often less intriguing than questions? If a probing into a why uncovers a bland, nothing-new-under-the-sun result, then the commonplaceness suggests an answer plausible if not definitive; more significant, the continual asking may turn up delights not particularly germane to the question. What follows is a stab at why I find making walking sticks so agreeable, and—if I didn't trip myself up—I hope the response has a touch of the existential.

With a Good Stick in Hand

Far more than I would like, my name as a writer stands linked in the minds of American readers with vehicles and roads, wheels and asphalt, thanks to my first book, *Blue Highways*. Since its publication, I've had little success in suggesting I'm more impassioned by feet and legs moving across natural terrain or down rural lanes or around city blocks. I love walking in all its variations: the stroll, saunter, tramp, traipse, trek, ramble, constitutional, cross-country hike, and—at certain times—the night walk, a kind of wakeful noctambulation into a route darkness can make dreamlike and salutary to the imagination. Whatever the nature of the hoofing, each outing is accomplished a single footfall at a time atop one's own shank's mare. How excellent it is to see the world reveal itself to one who goes afoot—and how much larger it is.

Even though built around a series of pedestrious jaunts in the tallgrass prairie of Kansas, my second book, *PrairyErth*, did little to dispel perceptions of me behind a steering wheel. The truth is, to get to know the three-million square miles of our land, I drive because I have to; but I walk because I want to, and, when I go on foot, I carry something nearly forgotten in our car-crazed nation and auto-damaged landscapes—a walking stick.

Viewing my approach from, say, across a meadow, you might take me for a fellow with a cane, but that would miss the mark because a cane props and steadies the infirm while a walking stick buoys the rambler—both in body and spirit. Once, in a conversation on this topic, a woman said to me, "Why, you're speaking of a *staff!*" No, madam. A staff is a pole serving to power a hiker forward as a third leg that transforms the bipedal into a tripedal. What's more, a staff reaches up to somewhere between the elbow and the shoulder, while a walking stick only to the top of the hip. Today, of course, a hiker may use two staffs, commonly highly technical and fully unnatural. I own a pair of sleek, graphite poles for long-distance hikes over

Etching of Samuel Johnson on his 1773 walking tour of Scotland

broken terrain, but that experience is something other than a stroll; in my mind it's the difference between writing with a pencil and clicking on a keyboard, both of which I do.

For a couple of centuries, some walking-stick shanks have been hollowed out to contain hidden swords, or tubes for brandy, or a spyglass, and some handles have been embedded with a small compass, all of these variations cleverly wrought gizmos. For me, I want only shanks and handles natural to a tree branch. Brass or chrome are inert metal in the hand, either too hot, cold, sweaty, or just plain slippery. A fine walking stick retains something of the living branch to suggest continually not the forge but the forest. Concomitantly, perhaps, my walks are down the woody lane (originally made of oaken planks) where I live, or they're across nearby open fields, or along an abandoned rail line not far distant.

When I walk in a city I like to mark out an area and hoof every square block (say, the inside of the Loop in Chicago), but I don't carry a stick because urban folk are likely to take it as a weapon. I once was asked in Atlanta, "Whatcha got that billy club fer?"

The nature of my work makes it tricky to distinguish vocation from several avocations except for one that clearly can be called only a hobby: making walking sticks. The initial and keenest pleasure is finding a branch fit to assist peripatetics. I look for raw material in roadside undergrowth or in freshly cut or fallen limbs. I trim and shape the shaft and handle minimally so the natural treeness remains. Retaining the bark, I brush on satin varnish or rub in tung oil before adding a brass or copper ferrule to keep the road from eating away the shank. Silver maple, aspen, cottonwood, sycamore, Osage orange, mountain mahogany, moosewood, hickory, black locust, apple. I'm always ready to try a new wood, one with requisites of overall straightness — but not machinelike perfection — and a strength allowing a nearly imperceptible springiness. My searches have yet to come upon a suitable sassafras or pawpaw or persimmon despite their abundance outside the front door.

The handle should provide a good feel in the palm and a sound grip for the fingers, and I prefer three basic shapes: the knob, the el, and the tee:

I avoid the crook because it's a less comfortable shape and it hinders the to-and-fro penduluming of the stick, which reflects the motion of the legs that somehow gets transmitted to the brain and helps create a stroll merry or meditative.

Solvitur ambulando, writes St. Jerome — "to solve a problem, walk"—but I leave problems on my desk and go out to partake and enter into things beyond vexations. My maxim is *Observatur ambulando,* and that means looking about and trying to avoid being diverted by keeping track of distance or paces per minute or any kind of mensuration whatsoever. To awaken the mind—and mix my measures—five meters can be as useful as five miles. (Besides, when walking I don't want anything mechanical—like a meter—defined as "the length equal to 1,650,763.73 wavelengths in a vacuum of the orange-red radiation of krypton 86." After all, one's tootsies get pretty good at determining distance.) The goal is to step away from selfness and integrate with otherness, something more difficult in a vehicle.

I inherited a single object from a great-grandfather, a man whose face I never knew although I did see Daniel's hand, so to speak, in a splendidly knobby stick he made in 1910 after a stroll in a friend's Florida orange grove where he cut a wonderfully curious limb and polished its bark to perfection. Before my father died, he asked what I might want of his, and I said only the old banjo clock and the walking stick. It was Daniel's craft that drew me into the world of stickery and inspired me to find and shape my first attempt out of a wind-broken aspen I came across in the mountains near Durango, Colorado. In the quarter-century since, I don't know how many sticks I've made for my use or given away to someone I believe will actually take one into the field. Like all of us, my friends spend hours atop four wheels; but when a walking stick stands in the corner by the door, always ready like a faithful canine to be taken out on a saunter, the lure to touch primal and sacred things of the earth can be strong.

THE MANICHEAN

This assignment answered a request to write a "celebratory essay with a distinctive eye and voice expressed in an interpretative style." After spending some time in southeast Oregon, I decided to try to show magnificence in a land whose very name is Misfortune and attempt to reveal beauty arising from severe austerity, a harshness inimical to human occupation, a place where inhospitality defines its virtue and goodness. I discovered, though, that a dualistic, syncretistic approach to landscape discomfits some readers.

The Old Land of Misfortune

It was a void on my road map, an implication of only emptiness here, and that's what drew me to southeast Oregon and the edge of a lake so shallow it's often little more than a fugitive damp. By at least one definition, I was in the most remote spot in the lower forty-eight states, that is, as far from an Interstate highway as one could get. From that place the nearest federal four-lanes—I-5 and I-84—are more than 160 air miles distant. My approach, Interstate 84, was, if you don't get lost in the maze of dirt tracks making up a fifth of the route, 250 miles from where I stood—the distance, say, from Grand Central Station to the Pentagon, from St. Louis to Kansas City, Detroit to Chicago. It's true that several miles east of Tonopah, Nevada, one can be equally far from an Interstate, but that location is along U.S. Highway 6 and any aura of remoteness is considerably reduced.

Because I live about two-thousand miles east, it had taken some effort to get into this heart of the Oregon high-desert indicated in my atlas by roads running around and even away from it. The Malheur—French for "misfortune"—is not the Oregon of sixty shades of green arising from rain, rain, rain; and here are no Pacific Coast sea stacks, no Yaquina Bay oysters or sweet geoducks, no espresso at the back of a little bookshop. This is the Other Oregon, the Big Empty, an immense space shaped and volcanically deformed before being turned into desert by the massive rain-shadow cast eastward from the almost-thirty-million-year-old

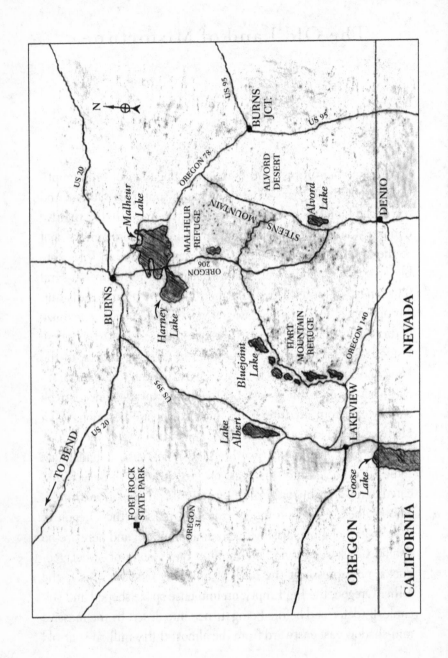

Cascade Mountains to the west. Precipitation does fall here, about enough to fill a lady's teapot.

That October I was walking along the northern end of Bluejoint Lake just below the high fault-block escarpment of Poker Jim Ridge, a wall of tenebrous basalt broken upward into the light of day by the great shoving of tectonic plates miles below. In a time when the rimrock there had seen fifteen-thousand fewer autumns, the ground I stood on was then twelve-hundred fathoms beneath a body of water that left its imprint in an ancient shoreline on a ridge two-hundred feet above my head. But, only a couple of generations ago, Bluejoint Lake was an unbroken expanse of cracked mud, the bottom of a predecessor basin at least six-hundred-feet deep and part of a concatenation of a dozen similar catchments and uncountable ponds lying to the south; today all are comparatively puny, evanescent lagoons that together mark the grave of a Pleistocene lake large enough to have swallowed Portland, had Portland been here.

The fascination of the Malheur depends on trying to see what it has been, how it was once so different, all the while remembering certain kinships and lines of descent: fire the father of liquid stone, volcanoes the mothers of risen valleys, and wind and ice the rods of discipline to shape the offspring. More than any other place I know, the Malheur bespeaks radical changes; any apparently subtle ones mere masks for grander upheavals. Under the Great Sorcerer's wands of weather and plate tectonics, things—mountains, valleys, hundred-mile-long lakes—vanish, come to light again, only to disappear once more. Sixty miles south, straddling the California line, huge Goose Lake dried up in the 1920s to reveal the indelible 1845 tracks of the famous Applegate immigrant trail striking a course right across the dried bottom strewn with bits of broken-down wagons. Then the lake rose once more to conceal history like a liquid Pompeii: Instead of molten rock and falling cinders, here it was water flow and rainfall covering a human past.

Despite their size, some of these residual waters can be waded shore to shore, and they are as noteworthy for their shallowness as transience, yet they exist today because once they were deep holes of the ancient lake; to slosh across a shallows now is, in effect, to walk the bottom of an inland sea. It's that kind of inversion, that impermanence, that irony of natural process, which marks the Malheur: What was deepest is now shallowest; what was fiery, flowing magma is rigid mountain; what was a juniper forest lies entombed under a hundred feet of dried mud now turned into a greasewood waste. To traverse this desert in any deep sense, one must move in time to gain an idea of the sweep of years revealing the topsy-turvy undulations of a nature that appears to flip-flop through the eons and toss the logic of creation bum over teakettle.

Bluejoint Lake lies in the Warner Valley which itself is another and larger bottom of a primitive lake; it helps to see these remnant waters as once bigger or smaller, deeper or drier, linked or disconnected — that is, as what's left of an ancestral body of water. The autumn day I was there, Bluejoint Lake happened to be not completely dry, and its perimeter was golden with bunchgrasses and shrubs creating a perimeter of marshiness waiting for the next chance to return to something like a greater deep. In the 1870s a government report designated the encompassing basin as swamp, but only fifteen years later a writer noted, "The principal portion of the valley is sterile, barren greasewood desert with only an occasional marsh or salt lake varying the monotony. It would be difficult to imagine a more desolate and God-forsaken region outside of Assyria, Arabia, or the Great Sahara."

The awesome reach of dried-up lakes and desiccated creek beds eastward is not so much a void as what might be better termed a *devoid* — at first glance, a waste devoid of all but gravel and scrub and alkali flats where the only moving thing is a column of dust, a spectral visitant waiting for wind and the dry rattle of serpents to give it voice. That blankness on a road map has no place for sensible humanity. Like a planet at inception, it's an igneous sprawl forsaken enough to make a Civilian Conservation Corps worker at the Hart Mountain camp in the 1930s confess, "The country is all right, but there's too much of it."

Life other than the reptilian seemed to have so repudiated the gauntness of the flat, I one afternoon found myself waiting for sundown not to escape the heat but to let darkness close down the overwhelming openness, and pull the shades of night across an immense window which looks into another time zone. Then, perhaps from the mountain behind, I could hear through the Plutonian blackness a different voice of the territory, maybe the dolorous call of a coyote, its song-dog belly thin with little but emaciated lizards and withered spiders, its nose coated with alkali, and its eyes ravenous. The sense of desolation was not one of simple abandonment as with the ghost town nearby; rather, this one was severe because, like the resident dust devils, it rose almost perceptibly to suggest people could never endure where they don't belong. Why would someone be out here anyway except to prepare himself for Hell?

Yet, in a land of inversions, why not the flames of Hades reflecting the pure fires of the Empyrean? Why not in a place that looks like the end of all existence, a realm to unnerve anyone who falls into imagining his own bleached and disarticulated skeleton, only a jawbone holding a few teeth to tell who he was? *You are alone. Go ahead, try it, call out for someone, shout until you have no more voice. There'll be no answer: not now, not later, not until some other fool hiker, much too late to help, happens upon your molars.*

But more reciprocity: What if someone *would* step out of the darkness? A someone to disrupt the forsakenness you're there to experience. Who, other than a shadow bent on evil? Who else would come into an overcooked land brought from the mind of an inexperienced godling in his first essay at creation, having a go at it and getting it all wrong, his unseen hand dividing the waters to let dry ground appear and pronouncing it good until it refused to bring forth a tree yielding fruit after its kind, an Eden gone awry, everything driven out except serpents, and the Inceptive Word saying on some third day, *This is no damned good*, and cursing deserts thereafter to be the dominion of demons and devils for the purging of souls.

Walk here in sackcloth to repent a life lived too abundantly, frivolously, and blindly in a nation too easy and forgiving of excess, in an era so accommodating one can ignore the universe being mostly a lethally dry void where wetness and life and light are exceptions. Here, one finds connection: ground too hot or cold, wicked lakes turned to salt, dry alkali beds raising mirages to taunt thirst, columns of dust dancing in satanic spirals.

But that's the short view because from such a place the incipient waters once rose and from them the *prima materia* and from them stamen and pistil, ova and legs and mind, words, music, theorems, walks on a moon that is a nightly presentment of planetary origins in its rocky desolation of first matter, a world forever hopeless of seed. The sharp stones here inscribe themselves into a hiker's soles, a reminder he didn't just wander without purpose into this stunted severity; he came deliberately, driven by that thing that killed the cat.

Beyond Poker Jim Ridge there were, of course, a few dwellers having dominion over wandering cattle, and farther yet a handful of other people offering gasoline, a meal, or a place to sleep. And schoolchildren too; some of whom will put in more than a hundred-thousand miles on a bus before they complete their final required year, and those others who get stashed up north in Crane at one of the last public boarding schools in the nation. Seldom are those young visible. It was difficult to think of any dwellers as residents because the territory did not really allow true human residence; instead it tolerated only passers-through, some merely moving along faster than others, and even natives born in the Malheur three generations ago have the look of itinerants, and so in reciprocity it was easy for them to tolerate my passage.

But being only a passer-through can sharpen perceptions and make keen the awareness that the traveler will leave and never be a resident, the place being better for his departure. Those dwellers are some of the descendants who responded to a newspaper ad for the Catlow Valley, the one immediately east of Warner Valley:

> 100,000 acres of choice sage-brush land in one of the greatest valleys in Eastern Oregon. We start excursions to settle this rich valley on April 1, 1910. We can settle 500 families on choice rich land. It will all be gone by Sept. 1, 1910. Will you join us?

In the valley—today holding only a single ranch and the ghost town of Blitzen ("lightning")—many dwellers stayed not even long enough for their newly born to learn to ride a horse.

One morning, under haggard clouds, I walked to a basalt ridge of fragmented and fallen blocks heaped up and spent like a collapsed and exhausted city. In the rubble of the old magma, from clefts, cracks, crannies, crevices, the toughest of plants struggled out a pitiful, creeping, briefly promising existence, trying to go as far as they could, like the dwellers, before the next cataclysm inverted things again. In his *The Encantadas or Enchanted Isles,* Melville writes, "In no world but a fallen one could such lands exist."

People of the Malheur share, if not a yearning, at least a respect for spareness and natural parsimony, and they dread congestion, touched as they are by their intolerance of any encumbrance other than space and weather. Had the early Spanish explorers of North America made it this far, they might have left one of their Texas toponyms here: El Despoblado, the unpeopled, and the dwellers would find it accurate enough, although today some of them might prefer a name like El No Trespasso. One fellow, upon learning I was a writer, asked me not to give away any secrets of his hugely hidden-in-plain-sight purlieu. He found subsistence sufficient but time too scarce, often tapping a finger to measure the moments before I would move on. "If you write about these here parts, you remember this—you say *it's one hell of a place.*"

The southeast section of the great rectangle that Oregon is composes about one-quarter of the state but holds less than one-half percent of its population. Outsiders, to be sure, look for ways to fill the land, and some are succeeding with usurpation up at Bend near the northwest corner of the Malheur quadrangle. No one I met here spoke of Bend respectfully; after all, they are old residents who know the old place names: Poverty Flat, Mud Lake, Starvation Springs, Deadman's Bedground, Skull Creek, Coffin Butte.

On the Oregon-Nevada line not far southward, in Denio, I asked a café waitress how to pronounce the name. "Duh-*nye*-oh," she enunciated, "but if you live here, it's just Denial." Indeed. The Malheur denies most of what Americans have come to believe they need, and in that denial, in that refusal, rejection, disavowal, and repudiation lies the essence of the dwellers, some whose ancestors by force took the place from the Paiute people. Of the dozens of names on my map of the territory, almost none is Indian and four of the half-dozen most important toponyms honor military men: Harney, Steens, Alvord, Abert. Westward fifty miles and just north of Fort McDermitt Indian Reservation, a highway historical marker mentions the Bannock War of 1878 in saying the Paiutes "ravaged the country [before] finally being defeated and dispersed." Across the last three words someone had sprayed in bloodred paint: SLAUTERED. The misspelled word unequivocally expressing the inverted views of dwellers red and white.

So: People killed each other over a land which still today is ready to do it for you should you make even the simplest of miscalculations: too little water, gasoline, protective clothing; too much cockiness, inexperience, anxiety. In the tiny café at Fields Station a little north of Denio, the owner keeps count on the wall of the annual number of burgers and milk shakes sold. There's no record of visitors who get lost or those who grow uneasy and certainly not those who find clarity of mind in a place capable of blowing away paltry sediments of a material culture cluttered with insignificances as if they were desert grit. Take that Missouri writer who went out after dark for a little ramble among the greasewood, and neglected to keep track of how far he'd gone until realizing he was probably lost, and feeling fear creep up his spine, and only then remembering to sit down to wait for the clouded sky to open and Polaris to shine through and set him straight.

One morning, sixty miles east of Poker Jim Ridge, I followed a loop road up the easy slant of the broad back of Steens Mountain, a route so gently inclined that eight-year-olds compete in an annual ten-kilometer footrace over a portion of it. To arrive *from the west* and motor up Steens is soon to scoff at calling this uplifted mass of basalt a mountain. Ridge is the word, or should be, never mind that it's almost ten-thousand feet high and that in June it's often icebound and called Snow Mountain.

Miles up the grade, sage changed to alpine flowers and mountain mahogany, and that to aspen copses, and then, abruptly, nothing at all grew, everything turned to weather-wrecked rock. Beyond, the ground fell away sharply as if the edge of a flat world where behind lay a horizon of snow and stone and ahead

A page from the Malheur notebook

was only air, air one-mile deep. How could a land risen so high fall so far?

Steens Mountain is another piece—a magnificent piece— of fiery under-earth thrust upward nearly two miles above sea level, only later to be eroded and excavated by its inverse elements, water and ice. Rock born of a burning River Phlegethon took its shape from glaciers crawling its spine, some of them reaching its shoulder to plunge off into a lake below; and when the ice was gone entirely, it left cirques twelve-hundred-feet deep and nearly three-thousand feet above the dried mud of another Pleistocene lake, now naught but a playa called the

Alvord Desert that stretches twelve miles north and south and seven miles eastward from the foot of Steens Mountain.

The desert below was a white expanse of alkali that makes the playa when wet look as if it's burning, and when it's dry the wind drives whirling carbonates washed down from the Steens to where there's a lake bottom but no lake, only a Tophet dazzlingly level and lifeless except on days city dwellers gang in to ride wind-driven sailers. The cracks in the hardpan could swallow most of a yardstick, but two tons of a truck will sink in less than an inch. In season there can be a few inches of actual water looking more like a fata morgana than what it is, and that's yet another inversion. The Spanish could have called the place a *Jornada del Muerto*, which today would mean little since we paved the roads to Gehenna with asphalt instead of good intentions, and you can take them at eighty miles an hour.

I went back down the mountain and on around it to the playa and walked onto the desert bottom crazed with fissures and glazed with sun. Far out on the heated hardpan, I watched a spiraling column, as if on legs, arise from nothingness and begin moving toward me, and I took off for the ancient shoreline where once ice rivers came down from the mountain. No wish in me to be an Elijah and ascend heavenward in a whirlwind. But I couldn't make it, and after several yards I stopped to let the brown eddy overrun me. The warm grit covered me head to toe like a shroud, and I got a mouthful of the dust devil, and spitting grit I said, *This is one hell of a place.*

IN THE GUISE
OF FICTION

First published in a women's magazine with a cautious if not downright socially conservative orientation, this story passed editorial muster perhaps because at the last moment and without my knowledge, it was labeled a "memoir." Of all the pieces in this book, "The Last Thanksgiving of Whispers-to-Hawks" most nearly belongs to that category, although its fictive guise, no matter how thin, makes it by my definition a short story—never mind that family members once present at our holiday celebrations (those who have not yet joined the choir silent) can readily recognize nearly everything here; I hope they will see not an affront but a celebration of things too long left unhonored.

The Last Thanksgiving of
Whispers-to-Hawks

To invite Uncle Billy to Thanksgiving dinner was to invite trouble, and not to invite him was to be accused of uncharitableness if not bigotry. So our parents extended invitations apprehensively but dutifully, their disquietude, for my elder brother and me, adding zest to what would otherwise be a meal of religious pontification and tired sermonage. While Uncle Billy was not a full-blood Osage, in our line he was the closest to it and, in my ten-year-old mind, a pretty good incarnation of Indianness. To him, Thanksgiving was a perturbation of that tribal blood — after all, the holiday celebrated the voracious beginning of one era and the long glide toward twilight of another. If for him Columbus Day was a time of sorrow, Thanksgiving was a day of lamentation. To ease his guilt in his participation, he liked to sow little upsets like dragon teeth that might grow into something larger in a boy's mind. His last Thanksgiving at our home in Kansas City, Missouri, was the first one after the start of the Korean War.

Uncle Billy—Christian name, Wilbert; Osage name, Whispers-to-Hawks—and Aunt Dorene arrived tardy in their bent-up Nash, the old fellow somehow managing to catch—or succeeding in hooking—his sleeve on the horn ring to set our sedate street blaring his arrival. Almost frail, but straight of spine, he escorted our aunt to the door of our house, loudly and unnecessarily hallooed their presence, and returned to the Nash. From the trunk he took a brightly beaded and fringed clean shirt, pulled off a white one equally fresh, and vigorously, elaborately, ceremonially, began wiping isopropyl alcohol across his thin chest and under his arms. He rarely used water to wash anything other than his hands and face and hair. From the kitchen window, I heard our grandmother calling as if choking, "Somebody! Somebody get him!" My father went to the door, in hand the lure of a highball held aloft.

Nodding, Uncle Billy stepped toward the house, stopped abruptly, returned to the still-open trunk, and proceeded to change his trousers. The kitchen, the windows now full of faces, lay in a silence presumed only in a crypt. My brother whispered to me, "This could be the best Thanksgiving ever."

Midway in drawing up his trousers, Uncle Billy paused to open again the bottle of isopropyl. Yes, this was going to be a good Thanksgiving. In the kitchen, the silence changed to gasps, all of which could be translated into spoken English as "Oh my god, the neighbors!" and Aunt Dorene rapping against the window. My father went again to the door, highball still in hand, and calling no louder than necessary to avoid alerting any neighbors not yet at their windows, "Wilbert! Not in the street!" Uncle Billy waved an assent and finished his midtown ablutions, hoisted his trousers, and buckled his belt. Our neighbor Mrs. Canton, who believed there was a link between her husband's balding and his cutting down a tree infected with Dutch elm disease, had come out onto her porch in order to miss nothing. Uncle Billy, stepping rather bowlegged to let the rubbing alcohol dry, waved to her and said warmly, "Fine day for the national gluttony," and came smiling into our house, a halo of isopropyl giving notice of his entrance. From our bedroom window, my brother whispered, "Country-Boy Indians, one. City Slickers, zero."

Whenever Uncle Billy came for a visit, the children would blow in out of nowhere like dust balls from beneath a bed, and we'd pat the old tribesman's pockets for small gifts: a carved peach pit, a willow-twig whistle, a walnut shell holding not a nut but a minuscule drawing of a horrifically toothed and drooling pig-man. On that Thanksgiving his little gifts settled the house and restored a calm in everyone except Mary Margaret whom we called Aunt Tott.

She was a good cook—her peach conserves were her annual birthday gift to me—but she had turned her life into a dried flower pressed in a hymnbook. Were such possible, she was a widowed maiden who had talked—or prayed—her husband into an early grave he must have found wonderfully peaceful. Soon after his funeral, she began holding forth about her own demise— only days away these past many years—usually in terms of claus-trophobia: For her, there was to be no lid on the casket. Only a thin tea towel over her face. The real reason, I once overheard my father say, was so that she could talk right through it to any of those six feet down who, inescapably, could not but listen. Although without meanness, Aunt Tott was a twelve-gauge Christian and there was no bucking her authority.

As if a cavalry lieutenant, she would pursue Uncle Billy up into spiritual coulees where she tried to force a surrender of any heathenism, pantheism, and idolatry she was certain he was inflicting on children. Of pure Anglo descent—her maiden name Tottenham—she was imposingly broad of shoulder, wide of beam, yet not truly corpulent, and she used her dominating size to oversee the spiritual condition of the household, particularly the young. No child escaped her inquisitions to ferret out false doctrines, or the pronouncements of heresies that leadeth only to damnation; to her, more than any other, did I owe the aware-ness that my ten-year-old soul hung in the balance at every moment. At each holiday dinner, to Aunt Tott fell the task of giv-ing the blessing, which was always a sermonette to correct, if not an adult's, then at least a child's waywardness.

When Uncle Billy was present she more than once mocked

the old notion that Indians were a lost tribe of Israel while pointing out that, like the ancient Hebrews, Indians were possessed by a Dark Power whose name dare not be spoken. They had been placed in the New World wilderness to test white men and prove the rightness in taking the land and making it fruitful. She made clear to my brother and me that, while Uncle Billy was not the D—l incarnate, he was surely a minion from down below.

On a holiday meal, if the other women evinced little more than masked apprehension of Uncle Billy's next piece of deviltry, Aunt Tott unfurled her guidon and—were it proper to say—girded her ample loins for righteous battle. On that Thanksgiving, she greeted him with a clear if unstated alarum to the household, an equivalent to "Circle the wagons, Christian soldiers! Here comes them pesky redskins!"

Uncle Billy, his highball now in hand, returned her summons with a raised glass—"To the ripe fruits of the mother ship *Mayflower!*"—and Aunt Tott gave out her distinctive sigh of a woman long put-upon by the ungodly, pleased to get it in so early. (There would be time now for a couple more, each a demonstration to assist the shaping of a child's soul.) My brother held up, for my eyes only, a sly two fingers on one hand, a fist of the other: Pesky Redskins, two; Fruit of the Pilgrim Fathers, zip.

In Uncle Billy were the remnants of an old carny man claiming to have played the role of an attacking Injun in Buffalo Bill's Wild West Show. Once, while the colonel slept, Uncle Billy claimed he snipped the famed goatee of the old Indian scout into a satanic forked beard. I believed the story until my father pointed out that Uncle Bill was all of six years old when Cody retired his show. Nevertheless, Uncle Billy's yarns depicted him more as a wily counselor and strategist than a combatant, the tales often accounting for his glass eye: It had been scratched out by a bobcat, shot out by a senile Indian fighter, plucked out in his sleep by a crow trained by evil-hearted Pawnee. Those are ones I remember.

On the Thanksgiving in question, he loped off into a Plains tale with a particularly dark cast before Aunt Tott, making it a point to listen from the redoubt of her adamantine belief, demanded a cessation of heathenism in front of children. Uncle Billy paused, reconnoitered her position, considered her fire-power, and surrendered, we thought, to tell about the Reverend Obadiah Wilson's most powerful sermon, a piece of brimstone that got the people in the revival tent so aroused they rose and thundered responses; they rolled and stomped and made such disturbance that the very ground beneath the pulpit collapsed and dropped the good reverend three feet down into an old Indian grave, and his hellfired soul had to climb out covered with the dust of an ancient Choctaw.

At the conclusion Uncle Bill raised the whistle—made from an eagle fibula and trimmed with a breast feather—he sometimes wore around his neck only to drop it. I begged him to blow it; Aunt Dorene passed him a glance, and he said, "I better not, boy. No telling what I might call up into this room."

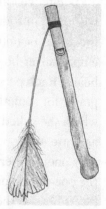

Eagle-bone whistle

Ever vigilant Aunt Tott said to the other women, "Now we have pantheism over there among the children. Rank, barefaced pantheism!" Because she from time to time also decried him as an atheist, I struggled to understand how many gods were the equivalent to no god. "Wilbert," she warned, "desist in front of young minds!" and with that Uncle Billy raised the eagle whistle and blew four shrill notes into the house. Quietly, he said to the boys, "Okay, my little braves, we'll see now."

*　　*　　*

When we sat down to the meal, Aunt Tott rose and stepped to the head of the table where my father sat, and in full apostolic authority she intoned, "All *churchly* heads bowed!" Preemptively, she aimed the sentence like a carbine shot right at Uncle Billy. As she powered up, slowly, ever so slowly warming to godliness, he pulled his spine painfully erect, stood, his old head lifted toward the chandelier, his scrawny arms raised with palms upward, precisely in the manner an Osage gives thanks. Before reaching his full position, he whispered to my bowed head, "If old What's-His-Name comes out from down under where you're looking at, holler."

The prayer moved from exordium on and on and through to the peroration. After her first words, as usual, my father and brother sat more bent than bowed, quietly shaking. With the last benedictory line, they raised their heads, faces crimson with suppressed laughter — not at the prayer but rather at its high tone and length.

Before yielding the floor to the baked turkey, Aunt Tott wished to introduce us to a new ceremony she had witnessed at the bishop's house. In the center of the table she placed an empty, silver bowl alongside an earthen crock filled with pinto beans. Each person was to pick up a bean, express gratitude or a prayer for something, and drop the pinto into the silver bowl — which she called a chalice. In order to force more soulful inquiry, an entreaty for personal or national salvation was acceptable, but only one per person. We were to continue until we transferred the one-pound package of pintos to the chalice.

As head of the house, my father, uncomfortably, was assigned the first bean, his token of thanks for the gathering. Around the beaning went, gratitudes for a plenteous table, for a touch of gout cured, a graduation with honors, successful cataract surgery, a baby sister, and so on until, running low on blessings, we all began more noting the remaining beans than listening to the thanksgivings. When I tossed in a bean in appreciation for my new BB gun, I had to remove the pinto and try again.

After his initial offering, Uncle Billy had done nothing but turn each bean into a wish—for a better fit on his upper denture, for less ear hair, for more on his head, for improved urinary flow, for death to tyrants. At his next turn, with the crock nowhere near empty, he stood again, picked it up, dumped the remaining beans into the chalice, and said, "With these little fellers from the earth—every blessed one of them—I hereby wish for a gold Cadillac and a thick slice of hot turkey on my plate!"

His abrupt response quieted the table. That surely was something close to what Aunt Tott had hoped to induce, because she pulled out a final pinto, apparently tucked away somewhere on her, raised her arm on high, and in full victory intoned, "With this tiny gift from Thy loving Hand, O Lord, I thank Thee for providing the young, the impressionable, those whose souls can so easily depart from the path of righteousness, we thank thee for this lesson in pagan mockery and greed."

My brother showed me two fingers on his right hand, one on his left: Pagans, two; Bean Counters, one.

The meal lurched on, powered by the good cooking. When it came time for the course of pinto soup always served last to honor the customary request of the old Osage, we learned this Thanksgiving we'd have canned-tomato soup, since Aunt Tott had usurped the pintos for her ceremony. Uncle Billy said nothing, but my brother held up two fingers on each hand.

The change in custom had again stilled conversation as we sipped at the tomato soup. Uncle Billy took the opportunity to rise and move next to Aunt Tott as if to offer a toast. Leaning over her as he spoke, he paused to rub his left eye, the one shot out by Buffalo Bill or stolen by a trained crow or whatever. As he did, the Dresden glass-eye dropped free and into Aunt Tott's soup before bobbing to the surface to stare redly at her. Looking heavenward, neither she nor anyone except my brother and me saw it. When Uncle Billy sat down, as if he'd forgotten what he intended to say, she—knowing the family maxim, *He who hesitates, listens*—resumed talking, all the while absently dipping into her bowl, the Dresden eye sliding away from her spoon, until a fatal dip caught the eyeball, and up it came, cradled in her spoon as she lifted it to her mouth. Glassily it looked down her throat, and it was then she caught the unnatural red gleam. For a moment she stared in terror as if the eye were her own, then she dropped it back into the soup, and cried out, "My God, Wilbert! This time you've gone beyond forbearance!"

He apologized unconvincingly and scoffed, "It's just an eyeball from a half-blind Indian." And then, perhaps remembering something from his missionary schooling, he said scripture he must have prepared for the children: " 'Hear now this, O foolish people without understanding, who have eyes and see not and have ears that hear not.' "

We boys were now standing to watch the slowly bobbing eye. Aunt Tott raised her soupspoon, took aim, and smote the eye, splattering us with tomato soup, and she retorted, her lips curling around her carefully formed words: "If thy left eye offend me, I'll pluck it out and cast it from me!"

In a quiet as if Judgment Day had come and gone, that was the end of the Thanksgiving meal. Later, my brother said, "I think the game's over, but you tell me the winner."

Such was the last Thanksgiving of Whispers-to-Hawks. He died the following March when his car hit a strip of black ice on Highway 99 just south of Bigheart, Oklahoma. He was driving a beat-up Cadillac he had, with a brush, painted gold.

The following November, Aunt Tott, now able to move unvexed and triumphant through the holiday, made her stained-glass pauses in her sesquipedal blessing of the meal longer than ever, long enough in fact for my brother to stand, lift his head toward the chandelier, arms raised and palms upward. I followed, and our father did not tell us to sit down.

APPROACHING
THE INEFFABLE

It's not unusual for a writer's brain to function visually as it draws up images the way some other minds fetch up numbers or formulas or theorems. In my case, that probably explains both my utter ineptitude in spherical trigonometry and my tenure as a photojournalist. A pictorial approach is a means of trying to comprehend things ultimately incomprehensible, and it suggests to me a Cro-Magon, in the light of a flickering, tallow lamp, daubing iron oxide and ocher onto a cave wall to make an aurochs. Despite certain insufficiencies, the ancient method of using visuals to share visions of what is mostly unfathomable can be as functional as other approaches to the great ineffabilities. After all, a writer's goal is to bring the reader to his shoulder: "Do you see what I see?"

Prairie and Plain

POINT OF BALANCE. A dozen miles northwest of Smith Center, Kansas, stands a narrow stone pyramid not much higher than a six-footer wearing a top hat, and from the peak flies an American flag. If the surface of this country were a uniform plane, the forty-eight contiguous states would balance delicately atop the flagpole like a ballerina *en pointe*. This place is the geographic center, and the people here take pleasure in the core of America being a stretch of their easy prairie hills which, only a few miles west, begin to merge with the High Plains. It's a land splendidly open, clean, uncluttered, a spot symbolically suited to be the heart of a spacious nation. Outsiders' comments about the tedious and cultureless prairie and plain do not usually annoy these Kansans, accustomed as they are to the old, blinding bias of woodland peoples who believe any place not marked by timber must be a wasteland of withered vegetation with intellects to match.

THE HAND INVISIBLE. If you would see what made the prairies and plains, look up. It's there in the cloudless sky, invisibly above as if a god: air currents, relieved of their wetness by the Rocky Mountains, move eastward over a land where the degree of evaporation just about equals the precipitation. These invisibilities create a place of equilibrium favoring plants that keep vital parts snugged in the damper realm belowground—

cooler in summer, warmer in winter—a place where winds cannot tear and rupture nourishing cells. To survive, the prairie plants send up only what they must, and they make it expendable. Let drought and wildfire come on, this native vegetation will idle underground while the trees wither and die and open the land to those waiting below as if in service to the unseen master hand.

TWO MILES SOUTH OF BAZAAR, KANSAS. On this upland, the trees—slippery elm, hackberry, walnut, cottonwood—keep to the vales where the broken limestone creeks run clear, and they leave the slopes and level crests to the tall grasses—big and little bluestem, grama and Indian grasses—and miles of wildflowers with names suitable to their blossoms: indigo, gay-feather, silver-leaf nightshade, shooting star, downy gentian. This long stretch of tall prairie is one of the last left in the country. Of the quarter of a billion acres of tallgrass once reaching from Indiana to just beyond here and from central Canada to Texas, only about 3 percent remains, most of it in these Flint Hills of Kansas. A traveler may now drive eight-hundred miles across the Middle West and never know what tall prairie means, even though it remains one of the very emblems of America. Let me say it: To know America one ought to stand at least once in grass running from elbow to a horizon that appears knee-high because everything in the Heart of America partakes of that far rim and its sky and openness and gift of light.

SIX MILES WEST OF FAITH, SOUTH DAKOTA. Overwhelmingly here, there's a sensation of being on top, a feeling of aboveness that comes not from elevation, for this is a place of undulating levelness, but rather from a horizon visible in all of its 360 degrees, visible even when one sits. You need climb noth-

Toole County, Montana

ing to see the slight curving of the earthen ball. This stretch of short grass along U.S. Highway 212 is not properly prairie but the eastern edge of the High Plains that lie beyond the ninety-eighth meridian where rainfall drops to twenty inches and dwindles with each westward mile as the elevation rises from twelve hundred feet to five thousand in a fairly regular tilting that most woodlanders will see as *flat*. Here, unlike true prairie, trees do not lie in wait to steal land from forbs, legumes, and clump grasses, those plants evolved to live in a realm where all is minimal except wind and sun, the primal abundances of the Plains.

THE RAIN SHADOW FROM PIKES PEAK. I have two memories of my first visit to the summit in 1952: the steep ascent up the cog railroad, and the vast, afternoon umbra the mountain cast down the eastern slope and across the foothills all the way, it seemed, to the great plane of Kansas where once plesiosaurs swam. Years later, when I learned about a phenomenon poetically called a *rain shadow*, I remembered that massive dusk creeping onto the plains. The metaphoric name is apt, for the mountains can stop clouds as they do sunsets, and it's those rock barriers that determine the life beyond them and seemingly out of their reach. As a stockade shapes the character of a fortress, so it is here: What gets kept out makes all the difference to what lives within. The annual precipitation in western Nebraska is fifteen inches, and in eastern Iowa it's almost three feet. That twenty-inch difference led explorer Zebulon Pike in 1806 to call the trans-Missouri west the Great American Desert, a term both then and now inaccurate in its implications of waterlessness and barrenness. Yet the description did serve briefly to give tribal peoples a few extra years of freedom before the great westering incursions of settlers changed everything. Believing Pike and thinking the absence of trees meant infertile soil, homesteaders were slow to take up this territory before the myth broke and farmers learned that bluestem and buffalo grass are often better indicators of fecundity than an oak or hickory; some settlers were led on by another skewed notion that "rainfall follows the plow," the belief that tilling grassland would change humidity and increase precipitation.

THE DESERT BREADBASKET. Pike, who understood little of the xeric world he passed through, recommended that the federal government seize the land west of the Mississippi River and trade it to Spain for Florida. In 1988, just four of the states in the "great desert" produced more than a billion-and-a-half bushels of corn, about one-billion bushels of wheat, and a half-billion bushels of soybeans. Never mind the rump roasts and cutlets.

THIRTY-THOUSAND FEET BELOW. From this Boeing 737, I can look down on some thousand-square miles of Nebraska and see a shape born in Thomas Jefferson's brain. Across the undulations of grasses and crops lies a great grid so insistent that only the most crumpled and dissected landform can interrupt it. His township-and-range system of 1785 brought a surveyor's tidy schematic to the country in order to help establish "clear" land titles and to take wilderness and turn it to the ends of white settlement. Below me is the largest physical expression of eighteenth-century rationalism in America, perhaps on the face of the Earth. A fellow passenger described it as "a lovely counterpane," but I have never seen much beauty in those cardinal-direction grids that so ignore, even deny, natural forms. It is, of course, convenient to drive across Oklahoma or North Dakota or Iowa and never lose a sense of direction as you travel, where the roads, fences, houses, and probably even the bedsteads and sleeping bodies lie only due this way or that. From nearly seven miles up, I can count the mile-square section lines of gravel roads or barbed-wire fences for half a minute and figure the speed of the 737. I can also wonder whether road travelers in eastern Colorado would see the beauty of the plains more readily if their routes followed not ruled lines but the sinuous arcs of the slight hills and the eccentric bends of creek beds. What if they traveled on roads expressing not an engineer but the land itself, on highways that call upon the full range of a dashboard compass?

CLICHÉ, SIMILE, ERRORS. Between the Ozark Mountains of western Missouri in the east and the Black Hills of South Dakota in the west, between the Cimarron River in southern Kansas and the Souris in North Dakota, the prairies and plains lie grandly sloped from the foothills of the Rockies almost all the way to the Mississippi River. It's a drop of some four-thousand feet or nearly four Empire State Buildings stacked one atop the other. The terrain is hardly a rampart, but covering as it does about eight-hundred horizontal miles, it surely isn't "like a pool table" except in popular misconception. This angled landscape is so roused with risings and fallings, with hills and valleys and stony encrustations, it looks as if a cosmic hand had wadded it up in frustration for its not being something else, and then in remorse tried to smooth it out again, only to be unable to quite flatten the crinklings: the western Ozarks, the Black Hills, Flint Hills, Red Hills, Smokey Hills, Sand Hills, Wildcat Hills, two disheveled and jagged Badlands, the Missouri Breaks, the Killdeer Mountains, Turtle Mountain, and a thousand and more bluffs, cliffs, ridges, knobs, knolls, humps, buttes, mesas, peaks, pinnacles, pillars, hogbacks, mounds, moraines, drumlins, kames, eskers, escarpments, cuestas, and even more valleys and vales and dales and dells, gullies and gulches, ravines, arroyos, draws, coulees, and bottoms. Pool table? Not even bumper pool.

THE RIVER. Only one watercourse touches all six of the Near West states. A deceptive thing of snags and sawyers and sand shallows, an unpredictable siltiness that eats its own banks like a dreamer chewing at his bedcover. The Missouri River shapes the earthly topography and political geography, the economics, institutions, the history. Initially, the Euro-American empire moved far up its contorted course into the plains, until people on the overland trails decided only its lower leagues were useful to reach a jumping-off place like Kansas City or Council Bluffs. First into the Near West by river went French explorers and voyageurs opening a way for Americans of many silks: Lewis and Clark pressing the quest for a route to Cathay, followed by soldiers, surveyors, scientists, writers, artists, and settlers beyond numbering. Against the current, in pirogues, canoes, flatboats, skiffs, keelboats, steamboats they came: Thomas Nuttall, Stephen Long, Prince Maximilian, John Frémont, Francis Parkman, and the three greatest early western artists: Karl Bodmer, George Catlin, John James Audubon. And in 1837 aboard the paddle-wheeler *St. Peter's* came a passenger named *Variola* that would remake the human face of the Great Plains: smallpox, decimator of native America. All of them—atop the great earthen Missouri, the longest river in the country before engineers meddled with it—all of them came into the middle country.

A MANDAN VILLAGE. A few years ago when the grasses had turned russet and the wild roses were bare stems thrashing thorniness in the wind, I was walking along the west bank of the Missouri River a few miles south of Bismarck, North Dakota. An early snow was on the way. Every so often behind me a car whipped up the highway toward the capital, and below, the water moved south, although its current was invisible in the reservoir formed behind Oahe Dam a couple-hundred miles downstream. The twentieth-century lay at a distance, but where I stood were grassy mounds of the Huff archaeological site, once a prehistoric, palisaded village of something more than a hundred houses, most of them aligned in tidy rows parallel to the river, their back walls to the north wind. People lived here more or less peacefully at a time when Europeans were sending men off to drive infidels from a presumed holy land, a kind of prefiguring of what would one day happen here. The native dwellings depended minimally on timber and much more on grasses and the soil itself. In those earth-contact lodges (architects would reinvent them a millennium later), the people ate bison, elk, deer, catfish, and mussels, and they grew maize, beans, and squash in gardens cultivated with hoes made from bison shoulder blades. What they called the river or their village or themselves, we don't know, but we can assume they liked the place because they stayed here for ten generations.

THE GRAND TOTEM. Were you to travel the Oregon or Santa Fe Trail in 1850, you would have learned to recognize, even from four miles away, nothing so quickly as a cottonwood tree. Great in size, comparatively numerous, marvelously useful and beautiful, the cottonwood is the totem of prairie and plains even more than the bison because, unlike the great beast, *Populus deltoides* is as abundant now as two centuries ago. Indians made canoes from it and used it to prop up teepees; Missouri River steamers fueled their way with cottonwood; homesteaders used it for rafters and posts in their soddies; game birds flew in to eat the catkins; bees made honey in trunk hollows; and travelers—red and white—climbed the trees to see what lay ahead or who might be coming up from behind. Without the cottonwood, life would still have proceeded across the plains just as life would have gone on in New England without the codfish, that eastern totem you can still see atop steeples and in the Massachusetts Statehouse; but I don't know of any plains congregation (or legislature) that ever put up a weather vane in the shape of a cottonwood, yet well they all should have.

BRED OF THE BLIZZARD. An improbable beast indeed—the head too large, horns too small, shoulders too high and rump too low, tail too short; a composite beast indeed—hooves of a cow, hump of a camel, mane of a lion, beard of a goat, the temperament of a dragon. Possessed of surprising speed, tremendous strength, an allegedly slow brain and limited vision, and its common name a description of what it is not: buffalo. Yet to aboriginals and Americans alike the American bison—evolved to withstand deadly blizzards of the great expanses—was the essence of the prairie and plain. The Indians of the high midlands built a way of life around it, discovering in it heat and light, fuel for body and sustenance for soul, and finding a use for all of its parts from nostrils to tail, from its scat to its spirit. White people put bisons on coins, bills, postage stamps, medallions, state flags and seals, mostly after trying to exterminate them like cockroaches. Before 1800 there were perhaps a hundred-million bison roaming America in numbers possibly making them the most abundant large land-animals on earth. A century later, naturalist Ernest Thompson Seton thought only eight-hundred remained. White men hunted them for hides and flesh, but mostly they slaughtered bison as a kind of implicit genocide of Plains Indians, the last holdouts against American absorption. Today, there are about a hundred times more bison than Seton's figure, and an alert traveler over the Great Plains may again see the beasts, if not in the millions that once stunned even the most wearied explorers, then at least as a symbolic presence. Never mind that now somebody owns every last one of them.

¿*HABLA ESPAÑOL?* At almost the exact center of Kansas is a small, brick museum and inside under glass lies a corroded piece of metal looking like a desiccated honeycomb, its medievalness startling in the vast wheat fields around Lyons. One of Coronado's men, so it seems, left that bit of chain mail behind in 1541 near the farthest penetration the conquistadors made into the American heartland. The horsemen, sweltering under their iron shirts and heavy morions, were hoping to duplicate the rapine and plunder of Pizarro in Peru. Led by two Indians who were kept chained and urged to yield up information by snapping dogs of war, the Spaniards searched the Southwest and central plains for rumored cities of gold. Had the conquerors been capable of perceiving Quivira as a metaphor of the economic promise of the territory, American history would be something much different, so changed that you would probably be reading this sentence in Spanish.

THE WARRIOR DIPAUCH. To fall in love with the land is, sooner or later, to ask what it was like before the twentieth century hit. Did the hills show as they do now, and did the river then turn just so under the bluff; and the first people, how did they spend their days here? On occasion there is an answer, as in the work of Prince Maximilian zu Wied, a German ethnographer, and his illustrator, Karl Bodmer, a Swiss painter. They ascended the Missouri in 1833 and created the fullest and finest artistic record of preconquest America ever. They saw and represented the place in its primeval aspect when Plains Indians had not yet much come to depend on foreign goods. Bodmer was a watercolorist who drew with the precision of a draftsman and painted with the genius of a master. You can check the accuracy of many of his landscapes today by comparing his paintings with the actual topography. Even more magical is a work like his *Interior of a Mandan Earth Lodge*. When paired with Maximilian's written account of evenings spent in the lodges where the travelers listened to tales told by the old warrior Dipauch, a viewer is almost present among the five Mandans sitting around the firepit, dusky winter-light slipping down through the smoke hole, long lances stacked just so, shields and parfleches and medicine bundles hung neatly, a bull-boat paddle leaning against a cottonwood post. Maximilian supplies the voices, the music, and dances, as he describes where the men sat, the gifts young warriors gave older ones, the tall and powerful dancer with an effeminate voice, and the women ceremoniously arising to the drumbeat and picking up lances and throwing aside their robes, and their discomfort as they hurried past the agog foreigners.

THE BEND IN THE TRACK. It's dusk, and the stone mass of Scott's Bluff in western Nebraska has gone indigo against the sky and seems to cast a shadow all the way to the distant train tracks which here make a small, almost imperceptible deviation from a course otherwise as unyielding from straightness as a civil engineer can execute. In 1905 a railroad altered its track bed by a few feet to avoid a single, forgotten and isolated grave of a woman pioneer who died in 1852. Somewhere between her New

York home and the Missouri River eighteen-hundred miles westward, she contracted cholera. Week after week, she lay upon a few thin quilts in the jolting wagon heading for the Valley of the Great Salt Lake. This halfway point accomplished, she died, and her family buried her in the sagebrush flats and marked the grave by setting into the ground a spare rim for a wagon wheel. On the iron felly a friend had scratched:

REBECCA WINTERS AGED 50 YEARS.

The rim, slicked by visitors' touches, stands today just ten feet from the Burlington tracks which shake only a little more than the grave when the freights pass every hour or so as they have for nearly a century. Of the many burials still marked along the great western trails, this one somehow moves me the most because of the grudging shift it forced in steel tracks that never want to get out of the way of anything, even mountains: the persistence of that small and pitiful ferrous arch and the bones below in the dry soil being jarred ever so steadily into the granular soil they are coming to resemble.

PRAIRIE TROGLODYTES. Henry David Thoreau, in his customary way of negative boasting, said his cabin at Walden Pond cost $28.12½ in 1845. Oscar Babcock of North Loup, Nebraska, in 1872 built his home of comparable size for one-tenth Thoreau's small sum. The Walden cabin had two windows and Babcock's only one, but both had a single door without a lock. Babcock cut his home into a hillside and closed the front with a sod wall, spending nothing until he put in the eight-by-ten-inch window, the wooden door, and the stovepipe. Living in a dugout like his, typically, prairie settlers as soon as circumstances allowed would build a sod house and, if the crops came in and a tornado didn't suck up somebody, eventually build a frame home, all three within a few feet of one another. Wooden structures didn't always make sense on a terrain exposed to strong winds, wildfires, severe cold and heat, and Indians bent on mischief. After all, dugouts and soddies, which can last a century, never blew away or caught fire, they naturally ameliorated outside temperatures by twenty to fifty degrees, and they were reasonably defensible. But even with a whitewashed front door they were inelegant, and bison or wagons in the night sometimes ran over the top of a dugout, and rain seeped through and was likely to drip for a couple of days. One homesteader said she had to stand at her stove with an umbrella raised to keep clods from dropping into the stew, and another family got lax with maintenance and found themselves one night buried in the mud of a collapsed ceiling. A plains mother jumped off the roof of her dugout but failed in her try at suicide. Men found it almost impossible to convince a missus who had known a real house in the East that she wasn't now living like the gophers just beyond the well.

THE CYCLONIC TRACK. If it's murder you seek in American history, look no further than the prairies and plains, the traditional home of solid and upright citizens, people who abide laws, are first to fight in a war and the last to join a social revolution. But Americans know that the greatest warriors — because of the odds against them — on the continent were the Plains Indians whose resistance became the soul of the Mythic West. (Once on the Great Wall of China, in a strange conversation, a Chinese man asked me about the ferocity of Comanches and whether they still conducted raids.) We know that tribal peoples of the plains were the last to cease the fight against the theft of native lands and the white corruption of their ways; we may remember that the final pitched battle between Indians and a federal force occurred at Wounded Knee, South Dakota — not in 1876 but 1975. For the settlers, in spite of not having a cause so just as the Indians', the history is even more crimson: Jesse and Frank James, the Younger Brothers, the Dalton Gang, John Brown, William Quantrill, Bloody Bill Anderson, the Bloody Benders, Wild Bill Hickok, Richard Hickcock and Perry Smith (*In Cold Blood*), Boothill, Bleeding Kansas. In the 1930s, a physician named William Peterson postulated in his book *The Patient and the Weather* that people living in areas of severe and frequent meteorological disturbances—Tornado Alley is here—are prone to aberrations like mental alertness, genius, comeliness, *and* to counterparts like insanity, feeblemindedness, and physical malformation. Should the theory have merit, who could have been surprised by the cruelty of a Nebraska serial killer named Charlie Starkweather?

AN EIGHT-FOOT PHARMACOPOEIA. In Missouri, south of Sedalia, the trees begin to thin out, the land to open, and something fine and rare appears: prairie never penetrated by a plow. On these virgin acres that haven't even been grazed in years, a hiker with a guidebook to plants and a sharp eye can find relicts high and low. Example: a slender stalk of bristly leaves and yellow flowers that look like small sun disks. Identification: compass plant, also called pilot weed, gum weed, and *Silphium laciniatum*. The Ponca Indians called it *makatanga* (big medicine) and the Pawnee *kahtstawas* (rough medicine). Because it aligns its narrow leaves with the poles, it gave direction to hunting Indians and westering whites, and to both it provided soft exudations that made a serviceable chewing gum. The Omahas believed that where this plant appeared in abundance lightning would also, so they camped at a distance and burned the dried taproot during electrical storms to allow rising smoke to deflect thunderbolts. The Pawnee pounded the long, carrotlike tuber into a decoction for general disability, and settlers (learning from the Indians) used it and a related species to treat rheumatism and scrofula in themselves and glandular enlargements in their animals. The leaves they brewed into antispasmodics, diuretics, emetics, and cough suppressants. For this eight feet of pharmaceutical utility, they needed no guidebook.

A PRAIRIE RIDDLE. The creature is so associated with the American prairie and plains as to be its totemic mini-beast, but its heritage is classical and biblical. Eos, Greek goddess of dawn, transformed her mortal husband into one so that he might have endless life—and the change worked, if you consider immortality to be an eternal withering of the human into nothing more than a cracking, disembodied voice. To Aesop the creature was a symbol of improvidence; Moses named it as one of the three things his people could eat in the wilderness; and John the Baptist in his desert journey survived on it (with a touch of honey). On this continent, Potawatomi Indian women ground and blended it with acorn meal into patties and roasted them on hot stones or sun-dried them to eat during winter; whites, though, could see them only as an airborne pestilence that came on like evil thunderclouds to strip off fields like bedsheets for the wash. Sometimes the things would even gnaw away on sweat-stained hickory handles of scythes and pitchforks. Yet, one alone, winging, leaping, stridulating, is a creature of distinctive voice and delightful name: grasshopper.

WHIZZ! It's one more thing the bulldozer, with help from rural electrification, has put the quietus on. You can now cross the seven-hundred miles of Iowa and Nebraska or roll through Kansas or Oklahoma and see not a single working windmill. Yes, you might spot a few derelict steel towers yet holding on to the helic blades, perhaps one continuing to rotate slowly on unoiled bearings dryly screeching as it grinds toward a final silence.

Even more than barbed wire, the American wind-engine allowed settlement and ranching in a land where water moved not so reliably in creeks as in aquifers below. Then, at mid-century, came submersible electric-pumps and bulldozer-gouged ponds, both impervious to windstorms and neither needing much maintenance. But lo! The white man's West was not the same without the interruption wind-machines gave to the horizon and neither is a rancher's utility bill which once reflected the frugal pumping of shallow waters. And more, gone from the western country of swiveling metal vanes with painted trademarks that could cast words—a virtual story of passion—into the prairie wind: Adam's Novelty, American Advance, Back-Geared Baker, Geared Gearless, Boss Vaneless, Defiance Oilomatic, Running in Oil Giant, Midget Wonder, Eureka Junior, Farmer's Friend, Terrible Swede, Lady Elgin, Gamble Long Stroke, Dempster Double Stroke, Irvin Screw, Whizz, Improved Climax, Happy Home.

THESE TWENTY EMBLEMS. Bits of essence, pieces of prairie and plains, commonplaces, definers, synecdoches, things abundant—or at least once so. But even where abundance has vanished, as I write now, they are for a while longer still on the land, and you have only to look in a certain cast of light to see them or perhaps only their pentimenti.

TO GO SOLO

For a writer in search of stories, traveling with a friend or partner—no matter how affable—can be a distraction difficult to overcome. Despite the assists from an additional pair of eyes and ears, other details potentially useful get inevitably masked or obliterated by a second human presence and vanish unnoted. I estimate it takes about two days of travel with a companion to equal reportage gathered during a single day of solo exploration. Call this near-necessity the loneliness of the long-distance writer.

A Fallen Yew, an Oaken Pillar, a Forgotten Birch

Of the several ways to enter a foreign land, mine has always been to plunge into its depths, immerse myself in differences that immediately tell me home is a long way off. When I arrived near London one warm early October morning, a fellow traveler and I moved quickly to hire a little four-on-the-floor, right-side-drive auto and, unwisely, took no practice tour around the parking lot. I steered us off onto the left side of a small highway and immediately got pulled into the vortex of a roundabout— a rotary—those paved circles that whirlpool racing traffic, sort it out, and send it along its various routes. A foreign driver watching for road markers may have to circle enough times to begin to feel like one of Dante's wayward souls being spun in Purgatory.

My navigator—a woman of pronounced Germanic heritage, whom I shall call Lucy—read the route signs fast and said, "Go right!" but since all exits were right turns, I had to circle again. I suggested she see the roundabout as the face of a clock and tell me our direction as if it were an hour. On the next rotation, she, a precise person and lover of digital time, called out "Nine-forty-five!" I interpreted that to be ten o'clock, which was wrong, and she said, "Try nine-thirty. Maybe nine-twenty-five toward nine-twenty-six."

Soon after, we entered a second rotary and explored its possibilities. She called out, "Three-twenty-two!" The road I did *not* want was, by nasty chance, the B3022, and so that's the one I

took. Once again on the correct route, I said, possibly louder than necessary, "Just the hour! Use just the hour hand!"

At least until Americans widely adopt the traffic rotary, the English roundabout gives sudden, full-measure introduction to national differences, but not of the sort I was hoping for. I wanted a prelude more felicitous; say, a pub snack to accompany a half-pint of ale should suffice. We found a traditional plowman's lunch—two types of hard cheese; pickled cocktail onions; small green salad; a whang of house-baked bread; and the capstone: a scoop of Branston pickle (a relative of chutney). English motoring challenges be damned, assisted by a dollop of Branston pickle and a half-pint, I sat back in full pleasure of differences and felt happily arrived. Ah, to be in England now that October's here.

To shake jet lag, about fifteen miles east of Winchester we turned off toward Selborne, a Hampshire village capable of inflicting serious quaintness-shock on an unsuspecting Yank, but I'd been there before and reckoned myself sufficiently inoculated to keep my wits and tame my ardor for rural England. We checked into an old inn, drew the draperies against the afternoon light and, meaning only to shake some jet lag, inescapably slept deeply until Lucy awoke me with a rattling announcement of "Hell's bells! It's six-thirty-eight! *P.M.!*"

In the quarter-century of my visits to Britain, the English have made some progress in the advancement of plumbing. It may be a result of their conversion to decimal coinage, requiring as it does less time counting in twelves and twenties and giving greater opportunity to evaluate the possibilities of twentieth-century plumbing. Yet, while their tellies pluck signals from satellites, their water closets and basins still ignore the convenience of a hot-cold mixer faucet or the economy of a shower rather than a tub. Nevertheless, near my bed was a small shower offering three selections of water: scalding, numbing, and a tepid trickle.

*   *   *

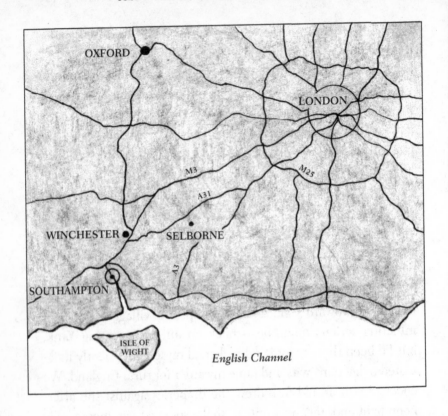

Village Selborne is quiet and fully English in nearly its every detail inside and out: thatched or slate roofs, orange chimney pots, ivied walls, and a church from the time of the Plantagenets (Richard, *Coeur de Lion*). It's famous because of an eighteenth-century book without characters (other than a turtle), plot, dialogue, or the slightest suspense; instead, it presents a text entirely of scientific letters composed by an Anglican curate. Any one of those details in America would doom it to oblivion, yet in England, Gilbert White's *Natural History and Antiquities of Selborne,* first published in 1789, has not merely never been out of print, it is the fourth-most-republished book in the realm, standing behind only—as you might guess—the Bible and Shakespeare. How it comes in after John Bunyan's *The Pilgrim's Progress* escapes me, but then salvation as a topic for me ranks just above, say, a documentary history of King James's Privy Council; White, unassisted by any lures of salvation, employs scientific observations to carry along his lovely sentences. Here are four about a mice nest he found in a field of "corn", i.e., wheat:

One of these nests I procured this autumn, most artificially platted, and composed of blades of wheat; perfectly round, and about the size of a cricket-ball; with the aperture so ingeniously closed that there was no discovering to what part it belonged. It was so compact and well filled that it would roll across the table without being discomposed, though it contained eight little mice that were naked and blind. As this nest was perfectly full, how could the dam come at her litter respectively, so as to administer a teat to each? Perhaps she opens different places for that purpose, adjusting them again when the business is over; but she could not possibly be contained herself in the ball with her young which, moreover, would be daily increasing in bulk.

At a time when belief in alchemy was not yet quite extinguished, his empirically observed and interpreted flora, fauna, and historical monuments, all presented in lucid and charming prose, stand without peer. My library shelves hold five different editions of White's *Natural History,* one of them a four-volume tooled-leather version which is about number three or four on my to-grab-in-case-of-fire list, all of this perhaps explaining the return to Selborne.

We walked down the lane to his spacious home, the Wakes, to see his garden and its ha-ha (a kind of sunken, invisible fence against roaming sheep), his sundial, penned manuscripts, and books before moving on into the village, with his *History* in hand as a guide. Selborne was quite recognizable from White's descriptions,

An eighteenth-century ha-ha

even after two centuries: written words, a living village, and wayfarers drawn into a long linkage—surely one of the higher ends of travel.

That night, after hearing about an eighteenth-century resident ghost common to such inns, I was suddenly awakened in the early hours when the shower noisily turned itself on for a full minute before shutting itself off. A groggy voice from the darkness: "Why are you showering at two-seventeen in the morning?" I said I was not in the shower, I was in bed. "So you're laying this off onto English plumbing?" and she was again asleep. Well, either it was one of the quirks of English plumbing or it was the ghost, but that leaves the question of how a specter gets itself dirty.

The next morning Lucy and I went up the lane to see the great and ancient yew growing next to the eight-hundred-year-old church belltower. The tree—White describes it, of course—had been there for about fourteen-hundred years; it was a sapling when Old English was the language of the land. Were I then traveling nearby, a curious fellow might have asked me, "How went it with you on the road?" but his words would have been, *"Hu lomp eow on lade?"* Or at least that's the way a host questions Beowulf.

When I first saw the yew a few years earlier, I measured its circumference at six arm spans. For a trunk so large, it was not a tall tree, perhaps sixty feet, but its limbs were massive and stretched out far laterally. In their shade sat not just Gilbert White but countless other people, some of whom spoke the language of *Beowulf* and others who must have laid eyes on Henry the Eighth.

I was talking to Lucy about such longevity in a living organism as we came in sight of it. Where its massive crown once was, where limbs the size of lesser trees once were, now only scraggly branches showed, things not big enough even for a walking stick. The great yew of Selborne, one of the most celebrated trees in England, had been blown over by a gale two years previous and was dead. Although villagers laboriously reset it after the storm so that it sprouted the following spring, the shock was too much. Older than the legends of King Arthur, it was now a twelve-foot-high stump shedding thick bark as beetles and borers chewed it back into dust. No matter how fine the church furniture that craftsmen were about to fashion from its huge boughs, the yew

The great yew tree of Selborne, England, in the nineteenth century

would now be milled lumber rather than a living link to what had gone before.

Some local antiquaries believed that sixty generations ago, near the entrance to an earlier church on the site, Saxons fused pagan lore and a newer religious belief by planting the yew as a symbol of Christian life everlasting. But if a symbol dies, then what happens to the belief it represents? Can a sanctuary bench holding village hindquarters symbolize eternity? (I have heard a sermon or two where that link is fitting.) Villagers took a waist-high cutting from the great tree and set it near the stump and called upon a woman in her ninety-first year and a boy in his first—the oldest and youngest residents—to add ceremonial handfuls of earth. Should that offshoot live as long as its parent, some writer might apotheosize it in A.D. 3400, yet another dispatch the ancient yew will have elicited.

The forecast called for Sunday to be "mainly dull," and I hoped the phrase described the sky and not our events under it, and, indeed, the English morning did begin so, unbroken clouds an evenly dismal gray like the inside of an old galvanized bucket. Lucy and I headed toward Wales, and, for a while, we endured the motorway, the whole time reminded that a man at the helm of an eighteen-wheel lorry cannot maintain self-respect unless he drives eighty-five miles an hour, eight-point-five feet off the rear bumper of a small Japanese auto. (Later, a traveling Londoner—not a trucker—told me in all solemnity that his rental car seemed rather sluggish at 110 mph.)

We left the four-lane at first opportunity to take up the English game of two-lane dodge-'em: In addition to dodging moving vehicles, I dodged parked ones, sheep, cattle, five bicycles (two of them pedaled by nuns in breezy habits), a stone barn thrusting a corner into the roadway, and a game of netless badminton using the road as a court. Then, to emphasize the travail in our travel, the weather got in on it with a drizzle that slowed us but no one else.

About the time I was trying to recall the reason I'd left the quiet of my reading chair at home, the answer arrived in Ross-on-Wye, a name that sounds as if it should be on a dinerette menu. In that fine village near the Welsh border, we passed a half-timbered shop selling antiquarian books—a place ideal for a mainly dull day. That's when I remembered my usual, nonpareil reason for visiting England: the chance to turn up a fine edition of some beloved book. This time I had in mind one I'd hunted for years. As remote as the possibility of finding it was, the bookshop did provide a reason to escape dodging and drizzle.

I asked the elderly proprietor, whose age had not removed his smile, if he might have a nicely bound copy of Samuel Johnson's *A Journey to the Western Islands of Scotland*. "You're wanting," he said, thinking, "a fine edition, perhaps full leather around vellum. Oh, that's a difficult one, that is." Shaking his head, he went to a glass-front cabinet, climbed a short ladder—"Not commonly found, that one"—stepped up on a chair so unsteadily I stood behind him at the ready. Still shaking his head and mumbling, he unlocked the case, fumbled among its disheveled shelves, head shaking, murmuring, "No. That's not—Oh my word! I thought possibly—" Shaking his head, grumbling. "My memory, you see, age—Oh, dash it all! Not here, not there. Confound it!"

Then he went silent. Pulling forth a small tome, quarter-leather with marbled boards, he said, "I do have this. Had it for some time, quite some time. I'm afraid it's rather dear." *But what was it?* He opened the book, studied it. "Oh yes, Mrs. Wilcox brought it in from the Barrington estate. That was, let's see, four or five years ago. Yes, I'm almost certain of that. The Barrington estate. Unless it was the Jordan estate. That was quite a sale too." *What was he holding?*

He rambled on so long he forgot why he was on the ladder and started to put the book back. I asked might I see it. "Oh, indeed!" And he handed down—ye gods and vestal maidens! It was Johnson's *Journey*! A 1775 first edition, no less, a book Johnson himself might have held. After years of looking, I could scarcely believe it. At last! The spine would need repair, but the interior was immaculate. Expensive, yes, but to me the price was fair. I said to Lucy something along the lines of being able now to go home, and she reminded me the ship didn't sail for another couple of weeks. Enough time to read on a day mainly dull.

We had tea and shortbread nearby in a café where the diners, in the English custom, sat sipping and whispering—not to keep secrets but to avoid disturbing, or sharing with, others. The aura in the place reminded me of a brass door-plaque I'd once seen in Norwich on the Strangers' Club: MEMBERS ONLY. The tearoom was ideal to evaluate a rare volume, to turn its goldenly aged pages, to discover a perfectly drilled, quarter-inch-deep tunnel of a bookworm, a touch of character bespeaking mileage through two centuries. The text employed the charming, if challenging, eighteenth-century practice of using the so-called medial or long *s* that looks like an *f*. On the title page was a minuscule inscription in faded ink:

For W Fanshaw 1818

Johnson was gone by then, so the writing was not his, nor were several brief and faint penciled notations in a cursive from another century, a touch no new book can have until it has survived the maws of time. The pencilings here and there "corrected" Johnson's use of commas but never his expression.

Lucy said, "Do you think you might put the book down and converse?" Of course, and I read her the Doctor's first sentence, changing only Boswell's name to hers and deliberately mispronouncing each medial *s* as *f*.

I had defired to vifit the Hebrides, or Weftern Iflands of Scotland, for long, that I fcarcely remember how the wifh was originally excited; and was in the Autumn of the year 1773 induced to undertake the journey, by finding in Mf. Lucy a companion, whofe acutenefs would help my inquiry, and whofe gaiety of converfation and civility of manners are fufficient to counteract the inconveniencies of travel.

"You're making that up. Let me see it." I passed the book, she smiled, handed it back, and I thereby gained, without further cavil, another ten minutes with Johnson.

The subsequent miles through drizzle into Wales now passed easily, my mind imagining a quiet inn with an easy chair by a rain-streaked window. Every so often I glanced at the wrapped

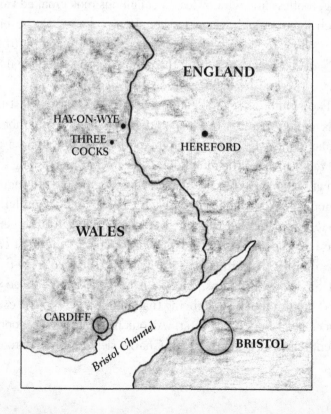

book on the backseat. Corpulent Samuel Johnson squeezed into a small Japanese auto on his way into Wales. Were a volume actually its author—as in "ten minutes with Johnson"—the oft-cantankerous Doctor would not be pleased. Maybe the most intriguing aspect of a book is that it will cover more territory, go more places, and slip into secret realms beyond any its author can accomplish.

With the last daylight, we crossed the border at Hay-on-Wye, a village famous for bookshops, ones I could afford now to overlook. We went down the Wye Valley and, five miles along, turned onto a lane in the hamlet of Three Cocks and, a couple miles beyond, came up to the four-hundred-year-old Gwernyfed Country Manor behind a low rock fence, its three-storey stone walls dripping wet ivy in the dusk. Near the ruin of the south wing, roofless and windowless, a caliginous rook croaked from a beech large enough to hold a couple of colonies of the birds. Lucy said, "To sleep with ghosts in this place is going to cost you," and correct she was, but the manor house looked ideal for a quiet corner to turn eighteenth-century pages.

The landlord, Roger Beetham, led us past cases of stuffed birds and up to our—there's no other word for it—chamber; to talk across it, we had to raise our volume. Beetham had a grizzled red beard and the mellifluous speech common among those who grow up speaking Welsh (one must be nimble of tongue to pronounce village names like Bwlch-Clawdd and Cwymllyfri).

He said, "We call this the Tudor Room because the ceiling once had Tudor roses carved all over it. Charles the First came here after his disastrous battle at Naseby in sixteen-forty-five to visit Sir Henry Williams, one of his lawyers, one of those who didn't do him much good, being that Charles went to the executioner's block four years later." As our host closed the door, he added, "Did I mention that King Charles slept in this very room?"

*　　*　　*

The next morning after breakfast downstairs I asked Beetham to show us the place. When he went to change his apron, Lucy said, "I don't think—in front of him—you should call our room the Headless Charlie Suite."

The house, built in the latter sixteenth century, served as the manor of the area for two-hundred years before the south wing went up in flames in 1780; according to local notions, the conflagration fulfilled a curse that fell on Gwernyfed when the first owner stole a small door and wooden porch from a monastery shut down by Henry the Eighth. The studded, plank door, which even a tall six-year-old must bend to pass through, is still the central entry. From 1780 to 1930 the manor served tenant farmers who took progressively less and less care of it until the Banqueting Hall lay open to the sky, and trees grew within the oak-paneled walls.

Wanting to escape city life in Cardiff, Beetham's parents saw a newspaper ad and bought Gwernyfed in 1964. Later, almost accidentally, they found themselves turning it into lodgings. In 1979 Roger and his wife moved from London to assume the role of proprietors. He had been a history teacher with no experience as a keeper of a bed-and-breakfast, but, like his parents, he too wanted away from urban life.

The rest was history, quite literally so, because Beetham began peeling away later wall and ceiling modifications to discover frescoes, carved roses, a spiral staircase with a newel made from a spar off a Spanish armada galleon wrecked on the Welsh coast, a twelve-foot-wide fireplace, and a secret compartment a priest might hide in to escape Henry the Eighth's anti-papal fervor. Roger also became curious about rather inexpert and uninterpretable letters inscribed on four wooden pillars supporting a minstrel gallery in the now-restored Banqueting Hall. Tradition held that Charles I carved a coded message for his second in command, Prince Rupert, who was to arrive at Gwernyfed after the king departed there in 1645.

Beetham struggled to decipher the message, ordinary capital letters, albeit some of them reversed or upside down as if to disguise their import. A friend went to work on it and, with the help of two guests who fortuitously were code-breakers for MI5, the British intelligence agency, the riddle of the ancient inscription finally came to light:

> Beware to whom thou dost disclose
> The secrets of the wooden poles
> In future wiser than before
> According to their kind ignore.

A military message? Something religious? Masonic? A riddle? A joke?

His knowledge of history led Beetham to a different interpretation: the Elizabethan amusement of writing verse in code, often hiding the poet's name among the words. Indeed, the Gwernyfed inscription contained six extra letters in this order:

I M W Y L S.

"An interesting detail," Beetham said, "and perhaps coincidental, but living eight or nine miles from here were friends of William Shakespeare. Did he visit?"

Studying the letters, Lucy blurted, "Whoa! It's like a vanity license plate! *I M WYL S!* Shakespeare *was* here! Did he also sleep in the Headless—I mean, the Tudor Suite?"

"I can't give assurance he did not," Beetham said, "but *I M W Y L S* is also an Elizabethan anagram for Williams, as in Sir Henry Williams."

"Nuts," she said.

The morning we were to leave Gwernyfed, a guest who collected antique bottles told us his wife the night before had perceived by her bed a ghostly "emanation, something cold."

A couple of hours later, on our way north, Lucy asked, "What would you have given for Headless Charlie or William Shakespeare to stand at the foot of your bed?"

Nodding, I thought, *Probably more than you really want to know.*

Our route lay, generally, along the current Welsh-English border, formerly marked by an eighty-mile earthen bank called Offa's Dyke after a Mercian king wanting to control the movement of people and goods in the eighth century. Some of the dyke was visible, but it required a keen historical imagination to see it as something more than an overgrown hump. That morning, the *Telegraph* carried a story about the impending opening of "the Chunnel"—the tunnel under the English Channel to France—the report focusing on widespread British grousing about it. While politicians and corporations wanted the link, millions of Britons valued their traditional insularity more; after all, a farmer here must gain permission to tear out a rural hedgerow. Among the British, something there is that loves a wall.

I was thinking about enclosures that morning because we were headed for Hadrian's Wall which once ran from the North Sea to the Irish Sea to separate what is now England from Scotland. It too was primarily a barrier to control movement of people and goods. While Offa's Dyke was now mostly a weedy berm, the Roman emperor's nineteen-hundred-year-old dressed-stone wall was elegant in places, rising and falling along a rocky escarpment in Northumberland.

Not far east of Carlisle, we took a room in a pleasant lodge, just south of where the wall once stood, so we could make jaunts to sites along it—Birdoswald, Housesteads, and, on a mainly dull and damp Tuesday, Vindolanda, a Roman garrison a mile behind the wall and twenty miles south of the present Scottish border. We walked around the stone foundations of what

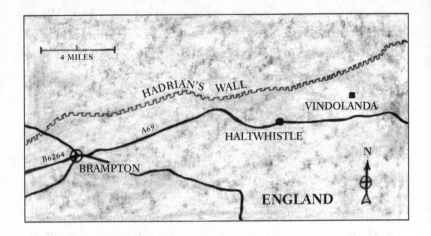

remained of ancient buildings, and tried to picture structures formerly atop them. At Vindolanda, one's fancy can get an assist from the reconstruction of a short section of the turreted wall done by the well-known archaeologist Robin Birley who grew up there during the years his equally famous father, Eric, excavated the site. I knew the Birleys' books.

While we were up on the rebuilt wall, Lucy asked what it was three men could be doing mucking about with shovels in a fenced-off pit outside the clipped grass of the fort foundations. The laborers wore standard English, working rain gear— Wellingtons and woolen sweaters. Seeing a pipeline in the fifteen-foot-deep mud hole, I surmised they were a sewage crew. By the time I came down from the wall, she was already at the edge of the trench. She informed me in a voice beyond what was required, "Your sewer men are actually archaeologists."

I pretended not to know her until one of them looked up to say, "Some days there's not a lot of difference."

Every so often the men, totally absorbed, stopped to ease a glob out of the mud, examine it closely, and cautiously place it in a plastic bag. When we were in the museum, Lucy motioned me over to a photograph and asked, "Isn't this a picture of renowned sewer-man Robin Birley?"

A fellow, possibly an archaeologist, scowled at me, and I was forced to reply to her, in my version of Cockney, "'Oo are yer, lidy?"

In the museum shop, I was buying Birley's book *Vindolanda,* his account of the Roman frontier post and the stunning discovery of hundreds of so-called writing tablets there, when this lidy comes up to me agin and her says loud ter me, she does, "The sanitation crew just popped in for a spot a tea."

Indeed, there sat Robin Birley, Director of Excavations. In what I hoped was a deft stroke to snuff further sarcasms, I took his book to him and asked would he sign it. He was in a jolly mood and pleased to accommodate: That morning the trench had yielded eight more tablets, each the size of an opened matchbook, to bring the total to almost thirteen hundred. Joining us was his wife, Pat, who had just come from the laboratory where she prepared the little slips, hardly more than shavings from a wood plane, for deciphering. Birley said, "One of them we examined today adds new material to our understanding of the Roman presence here. Things forgotten for two-thousand years."

In 1973 at the site, he made one of the astounding discoveries in European archaeology. While excavating the officers' quarters that predate the wall, he picked up a soggy square of something stuck together, and he gently pulled it apart. What he saw stunned him: wafer-thin wooden sheets inked with strange, unpunctuated characters in a language he didn't recognize. Almost immediately he took the artifacts to a nearby university, but by the time he got them there, the priceless rectangles had gone entirely black, the oxidized letters vanished.

He returned to Vindolanda to dig further. Along with fragile but remarkably intact wooden tools, pieces of fabric tents, and leather slippers, he found more tablets inscribed with carbon-based ink. Slowly epigraphists came to recognize the hieroglyphics as cursives in a language Birley knew well, Latin. With the help of infrared photography, he began reading the growing archive, a veritable library he was assembling from the anaerobic mud. The small, lettered slips were largely personal correspondence on bits of limewood or birch or alder incredibly preserved for nearly two millennia because, as Roman soldiers leveled old buildings for new construction, they covered the debris with clay to make a smooth surface, thereby sealing off whatever was underneath from destructive oxygen. The low acidity and temperature of the damp soil further helped keep them. Birley began to realize that those letters were the oldest—about A.D. 100—written material yet found in Britain and were in fact the earliest written evidence from ordinary hands yet found anywhere in Europe.

Among the cache was an invitation to her birthday party from Claudia Severa to the wife of a Vindolanda commander; a scribe had written the letter, but at the bottom was Claudia's own scribble:

Farewell dear sister.

Birley believed those words to be the earliest handwriting of a woman ever found anywhere.

The tablets from soldiers don't speak of religion or the empire. Rather they complain about money, bad roads, dishonest merchants, pink eye, and "wretched Britons." One letter says: "Two men have been held for committing an offense and have been lashed with rods until they were covered with blood. Can they be spared further punishment?" On another, a schoolchild copied out a line from Vergil and beside it the teacher's evaluation: *Sloppy.*

Birley said, "The people living here on the northern edge of the Roman Empire got their spelling and declensions wrong—which doesn't help us—but we have to remember that they wrote as they spoke, with no thought to style and no idea their humble words would be studied by people this far from their time. We've examined less than ten percent of the site, so there are surely more tablets here. Now that we know these letters—under certain conditions—can survive for centuries, imagine what may lie under York or London."

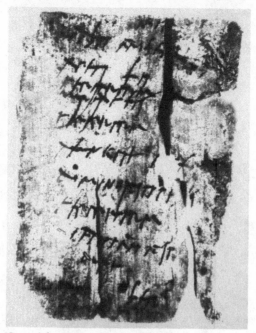

*One of the Roman "letters" found at Vindolanda
by Robin Birley*

When Lucy and I left, we walked past the excavation, the one Birley described as "a hole that's one of the richest archaeological sites in Western Europe," she, again with volume greater than required for my ears, said, "One hell of a sewage pit."

Mock on, I muttered, but remember, to the Romans, those old shoes and letters were trash, and she said, "You know, in spite of it all, even if it was late and delivered to the wrong person, the mail did get through. That hole's a two-thousand-year-old dead-letter office."

Once again returned to our homes, to thank her for help during our travels, I sent her a postcard picturing one of the Roman messages, and I signed it: *I M WYL T.*

THE GREAT
MISCELLANEOUS

"A Residue of History" with its very title continues themes appearing in several of my writings. It's an extension or maybe an analog to ideas that otherwise can be summed up by words like memory and connection because our bodies, our lives, and all around us are residues of the Great Mysterious Miscellaneous. As a concept, if not a word, residue should have a sweeter and grander connotation than it does. Perhaps residuum, despite its Latinate peculiarity, sounds more philosophical and spiritual, more like something we'd be honored to be a part of.

A Residue of History

There's something to be said for starting from the bottom —
a necessity in mountain climbing and bricklaying—but
I'm starting out from the lower end of the lower Mississippi
merely because I have a notion that this river, more than any
other in America, has seen as much go up it as come down: For
the 63,000 tons of soil the Mississippi carries down each day, it
has permitted people to ride it upward with loads of furs, cotton,
rice, sugar, coffee, money, petrochemicals, tobacco, jazz, pro-
nunciations, filé gumbo, the blues.

During most of the Civil War, gunboats worked the river
both directions, finally meeting near the middle of it to decide
with cannons whether our grandest navigable waterway would
sever the Union or bind it. After the Siege of Vicksburg, the Mississippi did indeed hold South to North as an artery helps link
legs to torso. To change my metaphor, this river is also a spine
holding us together latitudinally, and the ribs are the "stately"
tributaries: the Ohio, Tennessee, Kentucky, Arkansas, Illinois,
Wisconsin, Minnesota, Missouri, Kansas. I can think of no
other single physiographic feature in America that so brings us
together in both topography and legend. From the Canadian
border to the Gulf of Mexico, from the Rockies to the Appalachians, waters flow to this so-called Father of Waters, a misno-
mer if there ever was one since rivulets in Montana and New
Mexico, New York and West Virginia, and twenty-seven other
states and two Canadian provinces sire this river from sources

unnumbered over more than a million square miles. But it's useful to keep in mind the Mississippi is the offspring not just of rainfall but also of flushed toilets in Chicago, Indianapolis, Cincinnati, Pittsburgh, Chattanooga, Louisville, Kansas City, Minneapolis, Omaha, Denver, Cheyenne, Bismarck, Missoula. The Father of Waters is more accurately the great-great-grandson (or -daughter) of many forebears. If you walk along the levee in the French Quarter in New Orleans, you can see the contributions from almost half of our contiguous states flowing by. Nowhere else in America is the environmental apothegm "We all live downstream" more apt.

Toward sundown one May evening in New Orleans, I followed the levee and the flood wall toward the Robin Street Wharf where the *Delta Queen* sat ready. She was the oldest genuine steamboat still carrying overnight passengers on American waters. Built in 1926, she worked as a ferry on the Sacramento River in California until World War II, when she became a U.S. Navy yard boat. Then she got laid up for a spell. Sometime later, Tom Greene of Cincinnati saw a new life for her, and he bought the *Delta Queen* and succeeded in getting her towed into the Pacific, through the Panama Canal, across the Gulf, and up the Mississippi and Ohio rivers to be refurbished so she could resume carrying travelers — not on the modest Sacramento but on the biggest rivers in America. The *Queen* once again was full of polished wood and shined brass, and I'd booked passage to Memphis on her.

A little before dusk, the paddlewheel began to turn, the *Queen* blew her throaty and somewhat mournful whistle, her lines got hauled in, and we pulled into the current. The steam-calliope at the stern spewed cold condensate as the squalling growls and screeches slowly turned into notes, and the brass pipes warmed and cleared and blew steam into song: "Waitin' for the *Robert E.*

A sternwheeler on the Mississippi River at St. Louis in 1924

Lee," "Dixie," "Cruising Down the River." As I listened, in my mind's eye was a sepia, soft-focus photograph of a sternwheeler under way near St. Louis; my father took the picture in 1924 when he was fourteen-years old. Sometime later, in the 1940s, I found the photo in an old cigar-box still smelling of tobacco, and his image became an icon, a call to rivers I've heeded ever since.

Like a visitor from 1850, I sat in a rocking chair on the high sundeck to look down on the grim faces of automobilists grinding their way home. A woman at the rail asked me, "How far is it across the river here?" I guessed it was farther than it looked, and she, perhaps sensing not space but time, answered, "I think it's farther than that."

The industrial scenery made up in curiosities what it lacked in beauty, and the river from New Orleans to Baton Rouge was full of oceangoing ships from Singapore, Russia, Japan, Liberia. In the low sun, the deck of the *Delta Queen* shone and made the freighters appear tubs of rust and corrosion. Half an hour upstream, we passed a buoy marking the graves of two ships blown three miles upriver—against the current—by a 1965 hurricane before they foundered. In that stretch of the Mississippi, the depth can be nearly two-hundred feet.

Marine terminals and industrial docks began to thin out and in the dusk the factories and petroleum-cracking plants changed to black skeletal forms and then to distorted constellations of golden lights. From the edge of New Orleans to Baton Rouge, oil refineries and petrochemical works often alternated with eighteenth-century plantations, a few houses tumbling and some wonderfully kept: Next to the famous Oak Alley was Transocean Oil and near Houmas House was Texaco. A juxtaposition of eras.

That forty-mile section of river was the Côte des Allemands, the German Coast, an area settled by immigrants from the Rhineland some years before New Orleans was platted. Their German turned to Acadian French and their names changed from Schneider to Schexnayder, from Vogel to Faquel. Today the French has much yielded to English, and what had been rice and sugar lands were now occupied by Agrico Chemical and Matador Pipeline. The effects such side-by-side existence of industry and homes may be having on the health of the residents has made the Côte an environmental hot spot.

The next morning we pulled in near White Castle, Louisiana, across from Carville and its historic hospital where new treatments for leprosy were developed. I was at the rail with my binoculars. A man and woman paused to ask what I was looking at, and I said the Federal Leprosarium, and the woman said, "Oh! We don't call it that anymore. It's the Hansen's Disease Center." They were Ruth and Lloyd Carville. He grew up in the town that carries his family name, and he recently had retired from the local agricultural extension office. Carville pulled out his new business-card; in addition to the usual information was this:

> USED IRON & STEEL — BOURBON WHISKEY
> SQUIRREL TRAPS — CHIGGER REMEDIES
> W W II STORIES SWAPPED — EXCUSES INVENTED
> BARSTOOLS WARMED — MARTINIS MIXED
> WIVES COUNSELED — FISH TALES TOLD
> AGRICULTURAL EXPERT WITNESS

From a conversation that followed, it was clear he could have added:

> RECIPES FOR OKRA-SEED SOUP CONCOCTED.

About halfway to Baton Rouge we passed the little mouth of Bayou Manchac, a waterway the Army Corps of Engineers closed up even though it was once *the* route from there to the sea. The name comes from the Choctaw and means something like "back door," a tip the British took when they tried to sneak into New Orleans during the battle of 1815. The bayou had silted up to become only a ghostly presence. The power of the lower Mississippi is not its scenery but its omnipresent aura of things passing—up, down, away—and yet often remaining in peculiar fragments. To sit quietly in the dusk, atop the current, was to perceive remains, even in legend: North of there, at Parlange, a 1750 plantation has the usual resident wraith required of such old places, this ghost a young woman forced to marry an aged and hideous French nobleman; as the tale goes, she answered her father's demand by dropping dead at her wedding.

Baton Rouge, one of the farthest inland seaports in the world, is 250 miles from open salt water; the terminus is there because the U.S. 190 highway bridge is too low for ships to pass under, and so the forty-foot-deep channel the Corps maintains for seagoing vessels ends at that point, leaving the river northward to strings of massive barges moved by prodigious towboats (also called tugs although they no longer tug or tow—they push). From Baton Rouge, for miles and miles north, riverside industrial plants disappeared to turn the shoreline back to an older aspect of willows, willows, willows.

At two a.m. I roused myself to go on deck: Beyond the boat, there were no lights anywhere; in the darkness and near silence the *Queen* became a steamboat Sam Clemens would recognize. Standing just below the pilothouse, I could perceive our movement only by the whisper of the river slipping under the prow, and I understood how easy it once was to hear a leadsman throwing his weighted line and calling out, "Half one!" Throwing again: "Quarter less twain!" Pitching the lead forward once more, and announcing to the pilot a safe depth: "Mark twain!"

But the river I saw, while just as dark and quiet, was not at all Twain's river with shorelines stripped of timber for boilers, the muddy water snag-ridden, the currents erratic, channels less deep, sandbars and towheads more numerous. In 1882 when Samuel Clemens (by then he was also Mark Twain) took his last trip down the Mississippi, a couple of decades after leaving steamboating, he saw with some regret a river different from the one he learned, a waterway beginning to be shorn of the romance created by a steamboatman's defining challenges. He wrote, "The military engineers of the [River] Commission have taken upon their shoulders the job of making the Mississippi over again—a job transcended in size by only the original job of creating it." Yet he also saw a new myth and romance coming forth, a view he helped create: One afternoon on that final voyage, he turned his spyglass on a distant steamboat: To his surprise, it was named the *Mark Twain*.

Some seventy miles above Baton Rouge the engineers have met what some people believe to be their match. In 1831, at the former juncture of the Red River with the Mississippi, Henry Shreve, its first engineer, dug a channel so effectively that it now threatens to pull the big river a couple of miles westward and dump it down the Atchafalaya, a course to the Gulf 173 miles shorter, a change that would leave Baton Rouge and New Orleans and all the industry in between on a silty trough.

The Mississippi was high that spring, and as we passed the Old River Control Structure, the *Queen* got slowed in the hard current, and she moved to the eastern bank and away from the flashing amber warning-light. It couldn't have been, of course, but the river seemed to be shaking, vibrating, waiting for some stormy night to take up a new course, suck careless boats down into the Atchafalaya while remaking life for hundreds of miles around.

The next morning we tied up at low-lying Vidalia, Louisiana, along an ugly piece of riverbank, a necessity because a new gambling "boat" (floated but didn't move) had occupied the historic landing at Natchez, Mississippi. I took a shuttle across the bridge to the bluff town and wandered along the streets of the celebrated, antebellum mansions until I remembered it was not architectural elegance I was after but a muddied river. I walked back to the edge of the loess bluff and down steep Silver Street to Natchez-under-the-Hill which writer Bern Keating once called "the most wicked hellhole in the Western world" for its murders, thievery, mayhem, prostitution, and gambling. As far as I could see, only the last remained that morning in the person of *Lady Luck*, a new floating casino.

If the river engineers silted up history on Bayou Manchac, they washed it away at Natchez in 1933 by dredging a four-mile cutoff upstream that speeded the current and—like Hercules cleaning out the Augean stables—flushed downriver three of the four squalid, lower streets. Today, Under-the-Hill has only five remaining historic buildings, but they have been restored to create the new, American historical mélange of a "shoppe" selling sterling silver spoons and rattles for that darling baby to tourists who snap pictures of the half-sunk boats moldering away in a slough once a raucous street. On the veranda of a "saloon" one can sit with a beverage and try to imagine the landing when it was the first leg on the long and jeopardous journey up the Natchez Trace for boatmen who rafted their heavy cargoes downriver but, unable to overcome the current to get home, walked back to Tennessee or Kentucky. One pair of road bandits, so it's told, waylaid travelers until the rogues were seized and hanged and buried directly under the Trace so that their remains might never know quiet.

The *Delta Queen* continued upstream over water slicked by a windless afternoon, and the paddlewheel heaped up the Mississippi behind us as we passed Waterproof, Louisiana, a settlement the river has driven to ever drier ground four times. Since leaving New Orleans, we had been steaming betwixt generally parallel earthen dikes assisted on the east side above Baton Rouge by natural bluffs. Yet the levees were rarely visible from the water, and I had no sense of moving in a 635-mile-long trough all the way to Memphis. It took the Mississippi two-million years to cut out its broad bottomland which thereabouts can be seventy-miles wide but perceptible as a valley only when one is looking from a bluff. For the engineers, it took just a little more than a century to wall in the river and to try to lock it down. They have succeeded for now, so that the actual routes of, say, de Soto or La Salle or even Twain in many places lie "inland." Where the *Robert E. Lee* raced northward against the *Natchez*, today a farmer drags his slow plow, and where some Union gunboat sank, a tangle of willows and weeds grows.

*   *   *

At Vicksburg I could distinguish with binoculars the Civil War cannons on the high bluff. To reach a landing there, we left the main stem of the Mississippi for a "diversion canal," a piece of the altered Yazoo River once the Mississippi itself; but that particular diversion the engineers did not make: In 1876 the Mississippi shifted itself, as it naturally does from time to time, and moved on westward like a dissatisfied tenant, leaving Vicksburg with only a backwater called Centennial Lake. The Corps—at the suggestion of a schoolboy, so the story goes—then reworked the Yazoo to re-create something like a riverfront.

On the same day Lee began his retreat from Gettysburg, the Mississippi was once more open and free of Confederate restraints, and President Lincoln said that "the Father of Waters again goes unvexed to the sea." It was, of course, not so much the Mississippi that had been vexed but the humanity afloat on it and living near it. For the people of Vicksburg, the vexation continued from July 4th 1863 till after World War II: Their Independence Day was not a time for celebrative explosions but a call to honor memories by closing doors and keeping inside just as their besieged ancestors had done in caves dug into the soft face of the river bluff during the seven-month siege.

A nicely grizzled fellow full of lore, a Mister Boston, told me of a sunken boat a few miles south of Vicksburg and not far up the Big Black River from where it joins the Mississippi. "That old tub," he said, "is the steamboat *Paul Jones*." He waited for my excitement. I could only look blankly at him. "The *Paul Jones*," he said. "Come on! She's the boat Horace Bixby was captain of when he taught the river to a cub pilot you might know as Mark Twain."

When we regained the main channel and were moving again toward Memphis, a dangly-legged, goose-necked bird rose from the shore and flapped upriver, and Boston said, "That could be

Bixby right now. That's where the soul of an old river pilot goes. It transmigrates into great blue herons because those are the birds that know the river."

The sun dropped and glanced fiercely off the occluded water and shot it across with blazing streaks, and I propped back in a deck chair, feet on the rail in deliberate imitation of that famous photograph of Twain on his final river journey, the one he depicts in the last half of *Life on the Mississippi,* describing how the flow of the river steadied him while recent changes along it gave him discomfiture.

That's when it came to me that steamboat travel was not much of a way to explore the lives of the people living beside the water because, like the current itself, the boat keeps on rolling, and a passenger belongs not to the shores but to the Mississippi, which answers only to natural laws. Still, to travel a river is to become a momentary part of an eternal affluxion and see how it washes away earthen-borne life to leave only a rich residue of what we all belong to.

PROLEGOMENON

Sometimes writers bring out books underpinned as much by instinctive and spontaneous understanding as by anything they then might be capable of articulating. Only later do they comprehend their work more broadly and become able to address inchoate and incipient ideas: the why of a book. The piece that follows may be an illustration of such a development because now "Not Far Out of Tullahoma" strikes me as a kind of unintended prolegomenon to Blue Highways.

While I'm relying on classical Greek terminology, allow me to add a piece of Latin: This paragraph is a prolepsis. To interpret the vast changes in thinking and traveling spoken of in "Tullahoma" as an expression of nostalgia is an admission of not having traveled far or deeply enough in the United States: What's been happening along the American road since about 1980 has significantly reshaped the nation, sometimes for the better and sometimes less satisfyingly so.

Not Far Out of Tullahoma

Things were not much different for us in 1949 than they were for many other American families. My father, having hauled us around in the same Chevrolet through World War II, was ready for a new car, and Detroit was again capable of offering one. Six years earlier, manufacturers made a mere 139 civilian automobiles in the United States, and the following season only a few more came down the assembly line. But after VJ-Day, as gas rationing ended, the plants returned to making vehicles for citizens. Postwar prosperity in the United States eradicated not simply the privations of armed conflict but also the lingering ones of the Great Depression, and a new era began that would transform America — topographically, socially, economically — more than any other period since the arrival of European settlers. At the heart of much of that change was the highway.

To celebrate the end of the long, lean, and worry-riddled thirties and forties, my father bought an auto — his first new one although he was at the front edge of middle age — a Pontiac Chieftain sedan. He wanted it to get him to work in downtown Kansas City, Missouri, yes, but even more, to take us onto the open road because he believed almost devotedly a slogan of the time, "See America First."

For a few years, his preferred idea of a vacation, his two weeks and not a day more away from the law office, was to pick out a federal highway passing through our town — the one nearly at the exact center of the forty-eight states—and follow the two-lane to its terminus. Over several summers we followed U.S. 71 north to International Falls, Minnesota, and on a subsequent trip we took 71 to its conclusion at Baton Rouge. Then it was U.S. 40 east toward the Jersey shore; but the route to San Francisco, I later had to finish alone. The Atlantic City Boardwalk, the San Francisco Embarcadero, Paul Bunyan's North Woods, and Huey Long's statehouse became for me, by the time I was fifteen, not remote places but memories only a few days down the highway from home. Maryland and California were not like foreign countries across an ocean—they were just down the road, like our neighbors on Flora Avenue.

Six cylinders and twelve-hundred miles of reinforced concrete patched with asphalt created a sense of the United States and the varieties of being American that no social studies class could ever do. I believed in this country far beyond the morning pledge of allegiance or even the propaganda movies of the war because I encountered the land itself and the faces and voices that went with it. Highways led to native accents, regional cookery, local hopes and notions and ancient bigotries, the scent of a farmer's loam after rain, the smell of a Gulf shrimp boat. As different as the miles were, they still lay connected so that I could

North of Holbrook, Arizona

see the street in front of our house was a continuous strip reaching all of them. Highways made me belong to a nation that almost three-hundred-thousand citizens had recently died defending in battle.

If there was one book that led me to notions of American connections and helped me feel a part of things, it was a 1950 road atlas. After I'd traveled in that extension of our living room—the Chieftain sedan—and ridden in it along some of those mapped and numbered lines, the main routes in red and the back roads in blue, the atlas became a kind of snapshot album or personal diary. I could prop up in bed on a winter night and take a journey through certain parts of the country and see again stretches of territory that highway numbers or town names elicited: Manti, Utah, with its old stone temple improbably big in such a small place; Frederick, Maryland, with Barbara Fritchie's home; the buckwheat cakes in Plainfield, Indiana; the Civil War–replica hats (one in blue, one gray) from the five-and-dime in Vicksburg, Mississippi.

In those days, as we were leaving an older economy and social order dominated by rural life, we were still calling the Sears, Roebuck annual catalog, that fat thing city people only slightly less than rural residents depended on, the Wish Book. But my book of longings was something else, a Rand McNally with its seeming infinitude of highways, county byroads, parkways, and even something new with an old name: a turnpike four-lanes wide running through the mountains of Pennsylvania, the home of the most iconic American travel vehicle ever—the Conestoga wagon. President Eisenhower was about to identify the turnpike as the model for a vast national system of super roadways to be called Interstates, things that—as we heard again and again—would let us go coast to coast, border to border, without ever stopping at a traffic light. I was impatient for such a marvel opening up the horizon in front of the long, streamlined hood of the Chieftain.

Without thinking of the consequences of such presumably unfettered travel, Americans began year by year to put an increasing premium on speed as we came to value rate of passage rather than the nature of it, and our roads commenced becoming only means to a destination. If it was good to be able to move across Pennsylvania fast, then logically it would also be desirable to get in and out of those places that for so long had slowed travelers: hotels with the weary lugging of grips up to the fourth floor and cafés serving each order one at a time, cooked to suit a request for "sunny-side up," or "I'll take my noodle pie cold," or "Kedgeree with a bowl of hot blueberry slump."

Near the eastern end of the turnpike I saw for the first time one of those orange roofs under which lay more flavors of ice cream than I'd thought human minds could devise, and I considered the fake cupola as exciting as the Capitol dome not far away in Washington. I took a color photograph of the restaurant to prove to friends back home that I'd actually visited a real Howard Johnson's. How long would it take such a chain with vaunted standardized quality to get to our town?

Across the land, if something was faster than what preceded it, if it took less of our time to use it, then it was better. So, in our neighborhood, when the Dari-Delite (its soft-serve as genuine as its orthography) opened directly across the street from the old Duncan's Drugstore serving hand-packed ice cream, we gave up the infinite variety of an authentic soda-fountain for the limitations of fast-serve. We forgot the legendary concoctions of a knowledgeable soda jerk: juliets, Jersey fizzes, Delmonico frappes, Rex phosphates, and the top-of-the-line Ollie Moore (syrups of lemon, raspberry, and orange mixed with sweet cream and a raw egg, shaken, strained, poured over ice, and carbonated water shot in with force). The old collection I take this "receipt" from, *The American Soda Book,* says, "There is as much difference between the soda [water] of different stores as between the roast beef of different restaurants." A proud statement and often true. We could lazily drive right up to the Dari-Delite window, and get in and out quickly partly because there was but one flavor of ice cream, only three types of soft drinks, and three of syrups; even a simple fresh-squeezed limeade wasn't there. Then we could cart the stuff off to a drive-in movie, our feet scarcely touching the ground.

As the 1960s arrived, family vacations were changing how we saw and interpreted America. Each year we seemed to give up a little more of being travelers to become mere tourists for whom arrival is all, passives to whom travel is done rather than ones who do the travel. What lay between us and Yellowstone or the Everglades turned into miles grudgingly to be got through; small-town America — and cities even more so — became not possibilities for exploration or adventure but transient purgatories to be endured. Because our demi-generation believed so much in corporated destinations, Des Moines offered less than Disneyland, and some Six Flags over Uncle Shamland or Hokum Kingdum had a reality that real Six Rivers National Forest might struggle to match. At first we didn't perceive the fabricated history of theme parks to be akin to the roofs of the new Grabba-Burger chains, and we thought a Jeep ride through a Texas "ranch" to glimpse a zebra was a grander experience than an evening idle through an Arkansas woods in hopes of seeing a bobcat.

Today, sham-destination excursions seem logical: Americans are descendants of earlier travelers who, commonly, did not leave their indigenous lands to see new territory and meet the natives but rather to avoid strangers (Indians) and get to a *particular* place and, once arrived, take it up and rename it and remake it as much as possible to resemble where they came from. Think of them: new Yorks, new Jerseys, new Albions, new Switzerlands, new Mexicos, new Orleans. In us has lain a long and deep urge to recast the New World from the Old one. Nomadic hunters walking or boating across the Bering Strait and the Pilgrims sailing the Atlantic went not as travelers but as settlers set on landfall; the people passing through the Cumberland Gap or along the Oregon Trail weren't moving to see the sights but to reach journey's end. The American past, the most wheeled history on Earth, is not so much about wayfaring as it is about arrival — not that we've ever been all that attached to a place once we do set down.

Of the blueprints and tools we've used to lay out and construct this nation, none, it seems to me, is more important than maps and highways, and from the beginning we've shown our predilection to move as quickly and comfortably as possible, speed nearly always dominating comfort (consider when you next fly commercial air).

By the time President Eisenhower's grand Interstate scheme started to look complete in the early 1980s, many travelers began to see that a four-lane takes as much as it gives; after all, everything eventually tends to move toward temporary equilibrium. If you wish a metaphor for what happened as we autobahned ourselves, consider those famous little six red signs once adorning the two-lanes:

PEDRO

WALKED

BACK HOME, BY GOLLY

HIS BRISTLY CHIN

WAS HOT-TO-MOLLY

BURMA-SHAVE

Although advertising a product for men, the boards could have an entire family reading them aloud and watching the countryside closely for the next one:

SLOW DOWN, PA
SAKES ALIVE
MA MISSED SIGNS
FOUR
AND FIVE
BURMA-SHAVE

Those narrow signboards drew out travelers, lured them for a few moments to participate in their passage. But the four-lanes were too big and too fast for such reading, and in states that gave up scenic control of their highways, sky-sundering mega-billboards, readable a mile away, began sneaking up overnight like toxic mushrooms, and their witless messages advertised (for a while) booze and cigs, and later, vasectomy reversals, brassieres for large-topped women, ugly political allegations, religious dogma—all messages a generation of children yet to reach their nostalgic years may find difficult to remember as things that made them happily feel a part of America.

Independent cafés could rarely afford to move and set up along an Interstate, and so vanished hundreds of Mizzus Somebody's own blue-ribbon-at-the-county-fair recipe for corncob soup or nut pie à la Bama; gone were places with names like Jimmy Wall's Catfish Parlor and with it his secret batter and the hard-earned magic in his old cast-iron skillets. Menus no longer revealed a particular locale with its history, and they less often expressed a region and its culture. They had become, from one Swif-Stop to the next Git-n-Flit, lists of ditto food, and the best way to discover where you were was to ask where you were. To be sure, some of the road food of earlier times was of the gag-and-grimace variety because inconsistency was a certainty of two-lane travel. But, as in other things, the absence of quality gave not just meaning but memorableness to a good meal when it did turn up. Passion and memories often depend upon their scarcity—otherwise how should we know them?

Experienced wayfarers learned to laugh off the second-rate supper, aware that, were it bad enough, at least they would have a story to tell once returned home. I realized friends listened more intently to a tale of a wretched oyster stew in the U-Drop Inn than to an account of a five-star dinner or a stunning mountain sunrise. Part of the point of travel is to make home look sweet, otherwise we all might become itinerants with no one staying around to serve us green-chile stew—good or bad. Beyond that, the quest for savory road food, like those little red signs, drew us deeper into the country, made us a part of a place for a few moments. It was even rewarding just to learn the tricks of travel: To find a good grinder (the sandwich with a dozen regional names), don't inquire at the filling station—ask a librarian, bookseller, pharmacist, a teller at the bank. The old tourist-traps lured in only the lazy.

During the Cold War (if it was cold, was it a war?), politicians and corporations began claiming an Interstate system was necessary, if the need arose, for national defense to move munitions and weapons. And for a number of years when Americans were digging bomb shelters and their children were being taught at school to "duck and cover," we believed the "national defense" argument until it became apparent the four-lanes were there to move not rifles but radios, not bombs but baubles; they were there to sell autos, tires, and gasoline; they were there to push public transportation toward private transport, to give semitrailer trucks a publicly paid-for right-of-way. And we bought into all of it, perhaps driven by a new nostalgia for real highway adventure; we even turned truckers into instant folk figures, mixes of Casey Jones, Mike Fink, and Bronco Billy.

As we watched the Interstates dice up city neighborhoods and then move into the country and, like vacuums from Hell, suck the mercantile life out of a Main Street by pulling commerce to Interstate off-ramps only weeks ago woods and meadows, we could pass down mournful, vacated Broadways. With them, one more of the reasons for slow travel all but disappeared. It was harder to see how a particular place functioned and to understand how Fairfield did things that made it different from Springfield. Town centers turned into broken bones, the marrow gnawed out, and we were slow to see that a lunch at Qwik-Nuggets in Bangor would more likely put us next to a guy from Ohio or Delaware than beside a Down-Easter. The village-café coffee corner? Bye-bye.

Economies of scale and expediency had come to define much American travel: Plates of foodlike substance assembled in New Jersey arrived in cartons requiring only a microwave before reaching our table (if there was one), all of that stuff served up in places of reiterated vinyl-jug architecture where signs and chairs were made from leftover burger-boxes. Town after town embraced its strip of low-margin-high-turnover polystyrene food where the Big-Belly-Jumbo-Whopper *box* tasted about as good as what was inside. All that remained was to find a way to keep us in our cars, keep us moving through: Speed equals corporate profit. Hello, Drive-Thru.

And, at night, that framed repro-painting above the motel bed in Battle Creek—wasn't it the same one we'd seen a day earlier in Kokomo? People began to reminisce about once sleeping in a motor court where each room was a concrete teepee with a Magi-Fingers-Massage bed, twenty-five cents for ten minutes. And what about that cup of joe from a roadside stand in the shape of a two-storey coffeepot? Eateries that were not playpens but, well, just eateries where one might entertain a child with—oh my god—*observations* about the place and its people—waitresses and waiters, cooks and cashiers—all of it creating *conversations* that could show a child how to observe differences and converse with strangers.

So, we became a nation of movers who drove fast and long to arrive someplace that could just as well be where we'd started from; the main thing the open road had given was a tired back and bloodshot eyes. Something had gone awry in the grand Interstate scheme.

By the late seventies, vacationers began asking, "Why drive when we can fly?" and their rhetorical question had its point:

Wasn't it faster and easier to ignore the land between home and destination? And we had a new term—flyover country—one more way to detach from the actualities of our nation: the cop with the bad breath, the Samaritan who helped with a flat tire, the scent of sagebrush after a rain, a wheat field under harvest. We were getting good at deleting experiences, disconnecting from potential memories, and ultimately degenerating our lives.

About then a few Americans, seeing consequences, began trying to turn themselves from passive tourists back into active travelers who explore the genius of a place, searchers for the quiddity of Owyhee County or Hell Roaring Creek or the Rosebud Reservation, or an alley in Charleston. And as they headed off down some of the abundant and often vacated miles of American two-lane, those travelers started to uncover living fossils: a village still possessed of its mercantile heart, a diner grinding its own coffee beans, a clam shack so good the kid in the backseat stopped thinking of clams as slimy, a neighborhood tavern with a fellow or two who knew why Peculiar Street was so named, a nineteenth-century inn where one could sleep inside history. Before we might have realistically expected it, something new appeared: guidebooks to bed-and-breakfasts, historic hotels and lodges, real ice-cream stands, flea markets, catfish emporiums. Many titles of those guides employed words like *forgotten, hidden, secret, lost, mysterious, secluded, small, old, genuine.* Initially they came from amateur publishers, people who had witnessed the nullifying corporatization of the American road.

A number of Americans, driven mad by the Interstates, awakened. Knowing the frontier trails were gone but for broken traces and ruts, travelers began seeking highway adventures in a broadly settled and thoroughly roaded land now rarely wilderness but still similarly full of challenges and unpredictabilities to sharpen one's senses, whittle perceptions into keenness, and carve a lasting mark into memory. To escape the expressways was to have a chance at distinguishing Penn Yan from Mandan, knowing differences between the several Mount Vernons west of the Appalachians from the one on the Potomac, being able to differentiate the speech of coastal Carolina from that of the Piedmont, remembering in Rockport, Massachusetts, you might find creamed lobster but in Rockport, Missouri, the best dish could be bread soup.

Ike's Interstates don't much disturb me any longer because their 46,000 miles did not just open up three million miles of two-lanes; they also reminded us how to travel in ways that give a chance to enter the American landscape and to inhabit our heritage of history and place. I think that may be why, the week after next, I'll be headed for Tennessee. There's this place I remember not far out of Tullahoma.

North of Denison, Texas

A NEW ORDER

In 1984 I was sent to a corner of southeast Alaska, not far from Skagway and near the foot of the Klondike Trail, to look into potentially significant changes coming to the Tlingit people who have traditionally taken their livelihood from the cold waters of the North Pacific Ocean. I was asked to concentrate on relevant economic topics and perhaps a few social ramifications resulting from the return of massive portions of Alaska to native tribes. "But," warned the editor, "go easy on the totem-pole stuff."

Twenty-eight years later, the difficult and complex distribution of tribal lands continues in the face of various challenges, but the number of indigenous shareholders in Sealaska has grown by a third, to more than twenty thousand. Chris McNeil is now president and chief economic officer of the native corporation and, with his wife, has established a generous college scholarship for Tlingit, Haida, and Tsimshian youth.

Designing a Corporate Potlatch
for the Next Century

The crayon mountains I drew as a child always came out the same: a jamming up of apexes, a piling of triangles, each peak unsoftened by snow, every foothill crept over by spruces. Growing up on the edge of the tallgrass prairie, as I did, I'd never seen mountains like the ones I drew, and I eventually considered them only as impossible creations of a childish imagination, fantastical stones no traveler but the one who walks dreams would ever see.

In the spring of 1984, in the long light of a late Alaskan afternoon, *there*, rising before me, was an approximation of those crayon mountains, ones in living stone. Although I'd never before laid eyes upon them, they seemed like a remembered image, and a whimsy came to me that an ancestor or two of mine might have crossed the Bering land-bridge twenty-thousand years ago and walked down this very valley and seen the range. It was as if a genetic memory moved in my blood even though later ancestors had not stayed there but eventually continued on to the valley of the Missouri River.

I'd traveled three-thousand miles by plane and boat to talk to an Alaskan Native about those mountains and the descendants of the people who first saw them, and about their survival along the forested coast for at least ten millennia before Europeans began wandering in.

*   *   *

Chris Edward McNeil Jr.'s tribe is the Tlingit (*Klink*-it) nation, known for its artistry in carving totem poles and masks and weaving the famous Chilkat blankets. His forebears did not continue on southward into the continent but stopped right there to take up the land at least ten millennia before Europeans—including his Dutch great-grandfather—began wandering in. If such mountains could somehow reach me from across the generations and from so far away, they could surely hold the Tlingit people who have lived under the peaks for four-hundred generations.

We were standing in Klukwan, McNeil's mother's native village, on the graveled main street with its few bisecting dead-end lanes. Klukwan is not a pretty village, nor quaint, but with the Chilkat Mountains on the south and the Coast Range to the east, one can overlook the wrecked cars heaped to rust, and the clapboard houses in perilous leans this way and that.

The Tlingits chose this place for its jagged cordillera and for the Chilkat River running fast along the edge of the village. From the greenly gray snow and glacier melt, the people gill-net salmon: king, sockeye, coho. Klukwan is full of the deep gargle of ravens and, in season, the vertical drops of bald eagles coming to fish the Chilkat as the Tlingits do.

I was there to learn about land possession from McNeil, but it wasn't until I actually stood in the tumbledown river-village

A Tlingit blanket

under the mountains that I could understand the passion under-lying the Alaskan Natives' long struggle not simply to keep what is theirs, but to keep what keeps them. From that afternoon on, whenever I heard Chris McNeil speak of federal land-transfers and corporate earnings and cultural dispossession, I saw the Chilkat Mountains, so stony the snow could not scumble them, and the late-spring river ready for sockeye, and the salmon smokehouses of slab-fir sides darkened from alder fires.

During our conversation I asked him how an American Indian could possibly believe the old legal chestnut that "posses-sion is nine points of the law." In 1492, perhaps a million aborigi-nal people possessed about 3.5 million square-miles in the United States for twenty-thousand years; today Native Ameri-cans hold fifty-two-million acres, less than 3 percent of their original lands.

What truly—that is, *legally*—constitutes possession of property in America today? Certainly neither loving the land nor living on it for twenty millennia. In the case of Indians, McNeil offered, not even holding properly conveyed title is enough if ownership means having sufficient strength to deal with tres-pass. Armed might didn't work all that well amid intertribal struggles, and in the face of European encroachment, ultimately it proved futile.

But today, McNeil said, Tlingits and other Alaskan Natives—the term refers to Indians, Aleuts, and Eskimos rather than sim-ply anyone born in the state—have found contemporary sources of power through law and corporate structure, and are begin-ning to use them to possess what in their minds has been theirs since the days when Europeans were also living by stone tools. Alaskan Natives, he made clear, have never needed any govern-ment to tell them that their ancestral land belongs to them, but what they *have* needed was a government making land owner-ship clear to its agencies and any non-Natives casting an acquisi-tive eye toward indigenously possessed territories.

It did just that in 1971 with the Alaska Native Claims Settlement Act, legislation awarding almost a billion dollars and forty-four-million acres of land to various tribal groups as compensation for aboriginal property taken earlier by the federal government. Thirteen regional corporations, along with two-hundred smaller urban and village corporations, formed to manage the assets. The largest and one of the most successful of these is Sealaska whose holdings lie in the southeastern panhandle of the state, a place of dense forests and rich coastal fishing grounds. Sealaska, with total assets of almost a half-billion dollars, including nearly two-hundred-thousand acres, ranked number 745 on *Fortune* magazine's 1982 list of the top one-thousand industrial corporations in America.

McNeil's Tlingit name is Shaahakooni, but he's reticent about its meaning. He's thirty-six years old, a couple of inches under six feet tall, squarely built, his facial features manifesting both his Indian and Dutch ancestry. Speaking calmly with thought to implications in his words, he shows the mien not of a fierce warrior but of a sagacious attorney. He is general counsel and one of the five vice presidents of Sealaska. His wife, a Winnebago from the Great Plains and also a lawyer, has worked for a Sealaska foundation. McNeil's father, of the Nisga'a tribe in British Columbia and now a naturalized American citizen, separated from McNeil's mother when the boy was twelve, and he spent much time with his maternal grandmother and uncle in Juneau. It is the Tlingit way for the mother's brother to serve as disciplinarian and guide to a child. Uncle Judson Brown, once a longshoreman boss and now on the Sealaska board of directors, offered guidance to young McNeil by teaching him the obligation to assist his people. "He and my mother and maternal grandmother," McNeil said, "valued education as a way to help our people sustain our culture." They showed him a quiet pride to mitigate racism that can shape the way an Indian child comes to feel about himself. "But we were never overtly beaten down," he said. "It was more subtle."

McNeil, whose father wanted him to become a salmon fisherman, may become the president of Sealaska in 1991 when Native shareholders might be permitted to sell their stock to anyone—Indian or not. McNeil could be the man, say pessimists, who will oversee the dissolution of the last great aboriginal land-claims in America, and with them the core of his people's tribal identity.

Although early opposition to the Settlement Act came from whites, today many of them hope Sealaska will prosper. They realize that the Native corporations are part of the solution to one of the most snarled areas in current public policy. White thinking today is this: If tribal Americans become corporate shareholders, then the expensive and debilitating struggle between Indian self-determination and federal domination may find resolution. McNeil knows that little good will come from continuing the two-century-old economic dependence of red America. His people understand that the vaunted American sense of justice is not enough to end their dependent status; they now hope that the white-middle-class wish to end tax expenditures by making Indians earners and spenders will help them begin something new. In theory, that wish is a place where red and white, liberal and conservative thought can meet.

Chris McNeil sees his way as an attempt to find an "intersection between corporate life and Alaskan Native life," an integration that does not exclude one from the other. Such intersections have always been a colliding of values that every tribal American faces. McNeil does not say much about his own encounters with the agonies that so often curse the lives of Indians—poverty, alcoholism, ruptured families, racial scorn—but then, neither does he speak much about his master's degree with honors from Yale in political science, nor about his law degree from Stanford. Yet, under his words, it is all there.

* * *

On a drive north from Juneau to show me the cove where he once fished and smoked salmon with his father, McNeil pointed from the window of his BMW 528 to Seventh Street, his boyhood neighborhood. Although now condominiums, it was once a boardwalk settlement with houses on pilings above Gastineau Channel; toilets flushed openly onto mudflats for the tide to carry off the sewage. I asked whether it had been a slum. He looked surprised, as if the question were new: "I guess it was."

If McNeil has come close to finding that intersecting of ways, he knows many Sealaska shareholders—Tlingits, Haidas, and Tsimshians—have not. He understands that should enough of them fail to find a crossing of ways, Sealaska may not survive. His people's search for a union of cultures and values shows in the corporate symbol: conjoined heads of a raven and an eagle sharing a single eye, one bird looking east, the other west. David Katzeek, president of the Sealaska Heritage Foundation established in 1980 by the corporation, said of the search: "Let us be of one mind." Katzeek believes that McNeil may be the man to help create that unity of vision and purpose.

As part of the alternative service required by his Vietnam-era conscientious-objector status, McNeil began as the educational coordinator for the Tlingit and Haida tribes. Seven years afterward, he joined Sealaska and later helped establish the Sealaska Heritage Foundation. He came to understand the urgency of educating shareholders to retain ownership and keep the corporation alive, and he realized that many people, living on little, have had

Tlingit painting on a meetinghouse

to sell two-hundred-year-old ancestral artifacts. "If a family will give up a tangible piece of its heritage," McNeil said, "then what will it do with a piece of paper that has brought in less than seven-thousand dollars over the past thirteen years? Stockholder education has got to show the need for making decisions based upon an awareness of our distinctive culture, but that doesn't mean that Native identity and cultural survival depend only upon the success or failure of the corporations." Others are not so sure. Just because physiological bloodlines continue does not mean that cultural ones will keep flowing. A community must have an economic base, whether sea-otter skins or dollars. Yet many influential tribal elders, McNeil realizes, believe that the gap between heritage obligations and corporate assets may be irreconcilable. He also knows of the poorly educated who say, as they have for years, "It's our land. Why do we have to do anything at all?"

Much of McNeil's time goes to meetings in remote villages that can be reached only by ferry or seaplane. Once there, he listens to local voices call for immediate distribution of corporate assets. Says McNeil: "When the corporations began, the people had extraordinary expectations that Sealaska would solve most of our problems. But the reality is, while the corporation has helped, the overall economic impact has been marginal. No Native corporation can ever be a complete cure. In our peak months, even if all sixteen-thousand shareholders were qualified, we could hire only two thousand—at best."

Natives were turned into corporate shareholders by the Settlement Act of 1971 which extinguished virtually all Native claims so that Alaskan oil fields discovered a decade earlier could be opened. Although land claims began with the 1867 purchase of Alaska from Russia, it wasn't until 1929 that the aboriginal people took to the courts. They were spurred, in part, by the quest of the Alaska Native Brotherhood to end racial discrimination. (McNeil's maternal grandfather and his uncle Judson Brown were active in ANB; his mother, as a bright fifteen-year-old student, was put forward by the Brotherhood in a 1946 test case in Juneau to break down public-school segregation.) Because the Native claims effectively blocked oil-leasing rights, in 1966 Secretary of the Interior Stewart Udall placed a moratorium on all federal land-transfers, Native and white alike; his action became the catalyst to resolving the litigation. It clearly was in the interest of both the state and federal governments, as well as non-Natives, to quiet claims that could have prevented the leasing of oil rights for two or three decades.

The Settlement Act granted a hundred shares of stock in at least one of the Native corporations to every American citizen born on or before December 18, 1971, who could prove Alaskan Native ancestry of at least 25 percent. The shares are judgment-proof for twenty years, but they cannot be sold during that time. Eighty-thousand Alaskan Natives statewide received forty-four million acres and nearly a billion dollars in compensation. Not all aspects of the transfer have been answered, and some of it is tied up in satellite litigation.

"Because it establishes something that had not existed before," McNeil said, "the Settlement Act is a grand experiment." But what had *not* existed is much more than legal realty-titles: a genuine chance for American aboriginal peoples to free themselves from reservation ghettos and the domination by the Bureau of Indian Affairs. "At last," McNeil said, choosing the right words, "we could set our own destiny. We could seek values to guide us and form the core of our community."

As in any federal process, bugaboos and snafus abound. He spends his hours now seeking a course for the people, a task made no easier by a widespread feeling expressed even by Heritage president Katzeek: "There should be a better way than the Settlement Act, but I don't know what it is." In a 1983 *National*

Geographic story, an Eskimo shareholder in a financially weak Native company complained, "My shares in the corporation? Give me ten bucks and a six-pack, and they're yours."

Even though McNeil minimizes their views, cynical observers contend that such attitudes are just what many whites who supported the settlement actually wanted—corporations that will weaken tribal identities while eliminating their claims on the land. It could happen. If the corporations succeed and shares grow in value, what economically limited person would refuse to sell? If the shares are worth little or paying small dividends, why keep them? As has been shown repeatedly in the lower forty-eight states, an Indian without his homeland quickly loses his tribal identity, and with that goes his resistance to assimilation and his opportunity to contribute to the energizing diversity of America.

The Tlingit way of expressing realty ownership reveals subtle yet crucial attitudes: rather than saying, "This is my land," a Tlingit speaks of "the land of my grandparents." Every tribal member is a custodian of the heritage. McNeil showed me a recent open-letter from a stockholder calling for renewed determination to hold on to that heritage. She wrote: "The most difficult, almost impossible accomplishment will be to end 1991 with our heads facing the right direction, with the pride in knowing we accomplished the impossible—we beat them at their game, using their game board."

McNeil said, "One of the crucial flaws in the Settlement Act is its assumption that any shareholder owning fungible stock will want to keep it. In actuality, only people with a capital surplus can afford the luxury of accepting small dividends while waiting for stock growth." Also disturbing is the arrival of Termination Day in 1991 when shares of stock will be counted as assets in determining eligibility for government transfer programs like food stamps.

Should Sealaska—the wealthiest of the Native corporations—fail, the historical agonies of Indians of the contiguous states would be even more disruptive to Alaskan Natives. In America, Indians bring up the rear in per-capita income, life expectancy, and educational achievement. They lead in unemployment, child mortality, violent death, and alcoholism. Three of the five poorest counties in America are on reservations. What is more, this new idea of incorporation to help aboriginal peoples toward self-determination will have effects beyond the United States: Watching also are Canadian Indians and Eskimos, Norwegian Lapps, Mexican Mayas, Peruvian Quechuas, Australian Aborigines, Japanese Ainu. Although McNeil does not wish to exaggerate effects, he knows the waves of Sealaska may travel far.

The corporation began in 1972 with total assets of almost $79,000. Only seven years later it had grown to $162 million through additional governmental land-conveyances. Today it has nearly a half-billion dollars in its primary holdings of fishing, canning, timber, building materials, and a coastal water-transport service. Most of the timber and much of the fish go to Japan and Korea. "We work well with the Japanese for reasons besides market proximity," McNeil said. "Alaskan Indians and the Japanese traditionally have eaten similar food—raw fish, fish eggs, sea urchins, seaweed." He smiled at that.

But rapid growth and inexperience have created problems. In 1982 Sealaska lost $28 million because of unfavorable exchange rates, high interest, a poor timber market in Japan, and a botulism incident in Belgium that affected all American canneries. A year later, however, profits rose to nearly four-million dollars. All the shareholders know that should the corporation fail, it will not find rescue as did Chrysler. Katzeek said, "You need to keep in mind that any newspaper reference to Sealaska is followed by 'Native-owned corporation.' Now, when has anyone ever spoken of Chrysler Motors as a 'white-man-owned corporation'? If we fail, others will say it is because we are ninety-nine percent Indian-owned."

Ninety-nine percent owned, yes; operated, no. Sealaska employs only about 12 percent Alaskan Natives, although all of its board of directors and two-thirds of its corporate officers are tribal members. The company has struggled to increase Indian employment, but it takes time to train people, especially for management jobs. To that end, McNeil cites the shareholder intern program which seeks to prepare Natives for corporate positions, but so far only one person has risen from an internship to Sealaska employment. For some shareholders, the inability of the corporation to lower tribal unemployment significantly is more important than its new power to represent aboriginal interests in the statehouse or its help to village economies.

To many shareholders, the Sealaska Heritage Foundation, which has awarded almost seven-hundred-thousand dollars for student aid over four years, is the cement of the corporation. Younger people like the forward look of its educational grants; elders like its archives and programs to preserve indigenous languages, music, and crafts. In fact, many shareholders throughout Alaska believe that the ultimate purpose of the corporations is to provide an economic base for enhancing cultural survival. After all, Indians for centuries have resisted assimilation by believing more in the value of their origins than in the worth of a dollar.

Sealaska, then, has become a steward of Alaskan Native economic self-determination and cultural identity. In the face of continual threats to their existence, the coastal tribes have

Tlingit house painting of a bear

survived because they have been flexible in shaping themselves and their economy without losing their unique heritage. "Some of our people," McNeil said, "see any isolated village as culturally pure. It's even a last bastion to some. I don't believe that, and I don't believe any people possesses a life purified of outside influences. For a thousand years, my tribe has been traders, and trading inevitably mixes cultures. Our coastal people endured because they were not rigid." An old Tlingit clan song:

> *I am heading into a new land,*
> *I am heading into a new destiny.*

When McNeil and I were leaving the tribal house of his mother's family—the Killer Whale Clan—he mentioned another Northwest Coast Indian custom that's a precedent for cultural survival through an economic structure—the potlatch. Potlatches are of several kinds and serve different ends: celebration, competition, confirmation of status, stimulus for the arts. Before the coming of Europeans, a wealthy family wanting to commemorate an event—marriage, birth, death—would distribute its own goods to other tribal members. Excluding through deeds in battle, Tlingits changed social position only by sharing their prosperity. Still practiced today, the ancient custom provides economic stability and a linking of families and generations. Chris McNeil sees the potlatch as a metaphor of a traditional means for Sealaska to ensure the retention of lands and waters that feed body and spirit. It can be a sustainable engine of survival.

A TRIO OF POSTCARDS

Starting out for the Scottish Isles in the mid-nineties, I left with instructions to send back something like a trio of picture postcards which would run sequentially in three issues of a magazine — in truth, a clothing catalog. The editor phoned to say he wanted a close focus where a part stands for the whole. "Control any inclination to the encyclopedic," he said. "Synecdoche! Metonomy! Micro over macro!"

Just South of Ultima Thule

I.

On a map of the North Atlantic, the Orkney Islands look as if a cartographer dropped green ink from a careless pen, splattering three-score jagged splots around the northern tip of Scotland lying about nine miles south. The biggest droplet the Orcadians call Mainland although it is only twenty-three miles wide and a bit less than that in length; the Scottish mainland is, of course, only a portion of the British Isles, so, in short, the closest *real* mainland, peninsular though it be, lies almost 400 miles eastward: Norway.

In the Orkneys, even on Mainland, one can never get far from the scent of salt spray off the North Sea to the east or the Atlantic to the west, and all of the Orcades, except for the above-high-tide rocks, are deeply and prodigiously rent by bays, sounds, firths, and saltwater lochs. Nevertheless, it wasn't the omnipresent sea I felt there; it was *time,* and in those isles the sea is only the oldest visage of time.

Except for the faces of children and a few other things like heather blossoms or a plate of fish and chips, everything in the Orkneys attests to age, eras so far gone even the islands themselves have had eons enough to move from fifteen degrees south of the equator to nearly the sixtieth parallel, the latitude of the southern tip of Greenland, of what was once ultima Thule. Northern Europe and North America lay joined when these

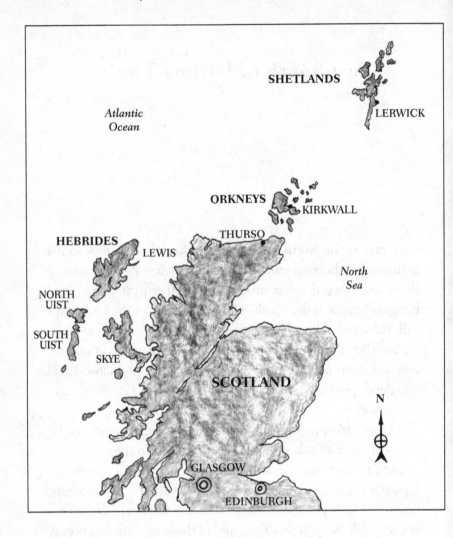

islands, such as they were then, sat in a vast freshwater lake called Orcadie. Should the fossil fish sleeping in their sandstone cribs for nearly four-hundred-million years awake, they would find themselves not in a warm equatorial broth but on the edge of the Arctic Circle. And, still, those fossils are new when seen from the basement rocks the Orkneys rest upon, granites and schist one-and-a-half-billion years old, among the oldest exposed stone in Northern Europe.

Like most travelers here, I didn't go for the so-called living rock; rather, I was there for other stones, the ones humans quarried and dragged from the ancient strata and then set upright or laid out in courses, labors begun and finished several hundred years before the Great Pyramids of Egypt started to rise. That people were even here in this tree-shorn land five-thousand years ago seems incredible not so much because of any real harshness in the terrain or climate, but rather because of the remoteness of the Orkneys. In my vade mecum for the trip, *A Journey to the Western Islands of Scotland*, Samuel Johnson writes, "Of these islands it must be confessed, that they have not many allurements but to the mere lover of naked nature." The Doctor was the chap who said, "When a man is tired of London, he is tired of life." He was, of course, a Londoner.

Yet, on the northern island of Papa Westray, directly against the blast and clamor of the North Atlantic, there's a settlement called the Knap of Howar, a few stone houses embedded in the earth a thousand years before pharaohs even began dreaming of laying up limestone into pyramidal tombs. Other than the Vikings, no one else passed through; the Orkneys are hardly on a crossroads to anywhere but the frozen north. Because those neolithic dwellings are small and as humble as the dirt surrounding their rock walls, they have a capacity, inexplicable yet consequential, to carry a traveler in time still further than those distant islands do in space. The power in the age of things Orkney can indeed transport visitors to some Thule of the mind and convey their imaginations into a realm beyond mere topography.

The greatest of the prehistoric Orkney monuments is on the west side of Mainland just above a sea loch penetrating a green and rolling moor and within sight of the large ring of ancient standing stones of Brodgar. Maes Howe, one of the finest chambered tombs in Western Europe, lies in an area of glacially

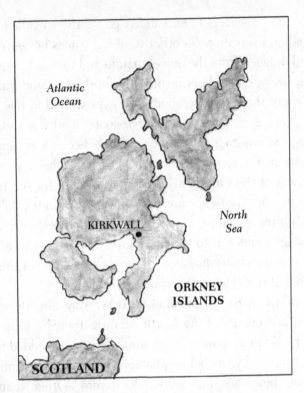

shaped hillocks, its grassy roundness making it appear as almost a natural part of the landscape until one sees it from the south, where a thirty-six-foot-long passageway opens to align beams from the sun at the winter solstice to strike the back of the chamber. Neither the claustrophobic nor obese happily enter the low and narrow and often damp entry-tunnel made of massive and rather regularly shaped flat stones. People must bend themselves in the middle, stumble into the darkness, each step taking them deeper, creeping farther from light, reaching more distantly into the past until the corridor opens into a small chamber that silences everyone as if it were airless.

In the dim beam of a flashlight, my eyes adjusted and things began to appear, creating what felt like a nether realm despite my being not *down* but merely *within*. The arch, the wheel, and metal tools were all still generations away when those stones went up. The tidy simplicity of the walls, long stones lying precisely parallel or at ninety degrees to one another, bespoke age and the silence made it resound. That far past was full of mortality: After all, for nearly five-thousand years the chamber was but a sepulcher. On his grand tour of northern Scotland in 1773, Samuel Johnson wrote in his *Journey*, "Edifices, either standing or ruined, are the chief records of an illiterate nation." So a visitor must try to read masonry.

The light played over the walls, flickered, stopped, and the past seemed to remember its voice as if it had been but waiting for someone to arrive from across the years. A yesterday is of no age and of every age, so it can pick its generation to speak from. Under the incandescence, time murmured from both four thousand years after the neolithic people built the chamber and from a millennium before flashlights existed. When the beam crossed the stones just so, from the walls emerged long and faintly etched lines wavering in the unsteady glow as if coming alive. At first, seeming to ramble across the sandstone, they appeared nothing more than adventitious scratches from one rock dragged over another; but slowly, like stick figures, they began to dance into orderly patterns composed in a backward alphabet lacking cursives and cross strokes. The scored lines showed themselves for what they were: runes, words scotched in by Norsemen who broke into the tomb in their perpetual hunt for plunder.

Those lineations constitute the largest collection of runic inscriptions in the world, and Maes Howe, its interior barely large enough for a dining table, is their library. As the Norse words wobbled under the uncertain light, they became voices to anyone who can listen with the eye. Some of the graffiti may have been left by raiders, surprisingly literate, who took shelter in this chamber during a fearsome snowstorm, an enforced stay in the close and darkened tomb that caused two of them to go mad. The words from vigorous men were at once surprising and predictable. Their Kilroys were there, of course, sometimes attached to the usual bravado of graffiti: "These letters carved by the man most skilled in runes in the western ocean."

And what else? Yes, that too: "Ingigerth the most beautiful of women" is, perhaps coincidentally, next to a crudely etched slavering dog. And: "Many a woman has walked stooping in here." And the simplest: "Thorni bedded." Those words, so much newer than the walls holding them, changed the mausoleum from a chamber of the dead into a shelter for the living, where more blooded passions found expression. That mixing of eras and peoples and vocabularies and moods turns Maes Howe, like other things in the Orkneys, into a time machine spinning travelers back through millennia even faster than the contraption imagined by H. G. Wells. And after stooping again down the long passageway and coming once more into the sunlight striking across the sea loch, visitors may feel they've returned from one of the farthest journeys they are likely ever to take.

II.

The Shetland Islands are not at the end of the earth—nor could they ever be, since globes don't have ends any more than they have corners, remote or otherwise—but when travelers reach the far extremity of the archipelago lying somewhat more than a hundred miles north of the tip of Scotland and smack between the Atlantic Ocean and the North Sea, they can be excused for feeling they have reached the ultimate back of beyond. That cluster of green hills and rock, stepsister islands to the Orkneys, although fifty miles north of them, has a sere and ragged beauty and often an appearance of some far place coming to an end, a land running out of terrain as it nears the Arctic ice. When Samuel Johnson made his 1773 tour through northern Scotland with James Boswell he wrote of the Highlands south of here in his *Journey*:

An eye accustomed to flowery pastures and waving harvests is astonished by this wide extent of hopeless sterility. The

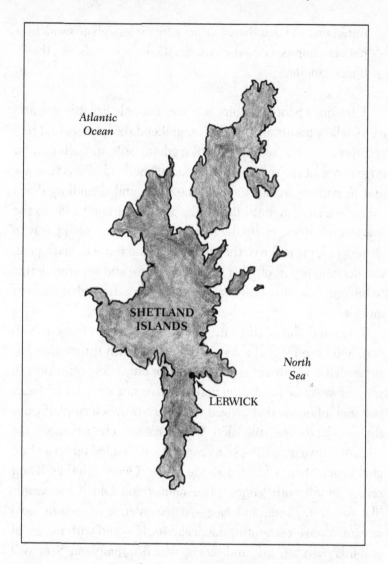

Atlantic
Ocean

**SHETLAND
ISLANDS**

North
Sea

LERWICK

appearance is that of matter incapable of form or usefulness,
dismissed by nature from her care and disinherited of her
favours, left in its original elemental state, or quickened only
with one sullen power of useless vegetation.

It will very readily occur that this uniformity of barrenness can afford very little amusement to the traveller, that it
is easy to sit at home and conceive rocks and heath and

waterfalls; and that these journeys are useless labours which neither impregnate the imagination, nor enlarge the understanding.

Johnson, a Scot will point out, was not only English, but also a city fellow hardly attuned to comprehend the massive and rugged terrain of the old northern kingdom. Still, to walk to a far edge of one of the sea-cuffed and rocky Shetland hills is to sense and to witness living things losing heart and dwindling down ever more steadily until life ceases altogether and yields to the inert: scrub trees, rarely the height of a tall horse, giving way to shrubs yielding to ferns, they to mosses, and those to black peat, the decomposition of what they once were, and it surrendering to broken rock without moisture or warmth except what weather gives it.

London is almost three times farther away than Bergen, Norway, and even Iceland is closer than the British throne that has somewhat uneasily ruled the islands for only a few centuries. In spite of years of royal direction and two fast decades of international influence that arrived with the North Sea oil-platforms, the Shetlands are still islets where natives cherish more the ancient Norwegian lines of a seagoing yoal hauled up on a shingled beach than a framed visage of the Queen Mother. Their sentences fill with Viking place-names and Old Norse words like *voe, rost, gloup,* and *haaf*—a sea inlet, a dangerous tidal stream, a wave-cut grotto, the ocean itself—and with names of seabirds: *bonxies, liri,* and *skorys,* which a mainland Scot will call skuas, shearwaters, and young gulls.

To celebrate the promise of a new year and the approaching end of winters that are not so snowbound as gale-ridden, the residents sing and roll through the streets of the largest town, Lerwick, during the ancient Norse-inspired *Up-Helly-Aa* celebration culminating with a torching of a replica Viking longship. A visitor wanting to make friends in a hotel bar will do well to comment on the fine Norwegian lilt in a native's speech, remembering never to take him for being merely Scottish. Ask not whether he descends from Robert the Bruce but rather from Sigurd the Stout. Those people were not plaid to the heart-blood as they were in, say, Inverness or Aberdeen; nor did their eyes fog up at the distant drone of bagpipes; although Shetlanders may live under the blue flag with the white cross of St. Andrew, it was tales of St. Magnus or Leif Eriksson that animate them. While a new economic order of big petroleum came in and remade their isles as fundamentally as the Vikings recast life for the endemic Iron Age people, a local fervor for things Norse increased and created a vigor of nostalgia that helped carry the islanders past the disruptions and dislocations of a long era ending.

I don't believe many of the Shelties—as they sometimes call themselves, after the intelligent and hardworking sheepdogs of these islands—consider that they live at the end of either a realm or an era, but it's difficult not to see it: brand-new shopping centers, supermarkets, two-lane highways, five-storey hotels, Indian and Chinese restaurants, and many faces with pigmentation whispering subtly if frankly that their ancestors never set foot in a Viking longship.

There was something else in a place redolent of the end of a thousand-year-long way of life which only haltingly turned medieval before slowly approaching our time: All across the sheep-eaten and wind-sundered slopes were dark and derelict crofters' cottages collapsing everywhere, stone ruins as abundant as boulders on the shore, and under each fallen, thatched roof and behind every broken chimney was the morose memory of what had gone by.

Yet those cots, clearly descended from Viking longhouses, permitted little nostalgia because they were cramped, dim, dank, and so primitive that the inhabitants—many of whom were still around to recite the story—shared the interior with their pissing, defecating farm animals. In exchange for fresh air, the people got strong vapors tinged with ammonia thought to create immunity to tuberculosis. With newer, less odiferous means of controlling TB, people abandoned the cottages for gray stucco dwellings that would look better in some derelict Levittown than against the sea hills of those handsome islands. Mainland Scottish visitors who remembered the Shetlands from just a quarter-century ago delighted in the new highways while they lamented the loss of a quaint beauty that the cottages—perhaps because they were of native stone and sat low on the slopes and thereby blended with the terrain—gave to the landscape. The only aspect remaining from the old crofts was the willy-nilly way they fell across the slopes here and there, unlike the new, two-storey suburban replacements which were mere sprawl. If there was inspiration in the harmonious lines of a longship or a yoal for a people wanting to rescue and reestablish a distinctive history before big oil mutated their heritage into something they could scarcely link with or pass on to a child, then the quiet and fitting way the ancient cottages, even yet according with the land, may serve to inspire the islanders.

Nevertheless, the old dwellings moldered earthward, while their owners went off to dig in public records for genealogical evidence to prove up their belief in Viking forebears was more than a wish, a longing that thinned with each generation like the terrain itself wasting down from scraggly trees to barren rock, a once vibrant urge coming to termination up there close to the end of the world.

III.

As my tour of the far Scottish Islands neared its end, and I'd gone on westward to a remote sea loch in the Outer Hebrides on the isle of South Uist, I found a small lodge on a slope above the water and facing the low coastal mountains. It looked to be a

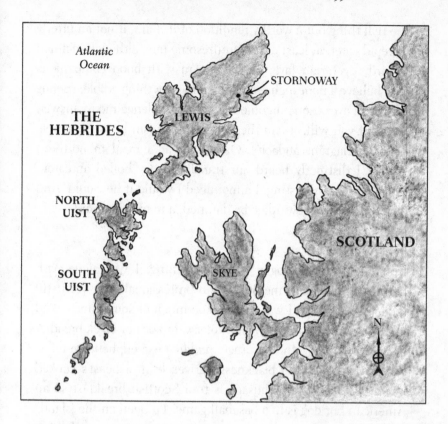

sweet little place to recover from my miles over land and sea, to return some spunk to my gait. In his *Life of Johnson,* Boswell quotes the Doctor: "There is nothing which has yet been contrived by man by which so much happiness is produced as by a good tavern or inn."

At breakfast on my next-to-last morning I realized I no longer could put off *the decision.* The time was near to order *it.* After all, even curmudgeonly Johnson believed, "If an epicure could remove by a wish, in quest of sensual gratifications, wherever he had supped he would breakfast in Scotland." The next morning would have to be the meal for *it.*

The kitchen of the little lodge was a capable one under the direction of Peadir, and he was fully equal to serving up not just the real thing but a worthy rendition of *it*. I am, if not an utterly intrepid eater, at least an adventuresome one, although inclined toward vegetarian fare; but when I'm with boon companions who believe a nonesuch red wine makes anything edible, friends who pore over exotic menu offerings to challenge me to answer, "I will if you will," I can then cross the chasm between simple risk and flagrant audacity. One night at a meal in northern China, I distinctly heard our translator say "boiled anteater." Thinking he was jesting, I announced I would if he would. And he *did*, so I did. Cowardice be damned, a man is his word.

In the morning, a foggy Hebridean thing, I was alone with nothing to challenge me other than professional duty, yet I still ordered *it*, figuring I was making too much of something called black pudding, a dish of no kin to, say, tapioca or black bread or even brown Betty. In this usage, *pudding* is a euphemism referring to tripe, and its blackness derives from a beast's cooked blood. What that flat sausage is to a Scottish breakfast so an American hot dog is to a baseball game. I'd been on the islands long enough to know that the Scots like to put names on food to mislead foreigners so they won't really consider leaving Des Moines to move to this beautiful, uncongested, boreal country. To mention a common one, the Scottish Gaelic word for *egg* is *ugh* (rhymes with *goo*). My first supper in the islands was quintessential national fare, something called *cullen skink*; I figured if an islander could eat little lizards so could any Yank good and true. It was delicious, ever more so when I spooned into it and found it to be not reptilian but cream-of-smoked-haddock soup.

I do confess, however, to passing up certain flavored crisps — potato chips — but it wasn't for want of culinary nerve; rather, I prefer to avoid silly foods imported from England — say, crisps with descriptive flavorings of prawn-cocktail, or chicken-and-dumpling, or bacon-and-baked-beans. I also admit to being satisfied with merely reading certain proprietary labels on canned goods in a Scottish grocery: Lunch Tongue in Jelly; Scotch Haggis (the second ingredient of this national dish was lamb offal, also termed "pluck and paunch"). I left them on the shelf near a tin of All Day Breakfast whose contents made me think a more accurate name might be All Thru the Night: beans, sausage, bacon, chopped egg nuggets, and mushrooms in tomato sauce.

No, indeed, the clever Scots would not drive me off their lovely wind-staggered islands by tricky names and unexpected ingredients more appropriate to zoo feed. I've tried soup of wild nettles—those nasty banes of path and field—and found it toothsome, not to mention my glee in chomping into a plant that has stung me from the cliffs of Dover to the northern Orkneys. After all, in eras past, in certain far places of the world, it has been an honored practice to eat one's enemy. Somewhere in America there must be a recipe for broth of poison ivy.

Still, on that morning, why did I linger over taking the first bite of my black pudding placed so harmlessly next to the poached *ughs* and grilled mushrooms? It started the night before. As I lay in bed and looked through my handbook to the Outer Hebrides, I came across this: "The nature of the land, the use of the sea as a food source, and the isolation of the islands are the main factors deciding the diet of the Hebridean." Recipes followed for fish heads and livers in oatmeal, boiled cormorant in stout, young gannet in ale. Then this one for sheep's-head broth: "Prepare the head the day before cooking. Using a red hot poker, rub over the sheep's head until a nice brown colour, remove ears, horns. Split the head longwise with an axe or saw."

A wise traveler waiting for Morpheus would have stopped there and taken up the phone book or the small print on the automobile rental-agreement. Oh no, none of that for me. I had to continue until I happened across a ne plus ultra, the very recipe for what would be on my plate the following morning: "Clean and wash one sheep's stomach inside and out. Mix in a bowl 8 oz. suet, 2 chopped onions, 8 oz. oatmeal, 1 pint sheep's or pig's blood. Place in stomach bag, sew ends, and boil gently for 2½ hours. Prick bags to prevent bursting."

As the thick muff of fog lifted to let a little sun into the breakfast room, I stared at my "pudding" and considered which of a sheep's four stomachs the cook used. I could, of course, have deferred to my semi-resolute vegetarian gospel by skipping breakfast to wait for a lunch of cock-a-leekie soup or a plate of clapshot. But, come, man! Isn't it a writer's task to enter realms of risk in hopes his report may serve others?

Finally, inescapably, I took up the exigent duty, reminding myself, *If they can, I can*. After all, at my request, Chef Peadir had specially made *it*. And so I took it. For three bites. Then the question arose: Wearied traveler I was, how could a reenergized step be worth this? At that moment I remembered Samuel Johnson's blessed sentence — "He that shall complain of his fare in the Hebrides has improved his delicacy more than his manhood." And I enjoyed the rest—that is, the other parts of my breakfast.

Once finished, and before Peadir could discover any loss of manhood, I wrapped the remnant of sausage in a paper napkin and went outside to look for Bob, the resident sheepdog. It took several minutes to find him because he was too deaf to come when called. At last there he was, dozing in the thin sunlight. Old Bob had that appearance aged sheepdogs get when their fur for some reason will no longer lie in place, giving them a perpetual dishevelment. I said he wouldn't believe what I'd brought him, and he didn't. Never raising his head, he had only enough interest to open one eye as I set the pudding before him; I waited, then pushed the black morsel enticingly close to his nose, although his sense of smell had gone years ago. He opened the other eye and with the slowness of arthritic age worked himself onto all fours, licked the pudding without passion, regarded the approaching cat, then me, and, with some fumbling, got the sausage into his chops and limped off I know not where.

I went up to my room, made some notes, loaded my camera, studied the map, got ready for a little expedition, and on my way out gave a thanks to Peadir for fulfilling my request. That's when something bounded past the kitchen door only to almost whip back the other way in full frolic. "Gad!" said Peadir. "What's gotten into Bobby? He's born again!" Perhaps I knew the answer, and perhaps I didn't. Quietly I went off up the brae, my step still listless as I tried to reevaluate potential secrets in black pudding. The Chinese believe in elixirs of rhinoceros horn and tonics of tiger-bone wine, and, damn it all, the Scots have blood sausage. No wonder the Gaelic word for "food" is *meat.*

As I made a slow trek over the heathered hills I knew I would have to face up to the cowardice of improving delicacy over manhood, and I also knew one of the rewards of travel is discovery of unconventional fare, especially when it leads to renewed physical fitness, even should it entail actually having to get down peculiar — that is to say, vile — provender. It was no longer a question of *could;* it was one of *must.*

That evening, as I sat at the tiny bar in the lodge and took a pint of fine ale in preparation for morning, something decrepit, disheveled, and dispirited limped past the open door. It was old Bob, as ancient and foot-weary as ever. The logic of his brief transformation came to me slowly, and when it did, I raised a toast to his health, *"Sláinte mhath!"* And then I did one to myself, and these were the whispered words: *This fellow, manfully, admits his delicacy.*

SOUNDED BY TRUMPETS SILENT

In San Francisco in 1987, I gave "Writing PrairyErth" as a talk before college English teachers, a group I'd been exiled from a few years earlier—not by them but by an anemic job-market. That turn of events was for the best, since my thoughts on restructuring the widely accepted canon of great American letters seemed, to the academy, misinformed if not radical. With "Writing PrairyErth," I hoped to provoke reevaluation, but my call to arms apparently was sounded largely by silent trumpets.

The urge toward otherness in this piece didn't seem to catch on, as suggested by the staggering rise of the memoir. Perhaps, in an age of pandemic self-absorption, a hushed response to opening outward was natural; but if autobiography doesn't ascend beyond the person portrayed, then its reach will probably forever be curtailed. Michel de Montaigne, in his attempts to get beyond the limitations of egoism in his Essais, employs self-deflating frankness of himself. Yet still, one can question the genuineness of his assertion "Thus, reader, I am myself the matter of my book; you would be unreasonable to spend your leisure on so frivolous and vain a subject."

Writing *PrairyErth*

Writing about America—if not American writing itself—
begins with the reports of European travelers: the journals
of Christopher Columbus, the account of Álvar Núñez Cabeza
de Vaca, the narratives of Pedro Castañeda (Coronado's lieutenant), Thomas Harriot, John Smith. Things may have changed
now, but my university education managed to keep those men—
as writers anyway—hidden from me. Our native literature,
according to my textbooks and professors of the late fifties and
early sixties, begins with works written by colonial citizens. While
I understand this approach, I find it a needlessly chauvinistic
one that misdirects us. After all, America was a literary subject
almost before it was a known territory. Were I teaching the literature of our land, I'd rather take my chances of catching an
inert sophomore's initial interest with the work of John Smith or
Thomas Harriot or Cabeza de Vaca than with something from
Michael Wigglesworth or Increase Mather or Charles Brockden
Brown, those worthies who were supposed to draw me in.

I attribute the slights to early American travel writing not to
Anglo prejudice so much as to the huge and overwhelming
national literary bias in favor of so-called imaginative literature
(fiction, poetry, drama) as though the clear and evocative record-
ing of fact requires no imagination. Try to think of Thoreau or
James Agee as unimaginative writers.

The *Harvard Guide to American History* gives a selective list
of about five-hundred accounts written by travelers in the United

States. These are books selected for their historical importance as well as their capable expression. To that list I can readily add another fifteen-hundred. A field containing two-thousand significant or at least worthwhile books, a genre that has come to shape even more than the novel our notions of who we are, where we are, and what we can accomplish, deserves the attention not just of our teachers but even more of young writers who are seeking new forms in which to represent their times. It's creatively destructive for so many of our future writers, regardless of genre, to work in ignorance of this long list of evocatively recorded journeys. (Let me add here that males on that Harvard list outnumber females by more than fifty to one. Such imbalance demands redressing.)

It may be, in part, that I'm attracted to the literature of travel and its relative, the literature of place, because for so long they also have been academic pariahs, and that's unjustifiable since no genre of our literature is so typically American. After all, seen in the light of human development, every American is a traveler or a descendant of travelers. And surely no nation has ever believed quite so completely in the necessity and curative power of moving hither and yon. From the time of the first crossings over the Bering land-bridge, mobility has been an elemental quality of our national experience. No wonder we've produced in just four-hundred years a literature of travel the equal of nations twice our age. I'm also drawn to nonfiction in its peregrinative mode because of opportunities it presents a writer in search of new structures. I see a sameness to much of our recent nonfiction, which I read as an alert to push further into the imagination as one would through a canebrake or dismal swamp.

I'm now in the last year—I assume, I hope—of a four-year project. In this new book—if you'll tolerate my calling what is still a manuscript a "book"—I'm writing about a well-defined piece of tallgrass prairie in our mid-latitudes. The work is a narrative account of a circumscribed place, a single county in east-central Kansas. After I began the project, I realized most of the truly lively writing about the Kansas prairie occurred in the nineteenth century: Washington Irving, Josiah Gregg, Victor Tixier, Miriam Davis Colt, John Gihon, George Brewerton. Those authors wrote at a time when Kansas was a topic frequently talked about in the eastern press as an unknown place of marvelous possibilities: a land ripe for agricultural and social experiments. (It was over social issues that the slavery question gave the state its epithet Bleeding Kansas.) If the territory was then a provocative topic, it is otherwise now.

Kansas today is a place seemingly not much suited to a writer in his right mind, because the rest of America assumes it knows all it wants to know about the state. But a region unknown because it's covered over by presumed knowledge—much of it distorted or downright incorrect—is just as ready for a reporter as one not yet explored. So, my work in Kansas is still a response to the thrall of the unknown, the lure of challenging ignorance—those classic motivations for a traveler. Viewed in this light, I'm following one of the very calls that pulled nineteenth-century writers into the region.

I must say, though, Josiah Gregg or Victor Tixier or Randolph Marcy did not have to face the question "So who the hell cares about Kansas?" *So who cares?* is always a writer's most fearsome uncertainty. Whatever the genre, a reader may begin to care if writers will look closely and report precisely and with imagination. If they do, they can reveal how maps today might still be accurately labeled with that traditional Renaissance inscription: *Here Be Strange Beasts.* A writer's assiduous examination should expose how little we see of a thing, how poorly we have understood it, how ineffectually we have let it touch our lives. It is such scrutiny that creates the traveler's ultimate excitement: the realization that if we but have the perception, we are perpetually strangers in a strange land.

After my fieldwork—*any* fieldwork—my task is then to discover the right voice with a distinct point of view, a persona who takes a certain tone in telling stories. With the job of finding an evocative voice comes the necessity of an appropriate framework to express it. The writer's search for perspective and structure can yield an excitement like that a traveler happens upon when a close observation reveals the extraordinary within the ordinary. In the instance of my current project, I've tried to let my explorations of the geographic territory lead me to a solution of the problems of voice and form. It took two years for a feasible framework to occur to me, but once it did, almost all of the organizational problems with the book were, in a stroke, solved.

Before I explain, let me say that I wanted this new work to avoid an approach I see as the major threat to good travel reporting today: a journey that exists primarily to express the soul of its traveler.

Of books well known at the outset of my tallgrass prairie explorations, two were nationally dominant: *Zen and the Art of Motorcycle Maintenance* (1974) and *The Snow Leopard* (1978). Both are fine works despite their following a parlous course capable of leading travel writing into memoir or fiction. In 1983 I used that very descent into self for *Blue Highways* where the narrator leaves his familiar surroundings and unwittingly at times heads off more into the country of his own interior than into the interior of the country. He neatly submerges into the topography of self for half the journey—and the book—before realizing the futility of that course. The narrator then begins to move from an inward-turning spiral—a conical helix—of his own self-absorption toward a reversed spiral opening outward toward other lives and new places. In *Blue Highways* the figure or pattern for this route (although not a true helix) is the Hopi "maze of emergence"—a glyph that has served for unknown millennia to remind the Hopis of the necessity to move away from self and into something other in order to become fully human. Otherness! Well might the Hopi maze be cut into the turf of every collegiate campus, chiseled into the facade of every library in this country.

The Hopi maze of emergence

The journey in *Blue Highways* is initially centripetal—an ever-closing spiral leading inward to a finite locus, a dead end. But as the traveler nears that central, still point, he begins to see the usefulness of—intellectually, emotionally—passing through it to another place where he can follow the lines outward, if not upward. I sometimes visualize the pattern by imagining the apex of a cone held against a mirror, where a traveler moves toward his own reflection but, to continue, must then follow the reflection on outward. (Centripetal motion, you'll recall, pulls an object toward the center while centrifugal movement throws it outward.) So, the movement here proceeds centripetally into the image of self and then from that still point—a potential cul-de-sac or nexus—the course proceeds centrifugally away from the center.

In my new book—the working title is *PrairyErth*—I want a course to lead outward from my own observations of a limited place into something larger. I've tried to go into the territory, into the tallgrass prairie, and continue on beyond. It is just that urge to move from self into (for want of a better word) non-self that has created difficulties. Whatever I've found in the prairie in the past many months may interest a reader not because it's lain undiscovered over the years, but rather because the narrator tries to perceive it anew and present it so. (In your mind hear the Plato-Pound conflict: "There is nothing new under the sun" versus "Make it new.") My question in writing this book has been: How do I steer away from self while depending on it almost completely for the discovery and formulation and presentation of the material?

My physical, topographical passage as a prairie traveler led—after two years—to a structural solution for the writer. The book covers only the 774 square miles of Chase County, Kansas. (For comparison, *Blue Highways* took on a good portion of the three-million square miles that are the contiguous states.) To guide my tallgrass searches and re-searches by car, horse, and foot, I used twelve U.S. Geological Survey 7.5′ Series topographical maps that cover the county almost exactly. One day while I was staring at those dozen sheets laid out on the floor of my study, I saw they looked like a grid archaeologists place over a site to guide excavation. It came to me: Wasn't I a kind of digger of shards, shards that would help me see and present that place?

That twelve-section grid, I realized, might continually provide an outline that would rarely match up with the pattern of my own perceptions of the territory. In other words, I'd have to leave my interior to travel, as writer, a course determined by an arbitrary, geometric schema. Because this shape would seldom— if ever—align with my own inner pattern, the grid could keep me fenced off from the temptation of the restrictive, encircling lines of self-exploration. Those barrier grids were continual reminders—invitations, actually—to excavate the landscape beyond my own interior topography.

But, having found a possible course capable of restricting self, I had to watch that the emblem did not then annihilate the self. Were I to write as a mere digger of test trenches, I would end up with a piece of social archaeology perhaps, but I wouldn't have the kind of literate evocation that was the inceptive urge. So, the struggle was to let the grid create a structure allowing the narrator's voice to inform and color. My hope is the pattern will prevent me from falling into the solipsistic black hole that is too often the death of potentially good tales of travel.

In this struggle against a writer's self overwhelming, polluting, and degrading the realm he wants to present, one monument of American reportage brilliantly overcomes it: James Agee's 1941 *Let Us Now Praise Famous Men*. It's splendid precisely because it resolves so originally and richly the centrifugal-centripetal problem of one writer's explorations. Agee employs the framework of a scientist in his purely factual descriptions of three sharecropper families in Alabama. (For an illustration of his method, see his descriptions of the Gudgers' beds or the Rickettses' fireplace.) With an objectivity quite the match of the documentary photographs of the people and the place made by his partner Walker Evans, Agee presents the details as precisely and fully as is readably possible, only then blending in his own vision and unique voice, thereby turning a sociological report into literature of the highest order. The book moves between the hard and flat side of sharecropper life in Hale County, Alabama, and the sharp edge of his passionate intelligence and imaginatively lambent prose. "Sprawling and overwritten," some naysayers have cried. Well, so is *Moby-Dick* and *Tristram Shandy* and *Gargantua and Pantagruel*. And what about *Tom Jones; Remembrance of Things Past?*

Although Agee's book has become a classic (even if the most unread of American classics), writers of nonfiction, it seems to me, have not much built upon his method or been enough inspired by his solution to the perpetual problem of the writer's self in its surroundings. Yet Agee's achievement stands squarely at the critical juncture between factual writing and fiction. He equilibrated self with its surround like a high-wire artist continually balancing to keep from falling to his death. To my mind, this equipoise between writing (and traveling) centrifugally or centripetally is the cardinal problem the so-called New Journalism tried to address. Its solutions, full of fictive devices (and ostentations of self), were dangerous to the survival of non-fiction, where its power—its very existence—depends always on the primacy of fact.

My book about the prairie will neither look nor sound like *Let Us Now Praise Famous Men,* but it was James Agee's perhaps intuitive recognition and conscious solution to the centrifugal-centripetal journey that started me on that course where I stumbled across a defining and delimiting pattern in a series of topographic maps. He was an architect of a threshold leading to a room more wonderfully spacious than I'd once imagined.

THE 3,170TH COUNTY

Although "The Smoked Ciscoes of Gitche-Gumee" makes no mention of it, my long pursuit of visiting every American county lay behind the quest for food of another era, and, to be honest, the hunt for the little fish seemed more a potential bonus than a goal. Cook County, Minnesota, manages to hide under the rather straight and regular Canadian border running from the western end of Lake Superior all the way to the Pacific. If you look at a map, you'll see how, out of 3,170 counties, Cook could end up being a finale.

The Smoked Ciscoes of
Gitche-Gumee

In the summer of 1949, just before my tenth birthday, I was serving in my usual role as navigator aboard my father's tub of an automobile, a vehicle large and black and not unlike a hearse—a fit comparison given that a year later he would nearly die in it when a drunken corn-farmer drove into him headfirst on a Missouri highway. But in the July before the crash, we were passing through the eastern edge of the North Woods of upper Minnesota. With a topographical abruptness hardly typical of the state, the road seemed to fall away as it rolled down a bluff; ahead was a distant skyline no longer of dark trees but one of a pencil line linking two radiant shades of blue. Which reflected the other, who could say? It was my first glimpse of a body of water showing no opposite shore.

With a road map in hand, I knew it had to be Lake Superior, yet how could a lake so far inland have a coast beyond the horizon? I was about to learn the Ojibway name for it: Kitchigammee, "big sea-water," or, in Longfellow's less correct if better known version, Gitche-Gumee. That so-called lake was the largest body of entirely fresh water on the planet, big enough for seventeenth-century voyageurs to consider it a sea.

At its deepest place, the tallest skyscraper on earth would vanish in it. More awesome than the somber conifer forest lying behind, here was a watery realm a boy from Kansas City could fill with creatures escaped from his imagination. The deep blue

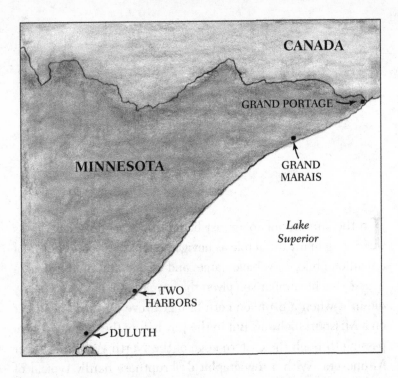

of its depths and the wind having at it bespoke remoteness and coldness even in midsummer, and, although I couldn't then have articulated it, I recognized the edge of something dangerously wild and intimidatingly mysterious.

Almost as soon as we turned southward from Minnesota Route 1 onto U.S. 61, the lake revealed its first enigma. Every few miles hand-painted signs cropped up, each advertising in one wording or the other:

SMOKED CISCOES AHEAD!

What a cisco was—smoked or unsmoked—I had no idea. My father, who had just taught me how to catch a walleye and who seemed to know boreal waters, had no answer either. A cisco might be a creature from the deep, some rarity, maybe an aberration of nature like those stuffed concoctions a traveler then could find exhibited for a dime along rural highways: jackalopes, a half fish–half frog, a three-legged calf, a two-headed alligator, even a merman (in Arkansas).

One of the few things that could move my father to stop and get out from behind a steering wheel was the scent of barbecue smoke across a road. In Kansas City, such a whiff usually led us to brisket of beef or so-called burnt ends laid over a slice of white bread. But along the bouldered rim of Lake Superior a little north of Two Harbors, Minnesota, the occasional wooden cafés hanging along its high edge and showing smoked cisco signs didn't look like the smokeries we knew. These had promise of unknown fare, the kind to make the labor of travel worth its undertaking.

We pulled into a rickety eatery held up by wooden posts seemingly insufficient in number and diameter to keep the place above the lake just then banging ominously far beneath the eastern café wall. The buckled floor was manifest warning that one diner too many might send the entire enterprise into the water. My father, a cautious man who sometimes wore a belt with his suspenders, stepped gingerly, as if testing ice on a pond, toward a table by a bank of windows giving onto the lake. Pasted to the walls were menus. Under the heading FROM THE LAKE, between listings of herring and trout, was a scribbled *When Available*, and there it was: *Smoked Cisco*. So, to my disappointment, a cisco was not a miscreation, not freak of the deep, but a small, edible fish.

I knew from my father's example that a jolly equatorial amplitude, a fulsome girth, does not guarantee an adventuresome eater, yet he could be bold—provided he had at hand one of his jingles like "S-M-O-K-E-D means O-K-2-E-A-T. Unless it's turned green." He ordered up two plates of smoked ciscoes as part of an expression of a belief he usually gave more utterance to than practice: From a mere vacation, one goes home older, but from true travel one returns changed by challenge. To him, an exotic dish provided the happiest of challenges, and when the food was, to use his word, scrumtudious, like the ciscoes, the richest of rewards. Of the highest order among travelers are those moments when a place and a comestible indelibly link to write themselves deeply into one's memory. That day, Lake Superior wrote itself into me.

That remembrance took me again to the North Shore of Superior in Minnesota a half-century later. I'd heard the little cisco was not faring well in the Great Lakes and to find a plate of them was increasingly difficult. One June morning I lit out for the North Country along U.S. 61, the North Shore Highway, a fine 150-mile stretch opened in 1924. I wasn't expecting SMOKED CISCOES AHEAD! signs, and I didn't see any, and hope dwindled as the miles came and went, and the roadside showed less and less developed as it neared the Canadian border. By the time I was running out of American territory I'd still not turned up a single smoked fish of any sort, not even a sardine. The coastal road opened frequently to splendid lacustrine scenery, and the hues of Superior, modulated by sky and proximity to shore, might have been decocted from gemstones: here flowing sapphire, there aquamarine, and once when I stopped to walk the stony margin and looked into a small pool I saw liquid chalcedony vibrating from the thump of the waves.

Superior, like its region, is an expression of water and weather working over rocks—hard rocks like granite, basalt, and gabbro. The coast is a gamut of steep and high headlands dropping to beaches strewn with stones from boulders to pebbles, the smaller pieces often wave-polished into spheres and ovoids, globets and orbs, colorful rotundities turned to cabochons a walker could almost right there string into a necklace. One may also find irregularities in startling shapes. In fact, at the decrepit café where I'd first tasted smoked cisco, behind a glass counter under the cash register was a small Superior beach-stone water-worried into the configuration of the head of an old man; had it been excavated from a cave or midden, a seasoned archaeologist would swear a human hand had crafted it.

The Superior visible today was probably created by incomprehensibly massive glacial lobes moving southward and gouging out stone softer than the adamantine igneous rock around portions of its margin so that the lake is the outcome of fire and ice, a place relinquishing its fierce origins but only slowly. Once, its waterline was almost double its present height above sea level, a fact one can readily discern in downtown Duluth in the steep, stairstep-like former shores of the ancient Superior.

The earliest voyageurs called it Lac Superieur, a name having nothing to do with altitude, size, depth, excellence, or (even today) with its comparative cleanliness. Rather, *superieur* refers to its position "above," that is, north of its four sisters. The uppermost margin of Superior is five-hundred miles north of the southern rim of Lake Erie, nearly the longitudinal distance of France from the Mediterranean to the Channel. For many residents of the Superior shore, its finest aspect beyond Duluth is a coast free from cities, and that means fishermen working out of sight of the breakwaters still drink straight from the lake, a detail I hoped would mean somewhere yet swam a cisco.

As the miles rolled under me with no sign of the fish—smoked, barbecued, grilled, steamed, baked, boiled, broiled, fried, poached, roasted, toasted, pickled, stewed, chowdered, coddled, curried, or, ye gods, even microwaved—my hopes forlorn, I at last fetched up in Grand Marais, a pleasant lakeside village. On its perimeter was a collection of brightly painted buildings rambling down to a dinky harbor where hung a faded sign:

FRESH LAKE SUPERIOR FISH

I followed its pointing finger to a newer board with elegant, gilded letters:

DOCKSIDE FISH MARKET
FRESH & SMOKED

Painted on the window of the shop door were two golden herrings, each smiling, and inside beyond them, behind the counter lay rows of smoked herring and other species, some not native to Superior. I asked for ciscoes. "Oh my," the clerk said in a kindness possibly trotted out to ease disappointment. "I don't have any. It's been some time. Years, I'd say."

At the market, the only commercial smokehouse on the upper North Shore, I bought two herrings and walked toward the dock, stopping to look into a fish shed where Harley Tofte, a man of middle years, bright in orange waders, was cutting his catch of that morning, eighty pounds of herring, each fish about twelve inches long and weighing a pound or a little more. He deftly and nearly bloodlessly opened the bellies of the sleek and fulgent fish, removed innards while leaving head and tail, and into a bin tossed each one now ready for twelve hours in his small smokehouse, the penultimate stop on a voyage from 150 feet down in frigid Superior to a warm dinner plate. I said I was looking for ciscoes, and he mumbled, "So am I." He scowled. "They've just kind of disappeared. What we get now is herring and lake trout and some menominee and whitefish. But ciscoes? Not a one."

Next door was septuagenarian Tom Eckel's cutting house where he, too, in orange waders was preparing what he'd just brought in, primarily trout. He grew up on a Superior island, something harder to do these days, and he was old enough to remember the area before World War II. His Gitche-Gumee pedigree was pure. I rephrased my question to reflect the sad news I was finding: Did he ever catch a cisco? He looked at me as if I'd asked "Did you ever catch a cold?"

With North Country politeness he said, "A long time ago," and returned to a plump fish under his knife. Then, because I just stood there waiting for more, he added, "I don't think you'll ever see the ciscoes come back—not in this area. Too many predators." When he put the fillet knife down a moment later he said, "But then, I didn't think we'd ever see the lake trout come back like this." Halfway through the next filleting, he stopped cutting. In Minnesota, a traveler learns conversational patience because the difference between a pause and a conclusion can be about a day. Eckel finished his muse and said, "The lampreys are under control, I think. Let's hope they are. I know I've heard that ninety percent of our fish right here are natives again."

Everyone's commentary about ciscoes was historical, recollections of what had been. Worse, in less than an hour, I'd just talked to two-thirds of the commercial fishermen remaining in Grand Marais. As I left the cutting house I pointed to a long black sock tacked to the wall. Tom Eckel said, "Found it in the belly of an eight-pound trout." When I reached the door, he added, speaking to himself, "Don't know what happened to the rest of the guy."

I sat by the lake in an easy breeze and opened my smoked-herring lunch. Excellent, but it wasn't ciscoes. On the road, optimism can be useful, and something Eckel had said gave hope for yet finding a cisco: He preferred to go after larger species, but fishermen along the southern end of the North Shore, near Knife River, places closer to the old café where I'd first tasted cisco, those boys down there might think differently. "Who knows what you'll find," he'd said. "Maybe a smoked sock."

After two days of wandering around Grand Marais and exploring the coast all the way north to the border at the Pigeon River, I turned around and headed southwest, my hopes further raised by a growing awareness that part of the difficulty in the search might be linguistic: One person's cisco could be another's chub (a name loosely applied), or a blind robbin, or (even more loosely) a whitefish. Who ever met a commercial fisherman using genus-species nomenclature to describe what comes up in the net?

I was looking for *Coregonus artedi*, the Latin name with a story attached to it: The latter term refers to a Swede, Petrus Artedi, father of ichthyology. After Artedi fell into a canal and drowned, Carl Linnaeus, coincidentally the creator of binomial taxonomy, wrote of his colleague: "Thus did the most distinguished of ichthyologists perish in the waters, having devoted his life to the discovery of their inhabitants."

A cisco is also known as a lake herring, even though it isn't a true herring but rather a member of the salmon family along with lake trout and various so-named whitefish of the Great Lakes. Overharvesting, pollution, the spread of invaders like lampreys and alewives all have affected smaller fish such as ciscoes and the larger species dependent upon them so that today certain fish have declined precipitously from their populations in, say, 1949. I also began suspecting that my quest would have gone better had I arrived in the autumn when ciscoes rise from the depths and cluster to spawn in warmer shallows. But, like a fellow whose inamorata slyly eludes him, I was drawn on by the challenge of the pursuit.

Late one afternoon near Knife River, I came to a beat-up tavern with a worn sign promising no ciscoes but at least smoked fish of some sort. The place was closed—it looked like for weeks—but I managed to raise Betty Kendall, the proprietor who lived next door in a trailer. The airless and dark barroom, redolent of years of cigarettes and spilled beer, was universally, dismally red—worn carpets, tottery chairs, ragged draperies—and decorated in hanging ball-caps and dozens of representations of Betty Boop, a comics character from an era Betty Kendall shared with her. Also a sign:

TO HELL WITH THE DOG
BEWARE THE OWNER.

By the look of things, experience suggested I should heed it.

Diffidently, I asked my question about smoked ciscoes. In weariness she said, "How many do you want?" Half expecting a laugh of derision to chase me out, I suggested enough to make a dinner. She disappeared into what I took for a closet and returned with several sheets of newspaper cradling golden ciscoes. She wrapped them. I asked were they fresh. "These were smoked yesterday at four o'clock. They come from over on the Wisconsin side." I recited a nutshell rendition of my quest, and she said about her late husband, Smokey, "He used to eat three or four while he was smoking them. You would've thought they were popcorn. Now, only a couple of fishermen in Knife River still go after them."

When I left, my wrapped ciscoes snug under my arm as if rare first editions of books long sought, I noticed across the road a second fish stand. It was shut down, but only a little farther along was yet another. I was in a hotbed of smokeries. Russ Kendall, brother of Smokey, had built his place as a proper market, small and plain but with appropriate glass-fronted cases, refrigeration, and a happy spread of smoked fish. He was old enough to know the cisco story through the whole of the twentieth century: from the time of abundance when a smoked-cisco stall would pop up about every fifteen miles of shoreline road, on to the near scarcity I'd been encountering. A local Ojibway showed Kendall's father how to build a smokehouse. Russ said, "People don't fish for them so much now because ciscoes are the most trouble and bring the least money, but I'll tell you this: They're good enough that, years ago, when this place was just a roadside stand and our catch was out in the open air before government regulations, one morning a cow wandered up and ate a couple ciscoes right off the table. Two days later the owner of the cow complained his milk tasted fishy."

* * *

That evening I unwrapped packages from three different vendors and began a celebration of a memory, a fulfillment of what Lake Superior had written in me some half-century earlier. On the table lay slender, streamlined creatures, fish of classic symmetry, their round eyes blanched from the oven. I cut along the back and pulled free the scaled skin once nearly luminescent but now turned golden by smoke. Flesh, the color of parchment, lifted easily from insubstantial bones almost invisible. The ciscoes were so delicate it seemed wondrous they could survive in the dark and cold and eat-and-be-eaten deeps they spent most of their lives in. They were tender and moist—"oily," people say on the North Shore—and reportedly rich with salutary omega-3 fatty acids. Their sweet delectability made finishing one almost a regret; even having a dozen others iced down, enough for several more lunches and dinners, didn't relieve my sense of impending cisco deprivation. But, beyond that, in mind was a wobbly café, a smiling father freed from a steering wheel, a smudgy window opening to a lake reaching out till it vanished, and I realized I'd followed a small, silvery, scrumtudious fish into a long corridor back toward 1949.

THE BECAUSE-IT'S-THERE ASSOCIATION

As a writer—and of late as a traveler—I prefer topics and places less frequented, as in "A Land for the Resolutely Curious." The Because-It's-There Association is an imaginary caboodle of those who recognize that any popularly supposed quarter of humdrummity (say, the state of Kansas) requires only an awakened curiosity to be worth a little exploration.

The venerable Delta Queen is now a permanently anchored hotel on the Tennessee River at Chattanooga. R.I.P.

A Land for the Resolutely
Curious

Among the variety of American travelers, those who visit a somewhere ostensibly lacking any feature other than mere existence aren't numerous, although perhaps they should be. The growing throng crowding national and theme parks and any piece of sand leading to waves anywhere can encourage a rambler to seek out the overlooked and presumed humdrum. Surpassing even the great Sir Edmund Hillary, this other kind of excursionist, resolutely curious, goes to a place *truly* "because it's there" and not because it's the highest mountain on earth. If the possibility of sixteenth-century-like discoveries—Vespucci, Verrazano, John Cabot—hardly exists any longer, the joy of personal discovery remains. A mundane locale, for one who's never seen it, can surprise and satisfy as much as those celebrated and hawked.

These days I'm usually out to escape famous American destinations, not because they're unworthy but because I've visited most of them more than once. After half a century I still dream of poking into every corner of America. From Underground Seattle to the turtle crawls in Key West, from the chamber of the Supreme Court in Washington to the bottom of the Deep Well near Chicago, from Mount Katahdin to the telescopes on Kitt Peak in Arizona, the lure of America is everywhere.

That's how, near the last Christmas of the millennium, I came to be aboard the venerable steamboat *Delta Queen* as she

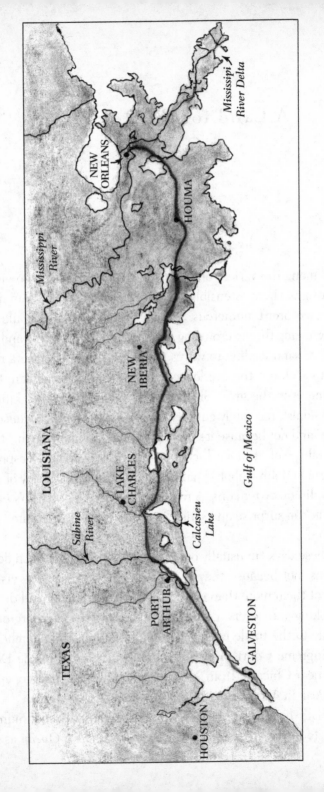

pulled away from the Twenty-First Street Wharf in Galveston, Texas. We were bound for New Orleans, 350 miles distant, via the Gulf Intracoastal Waterway, popularly called in its own territory the ICW. A few years ago, when one old pilot heard the *Delta Queen* was going to initiate an annual round trip on the ICW, he said, "What the hell for? Ain't nothin but an industrial ditch." To a member of the Because-It's-There Association of Not-Yet-Jaded Travelers, such words are traveling orders.

In a massive, wet lowland where humans for two centuries have dug and dredged uncounted miles of ditches — some wide enough only for a canoe and others for a span of barges — the ICW is the lone watercourse there called the canal. It runs about a thousand miles from the mouth of the Rio Grande below Brownsville, Texas, to Apalachicola, Florida, most of it sheltered from the open water of the Gulf by slender islands and spits and peninsulas; in that way it resembles the Atlantic Intracoastal Waterway running along the eastern shore. Nowhere else on the Gulf does the ICW get so far from ocean as it does between Galveston and New Orleans; over that route boats move entirely in a dug channel, something not true even for the Erie Canal which, by happenstance, is about the same length. Dredging the ICW made the Gulf coastland between those two cities effectively into an island, or, better, a chain of islands, the largest in the contiguous forty-eight states, a linkage unlike any other in the country.

Since its completion in 1949, you cannot in that section reach the open Gulf by foot or auto without crossing a bridge or getting onto a ferry. The entire ICW — elsewhere a conjugation of dug channels connecting dredged lakes and bays — is, in a nation of monumental navigational undertakings, among the most impressive constructions of the past century, the fulfillment of an idea that first appeared two-hundred years earlier. If engineers have not built the locks in the east Texas–Louisiana portion as big or numerous as those on the Erie Canal or on the Mississippi,

Ohio, and Columbia rivers, these lesser locks have managed to keep the central ICW from being absorbed or dissolved by the thousand swamps, marshes, bayous, lagoons, and drainage ditches along its miles. To see the difficulty, imagine digging a trench in a shallow pond. So many different watercourses cross it, natural and engineered, that a traveler can wonder why it doesn't drain itself into the Gulf, at one place only about five-hundred yards of low, sandy beach away.

Any passage humans create—whether footpath or super-highway—is never entirely benign to the land it traverses, but compared to other major arteries like the first transcontinental railroad or even I-95, the monumental Gulf ICW has untold capabilities to alter its natural realm, and that's the reason construction of an extension of it across Florida was stopped in the early seventies and later turned into a greenway. It's good to remember, though, that long before the canal existed, the Texas-Louisiana territory it crosses had been dredged and channeled for other purposes to a fare-thee-well.

Some time ago I came upon Jan de Hartog's *Waters of the New World*, an account of his 1960 voyage with several companions in a seagoing barge from Houston to Nantucket. His description of crossing the portion of the ICW that the *Delta Queen* would soon cover surprised me, coming as it does from a Netherlander who says of himself, "I have lived most of my adolescent life on inland waters of the Old World and most of my adult life at sea." Yet, this old salt didn't find the ICW a comfortable route separated from the perils of the open Gulf, although he wasn't bothered by the numberless canal hazards—heavy barge traffic, submarine pipelines, submerged pilings, cable ferries, pontoon bridges, drooping overhead powerlines, masses of water hyacinth, alligators, or the incredible and deadly suction created by tows under way. Rather, he was disturbed by a more ancient and less definable reason: a common European unease about American wildernesses extending in pieces from the

Adirondacks to the Olympic rain forest—and at times even into the Hell's Kitchen of a city.

That Old World response has been around at least since the Puritans who equated deep Massachusetts forests and their natives with natural evil; in their seventeenth-century minds, to subdue the dark wilderness and its inhabitants was to quell the Devil and to bring all into Christian luminance. In his chapters on the ICW, de Hartog uses words like *lonely, terror, hostile, desolation, creatures of the night, nightmarish country, the heart of darkness, a glimpse of purgatory, paradise lost, an atmosphere of something beyond evil.* Such language can lure a Because-It's-There associate into a five-day passage through a terraqueous place alleged to be riddled with shadowy creatures creeping a lost paradise beyond evil.

On several occasions, I'd been near that reported heart of darkness but by auto and foot and never into places only the canal can take you to. A road map of the region reveals an intriguing blankness of humanly unhabited waters surrounding much of the canal. South of the ICW, in the Louisiana parish of Terrebonne, for example, are some thousand square-miles without a highway. If such wildness was hostile desolation to a European visitor, its Cajun settlers found that *terre tremblante* indeed to be also "land-good."

The *Delta Queen*, built in 1926 and a National Historic Landmark (strange terminology for a boat), has a history of one narrow escape from destruction after another. Her fortune, for now, is mostly opposite the fate of her "brother" vessel, *Delta King*, now a hotel stuck to the shore in Sacramento, California. The lower Sacramento River was also home port for the *Queen* until 1947 when she survived being towed some seven-thousand miles down the Pacific Coast, through the Panama Canal, and up the Mississippi and Ohio rivers to a refurbishing in Pittsburgh. Because of her appealing lines, steam-powered paddlewheel, and rather long operating history, she's arguably become—along with the USS *Constitution*—one of the most beloved vessels in America. I'd been aboard her from New Orleans to St. Paul, from Cincinnati almost to Pittsburgh, and I know of few other vehicles that can so transport a traveler into our landscapes and history. She is, as her captain told me, "a time machine." To see from her historic decks the nineteenth-century Eads Bridge over the Mississippi at St. Louis, for example, is to catch a waft of time gone.

On an early December afternoon the *Queen* got under way from Galveston, moving at five miles-an-hour up the channel behind Pelican Island, and there she crossed the outlet to the Gulf called Bolivar Roads to gain the Intracoastal Waterway proper. To the starboard side lay a twenty-five-mile peninsula of sand which in places is barely broad enough to separate the canal from the Gulf. Beyond the abandoned lighthouse at Port Bolivar, she entered a twenty-two-mile-long channel that, but for one slight dogleg, deviated from straightness no more than a laser beam, our course lying between grassy shores and marsh, a few of them given to oyster beds.

Eastward was an old Indian graveyard, and everywhere

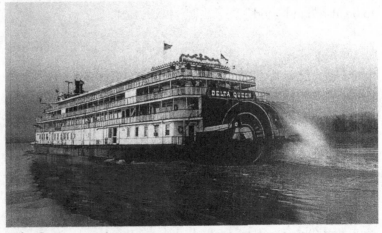

Delta Queen *in 1998*

dead-end drainage ditches, each parallel to the next in such a way that the peninsula was a place neatly and unnaturally scotched by water. From the highest deck of the boat, I could see at Rollover Bay the Gulf only a few-hundred yards distant, but from that point on I'd catch only rare glimpses of it. The canal bends twice at High Island—*High* there meaning twenty-five feet above sea level—to enter the country of Mud Bayou that drains Mud Lake through long, crooked, and unhurried miles even though the Gulf lies only eight-hundred yards south. The nature of slow-moving water is to turn upon itself, and, in that land of twisted creeks and bayous, straightness is the signature of human hands.

On the north bank lay the Anahuac National Wildlife Refuge, but, other than a few birds one might come across in a city backyard east of the Rockies, I saw no creature—of the night or day—whose presence was totemic to a vast and distinctive watery world; perhaps it was the wrong season or disturbance from our arrival. The *Queen* went under a bridge, a thing uncommon enough along the route to cause passengers to rise to see it. Once, cable ferries were the usual means to cross the waterway, but those boats are disappearing to leave overgrown and rotting pilings, a loss since lore typically gathering around ferry crossings shows little capacity to accumulate under steel bridges.

For a couple of dozen miles, save a single negligible jog, the canal ran straight eastward almost to Port Arthur, Texas; to those who delight in lines curved and sinuous, the route was not especially scenic, but before we could reach the end of the straightaway, darkness overtook us to offer better chances to encounter the Dutchman's nightmarish country. Yet with views from my observation posts along the rails obscured, any possibility of a nightmare would have to manifest itself in mere sleep.

I awoke just after sunrise to find us tied to the wharf at Port Arthur, a place remarkable for the near-total abandonment of its small commercial center. Given that the city bears the name of railroad magnate Arthur Stilwell, a man who confessed to founding the town on the advice of "brownies" appearing before him in the night, perhaps such is the economic fate of pixie-driven endeavors.

After a walk through the remains of Stilwell's dreamland, we were again under way and soon crossed the Neches River to reach the northern edge of a large spread of water I initially took for the Gulf but which proved to be Sabine (*Say*-bean) Lake, surprisingly shallow for its size. A long-legged horse could wade the four miles across that upper embayment. Even there, though, the canal lies almost entirely behind the protection of slender islands before it enters marsh again west of a refinery between two channelized bayous. The first Texas oil boom began in 1901 nearby at Spindletop Dome, something Stilwell's brownies may have had in mind when proffering advice to him.

Just below the docklands of Orange, Texas, the *Delta Queen* crossed the Sabine River as if it were simply a highway intersection. Ahead lay twenty-one miles of channel, once again as straight as a dredge can dig. Taking a vessel along such a course would seem simple enough, but the captain told me otherwise. While the ICW is essentially rockless, currentless, tideless, and a large boat cannot get lost, hazards of another sort are everywhere. He said, "On the Mississippi and Ohio, big boats have room to keep clear of each other, but down here we can just about shake hands when we pass. Then there's the bank suction the hull creates as it displaces water. A stern of a boat tries to go this way, that way. It behaves like the tail end of a dog with worms."

The haulage on the canal is largely petroleum and other chemical compounds like isopropyl alcohol, ethyldiamene, and caustic soda. There's also salt, scrap metal, and agricultural products, all of it moving on low — if huge — barges not built for the open sea. Beyond, in ports or in passes to the Gulf, I saw no ships on the canal, and in that way it is more terrestrial than nautical and resembles a wet interstate.

Where the Calcasieu (*Kal*-kah-shoo) River enters its lake, the ICW makes a sharp ninety-degree turn, bends a few more times, then straightens to pass through a flat world only about three feet above sea level, where pools and ponds and shallow lakes, often surprisingly circular, are sometimes hardly distinguishable from the marshes around them. Considering the thousands of miles of drainage ditches in the region, one has to wonder how much wetter it used to be. Before engineering, the area would have seemed a place just emerging from Noah's flood. A century ago, to find the way through channels that twist and shift like a line dropped overboard, along courses that appear only to quickly disappear into the reeds, cane, and willows, must have been a mosquito-blitzed nightmare.

(It's useful here to recall that *bayou*, *marsh*, and *swamp* are not interchangeable words. A bayou is a river; a marsh is a wet and sometimes inundated grassland; a swamp is flooded woodland. Along the central Gulf Coast, those distinctions are useful.)

At Gibbstown, noteworthy for its complete lack of anything you might associate with an actual town, such as a house or a human, the *Delta Queen* entered another huge marsh with a scattering of trees. Near its center lies Lake Misere, a lovely thing in the late autumn afternoon light and just then not deserving its name—unless transit was by canoe or bateau, as indeed it was for those who bestowed the name.

Beyond the debouchure of the Mermentau River into Grand Lake, the canal narrows. The ICW avoids the hundreds of lakes lying along its course as if they were islands because its builders, the Corps of Engineers, believed it easier to construct and more economical to maintain a ditch dug through what passes there for high ground than a channel dredged through a shallow lake. The canal in that stretch often runs for a dozen miles between a series of bays and lagoons lying just beyond a scrim of grasses or trees, the Gulf invisible to anyone at canal level. If you've ever been down an English lane between hedgerows entirely containing your line of sight, then you have an idea of passage east of Grand Lake. Happily, my cabin was on the sundeck, high enough above obscuring foliage to open to vistas I couldn't have seen from a small boat.

The challenge for a voyager along the straight runs is to avoid going numb to the miles of apparent sameness; this is a land for people who do not grow bored in crossing the Great Plains and who like places that challenge even Because-It's-There travelers to be patient and to look ever more closely; yet they too can begin to hope for a passing tow, a sunken barge, a bridge, a noisy rise of ricebirds—anything to disrupt the purgatory of rectilinearity.

In one limbo of miles through rice fields then in their seasonal pasture color, the wish for a bend, a twist, a deviation, a slight obliquity was like the cry of a parched throat on the Mojave. Just north of Grand Lake, our movement for ten miles, I must confess, was two hours of near deprivation and denial. Even though here and there the irregular and encoved natural Gulf shoreline to the south lay only a hundred feet away, it was invisible. During such passage, a wise traveler takes to a bunk, or a book, or a cribbage board. Others — members of the Because-It's-There Association—ignore common sense and do not.

No piece of earth appeared to rise more than a couple of inches higher than anything else, yet rises must have been there, at least in former times, because the place was larded with names for this *island* and that *isle*. I heard that the disappearance of those relict islets into a dryer landscape reveals the prodigious engineered draining. What a vertical mile is to the Sierra, so along the upper Gulf is an upright inch.

Verticality is crucial in the two kinds of locks and dams on the ICW: those to maintain the water level and others to prevent the sea from salinating the freshness of the bayous and marshes. Except for locks near the Mississippi at New Orleans, the rise or descent in those backcountry chambers can be the height of a chair leg, but here, as in baseball, it's a game of inches.

Vermilion Bay, a large inlet off the Gulf, is so shallow in places on its northern end that five miles from shore it's still only ten feet deep, making it possible for barrier islands nearly to turn it into a lake, yet even there the canal keeps behind a spongy strip of ground. At the east side of the bay is Weeks Island, a mined salt dome. After three days in the watery flats, I thought Weeks, although surrounded by land, looked indeed like an island, rising as it does two-hundred feet. In a terrain where natural height belongs only to trees — or grasses — that salt hump is a landmark.

At sunset of our next-to-last day, the *Delta Queen* made a ninety-degree turn and proceeded up a drainage canal leading to the Port of Iberia where new wharves had been built to make the inland Cajun town of New Iberia into a seaport. The narrow route nearly let trees in close enough to brush the gunwales; in fact, so near that a few months earlier a flummoxed squirrel had dropped onto the sundeck of the *Queen*. This was an area the Dutchman described as "nightmarish country." In the approaching dusk, a humped form waddled across an opening in the scrub, and someone shouted, "Beaver!" and there was a rush to the rail, enough to give a list to the boat, and the captain hurried forth to see what the stir was about. "Nutria, folks!" he called. "It's a nutria, an unwelcome invader!" But the year before he'd seen at that very spot a swamp panther, among the rarest big, native mammals in the nation. He said, "Now, that critter was worth tipping the boat."

Given the pervasive rot resident in such a wetland, even in a cool season, the air that December was crisp and free of the scent of vegetative decay, and in the tall marsh stood a few fishing and hunting shacks atop stilts, all the sheds closed up, and everywhere was an aura suggesting humans were temporary intruders and that no engineering could ever make it otherwise. Shovels and steel and concrete could not overmaster such a bosky ground, and the slap of a paddlewheel was a feeble thing pointing up nothing more than temporary transit. In a changing climate of melting polar ice, this land was on loan, and any true tenant had to be able to endure in a world six inches or six feet deep, where water bided time before resuming its long dominion. The place was not a nightmare but a vast quagginess, a trembling terrain challenging creatures with too much wetness as the Sonora does with too little.

New Iberia, Louisiana, several miles from its port, lies along the Bayou Teche, something too small for the *Delta Queen* to ascend, so the next morning I boarded a bus running alongside sugarcane fields and into town. On Main Street I bought a book about alligators by Edward McIlhenny, a conservationist and son of the inventor of Tabasco sauce. In a small grocery-café I sat down to a cup of Cajun coffee dark and thick like potting soil, and I read this:

> The deep booming roar of a twelve foot male alligator is a sound that once heard will never be forgotten. . . . When near these reptiles as they bellowed, I have felt a very distinct vibration of my diaphragm caused by the trembling of the air.

December is a time of hibernation, and so vanished hope to encounter any of those particular creatures of the night. The Dutchman's fears — or at least his adjectives and perceptions — just weren't holding up.

Not far from the old Evangeline movie house, I came upon Louis Dorsey, an African-American selling pepper sauce from the back of his pickup truck in hopes of sharing some of the millions that the Tabasco company earns from its plant just down the road. He offered a taste of his Brother-in-Law hot sauce made of three ingredients—two right from the parish: peppers and salt. "Don't know where the vinegar comes from," he said. I loaded bottles of sauce into my pockets as if they were saddle bags, and sagged back to the boat.

That night I could only try to imagine the complex universe of waters moving, twisting, swirling all about, not so much like cosmic clouds but like dark matter driven by dark energy. In the middle of the night we crossed the Atchafalaya River at Morgan City, a town according to some geologists destined to end up on the banks of or beneath the Mississippi when the big river at last breaks through the dam some hundred miles north near the mouth of the Red River and "captures" the Atchafalaya and thereby takes a shorter course to the Gulf. It's virtually impossible to speak of anything of consequence in coastal Louisiana without considering that under every prediction, perception, and piece of history is water.

East of Morgan City in the cypress swamps, I could make out only arboreal silhouettes just before dawn came on to erase any chance of mystery beyond that of existence itself. The boat passed antebellumed Houma, a seafood-canning town also supplying equipment to offshore oil-platforms, and continued into the morning, ever approaching New Orleans. The waterway still appeared too remote and thickly overgrown to lie at the edge of such a large city, but only fifteen miles from the great river-crescent there, new houses lined the shore only to fall away again, and the waterway returned to bank-side trees before finally fading completely into urban industries.

Near the Harvey Canal Lock, we approached a raised bridge halting rush-hour drivers who watched in surprise as the old paddlewheeler chugged before them, and when she blew her whistle—whether to them or the lock tender I didn't know—they stepped out to wave, inspired by a sound from an era before stalled traffic.

On the other side of the lock and across the Mississippi was the French Quarter and a bit farther the home wharf of the *Delta Queen*. We had steamed 350 miles through a realm only a boat can reach to reveal a coastal land neither a purgatory nor a paradise vanished but something better—a realm as enduringly wild as engineered yet still more disregarded than discovered.

ANCHOVIES
AND OLIVES

On assignment for a now-defunct culinary magazine, I wrote "Morning in Manarola" after a week of hiking along the Ligurian coast of northwest Italy. A key piece of the story was supposed to be local food, but about that topic I must rely on my tongue rather than any sophisticated knowledge of local fare, so I tried to build a village landscape around anchovies and olives. That's how other things, as they are wont to do in my work, crept in: secret suicides and so on.

Morning in Manarola

We travel to some places before we know where on the globe they are or that they even exist. Images arise in childhood imaginings, scenes that can express longings for a world more fantastic than the one we inhabit. All the while we understand such demesnes are impossible because common sense born of experience says hills can't be so steep, villages can't look like castles, and soon enough we learn that every place must answer to time and the devil. Yet, fantasy or not and however dormant, the wish to find those realms can remain until the fortunate traveler happens upon a fulfillment, often along the way to somewhere else. I think that's how one September morning I came to be sitting in a sidewalk café in Manarola, Italy, in a region called Le Cinque Terre — the Five Lands.

More accurately for today, they are five villages — Monterosso al Mare, Vernazza, Corniglia, Manarola, and Riomaggiore — lying along the exact edge of that northern thrust of the Mediterranean called the Ligurian Sea. Some eighty miles due south, French Corsica on a map points its finger of a peninsula directly at them to summon the attention of travelers: Here be phantasms. If ever a place seems marked out by topography for notice, it is the Cinque Terre.

The opposite has happened over the last thousand years. Even the Romans, known for extending empire to almost any place they could reach by foot or boat, little heeded this piece of coast, choosing instead to build their great inter-territorial

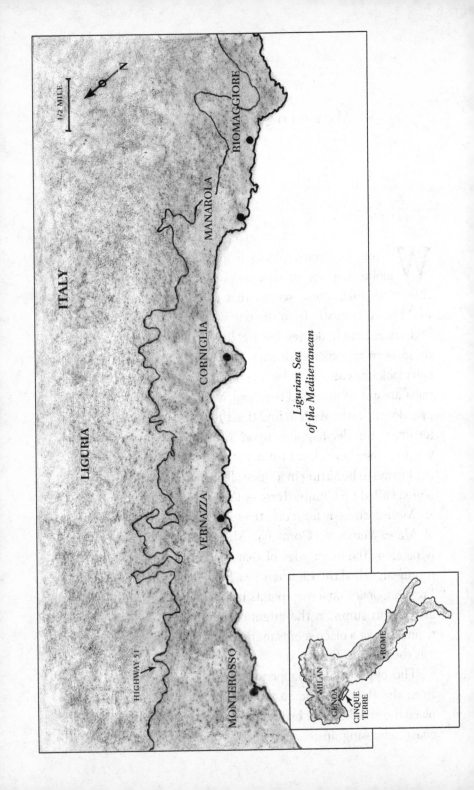

Aurelian Way on the easier, eastern side of the low—if rather rugged—mountains that trap the villages between rock and sea in a surround all but impossible for plows and wheels. Such a difficult steepness may serve birds and beasts, but humans? We're designed for life reasonably horizontal.

Over the years, a belief seemed to spring up that what ancient Rome ignored no one else should care about either. In that neglect the villages slipped through the centuries to arrive in our time like places from another era: gifts if not quite in plain view from the interior, then at least so from the sea to which they belong as Venice does its lagoon or Perugia its hill. Such isolation gave reprieve from the ruinous turmoil that has swept Europe since the Romans themselves let their empire fall into less dominant hands. Indeed, in the last World War, the people of the Cinque Terre could watch Allied bombers on the way to blast the harbor at Genoa forty miles northwestward from Monterosso and smear the town of La Spezia, only five miles below Riomaggiore. Perhaps it was the work of the Manes—from which the name Manarola may derive—the Roman embodiments of departed souls; if properly honored with lentils, bread, wine, and oil, the Manes were believed to bring protection, health, and longevity.

The five villages, survivors though they be, are not ancient by Mediterranean standards; rather, they are expressions of the late Middle Ages heavily doctored by the nineteenth century. One morning in a Manarola café as I fended off a drizzle with a *caffe corretto*—espresso "corrected" with a dollop of grappa—I couldn't visualize Augustus Caesar walking down the street, but I could imagine Dante on a visit from his Florence not far over the mountains, or Shelley and Byron in search of some bit of romance however defined.

Like its four sisters, Manarola shouldn't be here at all, not if the founders had followed horse sense and looked logically at the landscape, because there is no space for a hamlet any more than there's room for vineyards and olive groves on the declivitous and stony hills that come right to the sea like a door to a jamb. To solve the problems of a terrain running up and down rather than otherwise, Manarolans took to a cleft—you can't call it a valley or even a dale—cradling a spirited mountain-stream, and topped the rivulet with narrow pavement while leaving access points to the darkened water below that now murmurs under their feet like Manes from the netherworld.

Being denied a lateral landscape, builders chiseled niches from the cliffs in order to stack up shops and dwellings in such a way that Manarola, were you to turn it on its side, would cover about as much space horizontally as vertically. The slender, twisted lanes seem to rest more atop each other than to lie side by side in proper street fashion, so that someone looking southward out a fourth-floor window can cross the room to peer northward into the eyes of a stroller on the very next *via*. Architecture like this in an unexpected location gives each of the villages a distinct aura but one that could arise in a dream: Am I up or down? *Yes.* In the air or on the street? *You are indeed.*

Then there's the manner of the hamlets challenging the sea by setting foundations right against it, an offering like a pugilist who tenders his nose to a fist: *Hit me, sucker.* These abrupt stone rises of dwellings suggest more a complex of castles than a village, and of the reasons tourists come to see the Five Lands, primary is the peculiarity of ocean-beset buildings painted in warm Mediterranean colors. Here, not far from where the Riviera ends, life takes place around tiny harbors rather than beaches, and it's not about tanning lotion and sand but olive oil and cobbles banging against old walls the waves work to take down.

Some time ago, after seeing photographs of the Cinque Terre, I decided to discover whether such a place could truly exist. Although I arrived with several other hikers, I set out alone most mornings to toddle along the narrow and often slippery coastal path which in places hangs precipitously above the hard surf. I'd arrive in a village, walk it top to bottom, find lunch, make notes, then hike on farther south before catching a local train back to an old villa turned into a hotel in Camogli, a settlement rightly called a town.

The Five Lands appear, in the words of an Englishwoman quoting Alice's Dormouse, "much of a muchness," yet they are distinct enough to create preferences among travelers. Do you like fettuccine or linguine? Barolo or Barbaresco? For me the answer is yes and yes, but that morning in Manarola an open-front café called me to idle until the sun broke through.

Dingy gray, spotted street-cats, half feral and half mean, got themselves into compact hunches on window ledges or under low eaves to escape a dripping that was neither rain nor mist but somewhere betwixt. The dampness carried down along the lane a heavy, vinous scent of a winepress just rinsed after crushing white grapes glazed with red like a tippler's nose. When the weather changed, residents would again climb above Manarola to terraced vineyards like hanging gardens, where workers balanced burdens of picked grapes along narrow stone-walls that create plots, no more than ten to twenty feet wide, holding vines

Manarola, Italy

in a soil so scarce I couldn't imagine what sustained them beyond sea mist and sunlight. Across the narrow *via* in front of me were results of the labor: wicker baskets of grapes ready to be partly dried before going to the press, a method that gives the indigenous wine some of its distinction.

Down the *via*—hardly a street since it was so narrow a child's afternoon shadow could reach across it and rise a couple of feet up the wall opposite—and just above the harborette, fishermen had drawn up their dories on wheeled cradles and parked them like automobiles, vehicles here as unexpected as donkeys in Hoboken. To get into the villages, you typically must walk, or take a local train along a route of cliffs and tunnels, or you may arrive by boat.

The harbor is a bit larger than a baseball infield, and lies protected by a short rock-mole almost capable of quieting waves then in considerable aggravation after two days of a libeccio, the wind out of North Africa which blows fine, desert sand onto terraces to feed the grapes. Perhaps Saharan dust is the engendering agent, the *sapore* (to lift a phrase from an Italian kitchen) that puts the distinctive taste in Ligurian wine and olives. To eat of Liguria is to eat of the African desert.

A small place needs small things, and Cinque olive "groves" often contain only a half-dozen diminutive trees producing dark fruits hardly bigger than swollen raisins. If their flesh is thin, the flavor is thick; like hot peppers, the olives are little but potent with taste, proving the precept apparent here in so many ways: To reduce is to intensify. In Corniglia a day earlier at lunch, following a hilly hike, I ate twenty-eight of them and stopped simply because I'd emptied the bowl and knew still to come was pasta mixed with potatoes, a Ligurian specialty. When the waiter collected the dish of pits, he congratulated, "*Bene, bene!* You eada moa?"

After lunch, I took a glass of the signature beverage of the Cinque Terre, *sciacchetrà*, a white dessert wine, something I usually ignore, but I figured then it would keep me from a big almond gelato. The lightly sweet *sciacchetrà* had such a fine bouquet of pears I ordered another. What's better to a traveler than to have presumption knocked galley-west?

Although Italians usually drink down their little cups of coffee in a swallow or two, I lingered over mine that morning in Manarola in hopes the drizzle would stop. To ease the caffeine from a second cup and because the café specialized in panini, I ordered a sandwich of sliced tomatoes, fresh basil, and, according to the Englished menu, "olives sauces," although what I really wanted was my lunch of a couple days earlier in Vernazza where I'd ordered a plate of another characteristic food—fresh anchovies. While it's an exaggeration that I alone keep the little fish on the menu of two pizza parlors in my hometown, I do take to them as a Missouri farmer to Sunday fried-chicken. Expecting what Americans call anchovies, I was surprised to see set before me not minuscule brown slivers of over-salted fish but white fillets the length of my hand, seasoned with only olive oil, fresh basil, and a wedge of lemon. I should not have tasted them because now I'll never be the same, and memory will vex any wish to find them again. Rule of the road: Think long before eating in Paradise.

My Manarola panino was good, but nothing I couldn't assemble at home, and I paid more attention to the opening sky than the sandwich. A large man, florid of face, a white mustache dripping the last of the mist onto his chin, paused at my table and said, *"Musica?"* and, without waiting for answer, pulled a violin from beneath his jacket. Given the lingering dampness in his bow, the old tunes sounded more melancholy than artful.

When he finished, I lifted my "corrected" cup and asked, "Coffee?" In English, accented but mostly accurate, he said, "Your offer, *signore*, I"—pausing to recall the word—"accept," and sat down. He was a Tuscan from over the hills, but he'd spent much time on streets of the Italian Riviera, even down to the Cinque Terre. Said he, "I've lived also in America. I went to Toronto, but after a year I moved south to get a softer winter." That must be Florida. "Oh, *signore,* no, no! Detroit!"

His Christian name was Secondo. He leaned forward as if to confess: "I should be Terzo, Third, you see, but the first second boy, he died, so I got his number."

Off came his jacket in the warming day. Beneath he wore a carmine vest and a green Gypsy blouse full in the sleeves. Gesturing toward his getup, Secondo said, "This for the theater of the street. You look the part, you make a buck." I asked did he make good bucks as a strolling musician, and he said, "I do better now because I'm old. I don't play as good, not so strong as I used to, but I earn more because an old man working a street makes tourists feel *compassione.* The tourists know they're useless here except to spend a buck." He stroked the violin with hands seemingly too big for it, fingers I'd foolishly thought too meaty to pizzicato.

Manarola roused with sun, and trains began the hourly disgorging of fair-weather sightseers and young trekkers and vagabonds, one of whom ambled by and thrust a listless palm at us for a handout. Secondo said, *"Cerca lavoro!"* Get work. The kid slumped off. "Useless young. What's he good for? He's driftwood. He goes nowhere till current carry him."

I must have showed surprise at his response because he said, "In Detroit when they called me a useless drifter, I held up my violin to them, and I told them, 'No! Here's *my* rudder!'" With a single swallow, he finished his coffee more in annoyance than pleasure, and he said, "My father, Luca, music was his life — music was his death. He died with a fiddle in his hand. They had to pull it loose from his fingers. Gemma, his friend, she told me music of Tartini was too much for his age, but I know now he knew what he was doing. Today, *signore,* I tell you, just me to you, Tartini was his suicide. But no one knew, so he can get burial in the church." He held up his violin. "If I can die with her in my arms, I am happy, and maybe I get full mass too."

Secondo rose, thanked me for the cup corrected to enliven his bow, and he said, "Today, with your permission, no 'Devil's Trill Sonata.'" Why not? "For me, this isn't *the* day. I'm still strong. But tomorrow, who can say?" and he went up toward the depot, and I went down to the path along the broken coast. Somewhere farther, there had to be more fresh anchovies — impossibly, fantastically good, as if from a dream. If not, maybe tomorrow. Who could say?

SOMETHING OF A FIREFALL

When "Wandering Yosemite" appeared, it drew down a shower of
sparks like the now-outlawed firefall from Glacier Point. The com-
plainants were those who—as if there were a shortage of places for
amusement in the United States—see the great national park as a
windfall opportunity to make corporate profits off of preeminent
public land. What is truly in short supply in America are unthreat-
ened monumental mountains and valleys and their attendant natural realms. I have trouble imagining later generations castigating
ours for failing to leave them enough commercial developments.

Wandering Yosemite

When I go in quest of place, my writer's mantra comes from the title of a play based on Christopher Isherwood's stories: *I Am a Camera*. With eyes for a lens, and memory and notebooks for film, I begin to record a locale like Yosemite.

BUTTERFLIES. So well hidden in the Sierra is this valley, Euro-Americans did not enter it until 1851 when James Savage, operator of a trading post along the Merced River in California, directed a militia band called the Mariposa Battalion to threaten or brutalize the native residents of the valley into submitting to the increasing incursions of gold miners and settlers. On their first night, Savage's men camped near the meadow below Bridalveil Fall. The next morning the Indians, the Ahwahneechees, had disappeared but for an elderly woman who said, "I'm too old to climb the rocks." When she refused to reveal where her people had gone, Savage (as if to fulfill his name) torched the bark homes and the food caches of the Indians, and thereby began a forced and merciless dispersal completed in less than two years. *Mariposa* means "butterfly" in Spanish and *merced* is "mercy," but the name Yosemite is probably a corruption of *yo-chee-ma-te* or *yo-hem-it-teh*: "They are killers."

THE DRINK BOX. At the middle of Yosemite Village in the deep valley of the upper Merced River is a soft-drink machine

El Capitan, Yosemite Valley, California

and on its front a large, posterized photo of a golfer about to tee up, his electric cart at the ready, and beneath, the imperative DISCOVER YOUR YOSEMITE. I had just come from talking with Ranger Scott Gediman, who told me, "National parks aren't for entertainment." Yet within the Yosemite boundaries are the golf course, a refrigerated ice-skating rink, a ski lift, ski-board runs, a campground television-parlor, kennel, pizza stand, and an annual costumed pageant reenacting an English Christmas dinner. As I tried to make note of the pop machine, I was jostled by a passing crowd bestrung with gadgets as rock climbers are ropes, clamps, and pitons: cell phones, MP3 players, pagers, cameras, camcorders (often operated from moving cars). I dodged baby-strollers hung with diaper bags, and moved aside for a tandem bicycle pulling a trailerette hauling two barking dogs the size of large rodents. The throng wore not hiking boots and field shirts but flip-flops and halter tops, and the faces licked ice-cream cones and munched tacos and talked of baseball and reality television shows. Was this a mall or a valley world-renowned for its natural wonders and its eight hundred miles of trails? Within an ace of the drink box were two hotels, a large superstore, jail, post office, ATM, parking spaces for five thousand cars, and enough asphalt to pave half of Fresno.

HERCULES AS A PARSNIP. It's for mountains and rock and water not grassy flats and cow parsnip that people presumably come to this oldest federally established park where the Merced River descends five thousand feet from a cluster of Sierra peaks into a deep trough; within seven miles are a half-dozen of the most celebrated natural features in America: El Capitan, Half Dome, Yosemite and Bridalveil falls, Glacier Point, Overhanging Rock. From where I walked near a verdant and spongy meadow, I could see only a couple of the sights because cow parsnip blocked the view. The genus name, *Heracleum,* derives from Herakles, the mythic Greek hero whom the Romans called Hercules. At more than seven-feet high, that mighty parsnip is a wild carrot with rhubarb-like leaves each of which could wrap a roast chicken. Later, when I told a botanist that the plump, aromatic stalks made me want to munch one as if it were celery, he said, "The Indians ate them, but snacking on wild plants in a national park is illegal."

THE SUPPRESSED REPORT. In 1864, at another Yosemite Valley meadow—when they were more extensive—Frederick

Law Olmsted camped while employed by a New York mining company that hired him away from his job designing Central Park. He was managing a large holding near present Mariposa, California, where the gold-rush bonanza was giving out. The father of American landscape design imagined wealth of another sort, a stunning cornucopia to enrich the work of artists and natural scientists and, as significantly, the spirits of those who would visit. By chance, the month before Olmsted's stay in the meadow, President Lincoln signed a congressional act establishing a grant to preserve two areas of what today is Yosemite: the valley and a southerly grove of sequoias. After his expedition, Olmsted wrote a report for the California legislature then superintending the grant; the document is a landmark expression of the principle that a government should set aside places of signal natural magnificence for its citizens. Central to his reasoning is this sentence:

> If we analyze the operation of scenes of beauty upon the mind, and consider the intimate relation of the mind upon the nervous system and the whole physical economy, the action and reaction which constantly occurs between bodily and mental conditions, the reinvigoration which results from such scenes is readily comprehended.

Olmsted's report and its timeless guidelines never reached the legislature, and remained unpublished until 1952; all the while commercial endeavors arrived in Yosemite Valley and metastasized.

THREE-THOUSAND FEET OF AIR. Per square foot, it's possibly the most famously photographed small rock in the West. About the size of a picnic table—for which it's been used—Overhanging Rock at Glacier Point has also served as a "parking space" for a horseless carriage and, later, a Pierce-Arrow and a Studebaker. It's been a stage for a pair of dancing ladies in hoop skirts, a veritable magnet to backflipping daredevils and to the simply foolhardy. The pointy ledge is famous, one could say, for nothing; that is, for what lies beneath it: some three-thousand feet of nothing but air unless you count at certain moments rain-drops or snowflakes. The view from behind the railing near it looks into the valley and on toward the mountainous miles beyond and offers arguably the most spectacular vista in

Overhanging Rock at Glacier Point circa 1900

America. It's an excellent place to try to comprehend the evolution of Yosemite from deep oceanic sediments into tectonic plates lifted, shifted, subducted, and melted into granite, then solidified, only to be raised once more and deformed, dissolved, deepened, and dislocated by water and ice. From Glacier Point one sees a grandly contorted display of the four elements of the ancient world—earth, air, fire, and water—where water is the chisel, gravity the hammer, and the sculptor your notion of the originator of all things.

WHEN OWL HOOTS FAIL. Far from the crowded valley stands a tree trunk to match the photographic fame of Overhanging Rock. To attract tourists—and perhaps help them comprehend the immensity of a sequoia—a couple of sawyers in 1881 cut a huge notch through the base of one, a hole large enough to allow a triple-team stagecoach or a Stanley Steamer to pass through its heart. The gimmicked tree, the Wawona Tunnel Tree, more than two-thousand years old, indeed drew motorists with cameras—and pocketknives—and initiated a fad in California of cutting huge holes through large trees. The size of an upright sequoia, by volume the largest living organism on earth, is difficult to conceive, and one can argue that for the most mobile nation in history, driving a wheeled vehicle through is an effective illustration of size—and age—and is a somewhat better one than, say, felling the largest sequoia of all and turning it into 175 miles of two-by-fours. In Yosemite it's almost axiomatic that an increase in elevation means a decrease in the crowd, but the legendary Wawona giant couldn't go high enough to escape the fascination of tourists, and the tree is today only a stump; like an old outhouse wall, it's carved with uncountable *Kilroy Was Here*s. Incidentally, the Ahwahneechee word for a sequoia is *wawona*, its pronunciation thought to imitate the hoot of an owl, the guardian spirit of the big trees.

Wawona Tunnel Tree, circa 1890

SAVING THE PARK. Although Euro-Americans were slow to find Yosemite Valley, it took tourists just four years to arrive following Savage's expulsion of the native residents. Only months after the initial visitor, the first hotel, a ramshackle thing, went up at the foot of Yosemite Falls, and boulders were getting painted into billboards advertising patent medicines. Despite the area being in the hands of the national government, squatters — many of them failed gold prospectors — moved in to put up more facilities and begin farming the incomparable valley. Yosemite was on its way to the commercialism so evident around Niagara Falls or Stone Mountain in Georgia or Pigeon Forge in Tennessee. Valley businesses passed down from squatters are still in the park in various permutations even though some of their enterprises have been slowly curtailed: The Cadillac dealership is gone, as is one of the golf courses, and also the once-famous firefall wherein burning embers were shoveled off Glacier Point to create a three-thousand-foot shower of orange coals.

In the parking lot of the luxury hotel, the Ahwahnee, I saw a bumper sticker: SAVE YOSEMITE FROM THE PARK SERVICE. For the past two decades the National Park Service has laboriously created a plan laying out a future for Yosemite — particularly for the overrun valley — that seeks to balance tourism with sound conservation. The blueprint is sensible and thorough — 2,300 pages and twenty-seven pounds. At its core are two changes: The first is moving facilities that do not *need* to be in the valley to just outside the park, thereby returning the deep heart of Yosemite into something closer to its native appearance before the arrival of Savage's militia. The second may be more difficult: persuading tourists to use public transport instead of private autos to get around the narrow valley. Shuttles would reduce parking lots and eliminate not uncommon two-mile-long lines of stalled traffic. In the words of Superintendent Michael Tollefson, "Our goal is to have a smaller human footprint."

The Park Service has listened so long to various and often conflicting positions it has become hamstrung by minor voices often arguing for historical precedent (an approach that would have negated the abolition of slavery, suffrage for women, and child-labor laws). *Precedent* here often means a status quo to serve not the common citizen but the direct pecuniary advantage of corporate enterprises. Even a few environmental groups have questioned some of the proposals. Olmsted, in his precocious 1865 report, put it cogently:

It should be remembered that in permitting the sacrifice of anything that would be of the slightest value to future visitors to the convenience, bad taste, playfulness, carelessness, or wanton destructiveness of present visitors, we probably yield in each case the interest of uncounted millions to the selfishness of a few individuals. It is an important fact that as civilization advances, the interest of men in natural scenes of sublimity and beauty increases.

THE VIEW FROM A DOME. In a quest to experience a Yosemite matching my expectation, I headed toward the heart of the almost twelve-hundred-square-mile park to one of its signature formations, a granite dome, this one comparatively small and so undistinguished it bore no name on any of my maps. I liked the notion, even though an illusion, that this outcropping in the Cathedral Range was ordinary and unvisited enough to have escaped notice by cartographers, and that raised the question of whether I should be there. A ranger answered it: "The problem isn't so much total visitors—it's the concentration in a few places."

Zigzagging an ascent was like climbing the back of a mythically enormous turtle whose carapace was glaciated, white granite flecked with black biotite. I was walking what was once the floor of the Pacific Ocean, once rising magma, once the basement of numerous glaciers that left both polish and incised striations. I was on a hike *up*ward through time, a geologic trek skyward. Halfway up, an assemblage of small stones, a writ, dispelled any illusion of no one having been there since the last Ahwahneechee passed: LOVE. Considering the Ahwahneechee point of view, the word was ironic, and I pushed the graffito back into natural randomness.

I weaved upward among glacial erratics as big as bison, all of them waiting for that last, grand slide down. Scattered among them were stones the size of quail eggs unlike the bedrock in color, texture, and shape: Those smoothly rounded gravels had been carried to the top from some distant glacial outwash at least ten-thousand years ago. That dome, so apparently solid and immobile, was of course still in movement: sandy grit forced up, boulders waiting to roll down, and—with the rest of the Sierra— the entire hump was continuing to rise a foot every millennium. I stopped to admire a peculiarly gleaming pebble that before my eyes got up and hopped away. Camouflaged to match the mountain, a frog was a thousand feet above the nearest standing water.

Conifers, mostly Jeffrey pine, had found crevices the width of a broomstick or a human hand and were drawing out a weather-tortured existence and twisting themselves into lovely grotesqueries. Clustered in the few places of scarce soil and shelter grew penstemon, Indian paintbrush, stonecrop, Sierra wallflower. Life, both rooted and legged, was extracting itself from a rock more barren than not, more hostile to organisms than otherwise.

Then I arrived on the top, prepared for a jolt of some contemporary intrusiveness to open: a long view of a valley parking lot or a gridlocked intersection. A jolt there was. To the east rose the magnificently jagged peaks of the snowy Sierra and to the southwest was the totem of Yosemite, Half Dome—but not its oft-pictured side. Rather, it showed only its humpy hindside. Looking at it was like watching a Shakespeare play from backstage where old and familiar lines seem different, strange, new. I'd found my Yosemite in its grand beyondness etching itself into memory as if crags, knife-edged rocks, the spines of pinecones were inscribing images. If my ascent was like a journey in time, what would a hike reveal in a half-century? In an eon? If the mountains were going up, where was the rest headed?

READING MUIR. My last night in Yosemite I happened to read this passage John Muir wrote almost a century ago:

The regular tourist, ever in motion, is one of the most characteristic productions of the present century; and however frivolous and inappreciative the poorer specimens may appear, viewed comprehensively they are a hopeful and significant sign of the times, indicating at least a beginning of our return to nature; for going to the mountains is going home.

ONE SWEET TALKER

In late 1987 the offer of an assignment to do a story on what turned out to be a place I'd long wanted to visit came my way, but with the unappealing proviso to write something "free of complicated expression and overt environmental, social, political, or ethnic topics." I asked what would be the point of such a story. Replied the editor, "Beyond the challenge to a writer like you, a good point might be a first-class, round-trip flight with all additional expenses paid for three weeks." To where? "New Zealand," she said. The woman had a way with words.

Into the Antipodes

Consider what must be the most well-known topographical outline of any nation in the world—the boot of Italy. Move it to the South Pacific, turn it upside down so that it's poised to kick Australia sitting like a deflated rugby ball to the west. That musketeer's boot, though severed, is the twin-island-nation of New Zealand. Nowhere else in a region called "down under" is the other term for it—the Antipodes, "opposite feet"—more appropriate than for that buskin. As if to confirm the reversals, even the Man in the Moon and the constellation Orion the Hunter stand on their heads there, and the Big Dipper and North Star never show themselves to correct this seemingly topsy-turvy world. Instead, old-style mariners turn their sextants the opposite direction to sight the Southern Cross for a bearing or they read a compass answering the magnetism of the South Pole: While the magnetized tip seems to respond to the pull of north, it is actually being *pushed away* from Antarctica.

One mid-December evening, I was standing on the instep of the New Zealand boot, on Queen Street, the main mercantile thoroughfare in the largest city in the nation. Auckland is a place of wharves under low hills, and a bay greenly occluded like old jade. Where Queen and Shortland streets intersect, the White Lady pie cart sat every suppertime until early morning. In truth, the "cart" was a bus-like contraption dispensing "burgers"—beef or egg or vegetarian—and ham-and-pineapple sandwiches, rump steaks, and even a salad or two. The White Lady hadn't

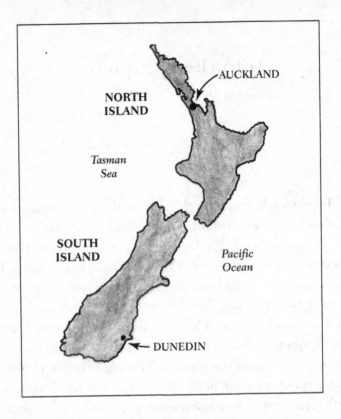

sold English-style meat pies in several years, and that shift from flesh pies to so-called burgers is a capsule history of post–World War II New Zealand where British names and customs remain, but products and attitudes, more and more, can suggest America or Japan. The automobiles parked around the White Lady, if older than five or six years, were Austins, Vauxhalls, Jaguars, but later models were Hondas, Toyotas, Datsuns. New Zealand, in its outward aspect, now resembles the mother country only slightly more than does Canada. Let me except speech: While I waited for an egg burger, a young woman, her Polynesian features glowing in the streetlamp, ordered a beef burger; in an Eliza Doolittle voice, she said to the frycook, "Oy luv ya ambuh-gahs, mite." Indeed, the egger was good, although the slices of pickled beets were more curious than tasty.

As I ate, I formulated a route to follow a line north from the pie cart into the human history that lies so lightly atop the land (humans have been here scarcely a thousand years) and then drop south along the broken backbone of mountains that dramatically form the New Zealand landscape.

Along the way I wanted to do some walking to get the feel of the place and, more particularly, in a land of unique ornithological richness, to see birds quite unlike those in the Northern Hemisphere. Not just kiwis and penguins, but also birds bright of name or colors: yellow-nosed mollymawk (an albatross), rosella, mud peep, dancing dolly (also called the Jesus Christ bird; why, I didn't learn), blue billy, wandering tattler (the writer bird), and maybe—if lucky—one of the iconic *k* birds: kookaburra, kakapo, kokako, karoro, korimako, kotuku, kaki, and of course kiwi. For some inexplicable reason, I especially wanted to see a rifleman, a modest, almost tailless wren able, if it chose, to nest easily in a shirt pocket. The decline or extinction of native birds that marked the nineteenth century in New Zealand suggests a traveler should get to the seeing while the seeing is still possible.

I set out for the Northland, the toe of the boot, where both Polynesian and European settlement began. Highway 1, an asphalt two-lane, followed the Hibiscus Coast of green bays and easy hills, the land at one moment appearing subtropical with tall palms and kauri trees, then at the next view seeming temperate with pines and myrtles. On that day, the grandest vegetation was the pohutukawas, called the New Zealand Christmas Tree, a broad spreading of feathery, crimson blossoms which, as if in celebration, often open briefly right around the twenty-fifth of December. On a day of sunny sky, warm air wafting over green fields, from my car radio came a carol, something about the weather outside being frightful. Another piece of topsy-turvydom in a realm where Santa needs not runners but wheels.

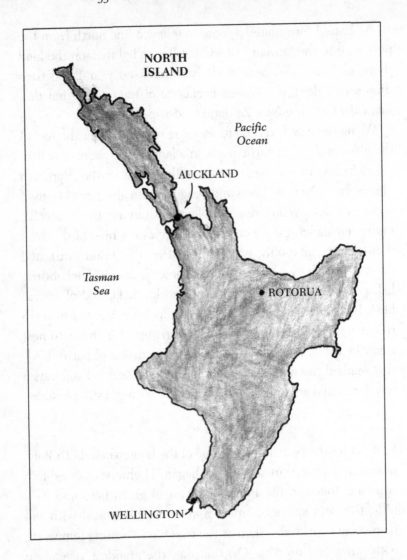

Puhoi is a village with its heritage of Czech immigrants showing in a wayside shrine and crucifixes tacked below the eaves of red-roofed buildings. Just beyond the ten-by-fifteen-foot library, I took a Devonshire tea, now more common in New Zealand than in Devon: scones topped with heavy cream and strawberry jam, a meal that made up in caloric potency what it lacked in volume; more than enough to make me regret it all the way up to Waitangi, a historic reserve, on a coast of sand beaches and rocky interruptions and green headlands rising out in the Bay of Islands.

Across the water was the town of Russell, once the center of European settlement in New Zealand and known as "the Hellhole of the Pacific," named by sailors who jumped ship, released convicts from the Australian penal colony, and the usual lusty characters attendant to whaling ports. In pursuit of sin, to the Hell-hole soon followed missionaries with, according to one Maori native, "faces so solemn they looked like a relation had just been eaten." The waterfront was alive with the descendants: excursion fishermen and people booking a chicken-and-champagne lunch cruise.

The European incursion that started at Russell in the late eighteenth century brought the inevitable clash between whites and the indigenous Maori, a conflict that spread through the islands and was not formally ended until 1840 across the bay and just west of Russell at the Treaty House in Waitangi. There, New Zealand formally became part of the British Empire. Without full cognizance of what the treaty implied, the native people accepted sovereignty of the royal crown, a Caucasian hegemony that still chafes many Maori.

The national reserve at Waitangi ("weeping waters") is seascapes, clipped grounds, and restored buildings like the Maori Meeting House. Although only a half-century old, it's splendid with dozens of carved and colored rafters and pillars radiating the ancient life, and the exposed roof beams painted in interlocking, white designs to give a sense of standing within the rib cage of a monstrous sea-beast—perhaps just what the seagoing Maori, arriving generations gone from far across the Pacific, intended. They built wooden war canoes holding 150 men, and at Waitangi one boat that still puts out to sea each year on Treaty Day is more than a third of a football field long.

The road north went into the orchard country around

Kerikeri, a high-street town with what may be the tiniest and most picturesque waterfront in the country. Only 120 miles from the northernmost tip of New Zealand, I began feeling grounded enough in a few basics of its history to start a thousand-mile drop southward toward the farthest end where one can almost smell the Antarctic.

At Kaikohe I took the smallest road I could find, one without a number on my map, and wound through modest valleys and compressed canyonettes, following for miles courses of streams that made passage seem almost like a little voyage. There was no other traffic, a good thing since even passing a goat cart on the narrow road would have been, if you will, dodgy; it was a region of pastures and farms rather than the vendors and motels of Route 1.

I did what I could to avoid, again if you will, a crash course in the language of the New Zealand highway signs: METAL ROAD (gravel), SLICK ROADWAY (paved), GREASY IF WET (slick), SLIPS (falling rock). Typically, bridges bore English names and streams Maori ones with a Polynesian piling of vowels. The route forced attention: Even along precipices, the road was without guardrails, instead turning the job over to trees and rocks crowding the shoulder. I had a better chance of glimpsing a Dieffenbach's rail (last observed in 1840) than seeing a guardrail.

Along the grassy lane, tethered goats nibbled like hooved lawnmowers, and wedge-shaped walls of stacked, volcanic stone kept in sheep, and high fences contained domesticated red deer, future venison steaks holding heads steadily to the grass as if grazing cattle rather than continually jerking them up like their nervous wild kin. Sheep trails cut the hills into terraces, and the valley filled with dozens of shades of green as the sun dropped and illuminated a pied fantail which the Maori call a piwak-awaka, a name more colorful than the bird.

*   *   *

Rotorua, a hot-spa town known for "thermal holidays," sits amid a volcanic zone. Because the day was Christmas, the place was nearly deserted, the emptiness filled only with the scent of sulfur steaming from rocky vents all about. In the vacant streets of early morning, the air redolent with hydrogen sulfide, it was as if the Second Coming had at last indeed come and gone and left behind a land emptied of everything but vaporing pits opening to a chthonic afterworld.

At the edge of town is the Maori village of Whakarewarewa— locally shortened to Whaka—with its fractured rocks and steaming mudpots, geysers, and pools of Hadean waters. Residents use the thermal upwellings for heating, cooking, bathing, and laundry. That Christmas morning, a Maori woman with skin like polished mahogany was boiling her holiday ham in a natural pool, and in an exhalation from a crevice nearby she cooked a plum pudding. Later she would add to her meal a cranberry sauce with stuffed muttonbird (a shearwater), fermented crayfish, and preserved corn in strawberries and cream. At her children's insistence, their day of crossed traditions was to conclude with high tea at an American chain hamburger-stand.

When she told me that, I grimaced in the manner of an ancient Maori mask: lips pulled back, tongue thrust far out and down, eyes wide. As chance would have it, she happened to work with the Rotorua culture-center and did not respond kindly to what she explained was a sacred expression, one not to be linked with burgers and fries. Called *pukana*, for centuries the Maori have carved it in wood to show defiance, challenge, aggression, but also beauty. She said, "We've survived the impact of Western civilization, the power culture, because we'll take on anything, but what do we do about American fast-food? But, for today, seeing how it's Christmas, I'm not going to growl about it."

From the vents vapors rose above the trees, and it seemed the land itself burned rather than the magma below, and gray mud-pots jumped and croaked like frogs, and a geyser called the Prince of Wales' Feathers blew out a hissing, twenty-foot headdress of sulfurous, watery steam, while a small encrusted basin named the Brainpot lay in a bluish, quiet heat, a proper place, the Maori once believed, to cook the heads of enemies, or perhaps Polynesian children wanting a Christmas high-tea at an American franchise.

Because Rotorua is known for *hangi*—traditional Maori feasts cooked by Vulcan—that Christmas night I partook of one offered to outsiders: venison stew, lamb, green-tipped mussels, white potatoes, sweet potatoes, squash, squid-and-crab salad, steamed pudding. During the feasting, eight Maori performed traditional dances with music, the stiff-leaved skirts of the women wonderfully clacking in time to the foot-stomping men, the performance punctuated with *pukana* after

Maori mask

pukana that might have been aimed at an ill-informed foreigner.

My route lay through closely cropped hills where lambs grew like wildflowers, Scotch broom yellowed fence lines, and Lombardy poplars cast skinny shadows into the morning. On a walk along a marsh I glimpsed a blue flash from something making a jaunty step through wet grasses; it was a pook, a gallinule also called Old Swampie. Nice, but I'd still not come upon any totemic *k* birds or a rifleman.

Lake Taupo, the largest lake in the country, sits near the instep of the New Zealand boot like an eyelet, and a few miles to the southwest is Mount Ruapehu, a big and snowy active volcano surrounded by Tongariro National Park. Symmetrical Mount Ngauruhoe rises to the northeast, and between the volcanoes lies an expanse of tussock grass and heather; there I stopped at the grand lodge of the north island, Château Tongariro offering a big-windowed parlor and a buffet lunch of European fare generally free of pickled beets in unexpected places.

I hiked off under the fire mountains and toward a stretch of shattered volcanics cut by streams intertwined with fingers of beech forest. Despite eighty inches of annual precipitation, the woodland wasn't considered rain forest, but the green dells were thick with mosses covering rocks and logs and anything else that might pause a little too long; to sleep overnight there could be to arise as more a mushroom than a man, a strange thing in such a volcanic land. The track to Taranaki Falls went through tussock scrub, into richly verdant sloughs, across more scrub, to descend an eroded wash lined with blanched roots. The late December air blew moist and warm, and birdsong seeped from the damp shrubs, and twisting streams purled, bubbled, splashed, trickled, dripped, and frothed over and around rocks pitched from the volcano ahead—more confusions of fire and water.

Halfway to the falls, a dun-colored bird rose from the heather like a tossed clod, cut loose with a sharp song, and kept it going, rising into the wind, higher, singing, higher, still in song, climbing almost to the low clouds scudding into the mountain. For five minutes the show continued, then the small drab thing, yet in melody, dropped back into the scrub and sat silent. Never before had I witnessed the aerial show of a skylark, a creature unable to find suitable habitat in the topographically wide and varied United States. Much of the flora and fauna Europeans have brought into New Zealand has proved deleterious to native species, but the English skylark is a sweet exception. Although living harmoniously with native birds, it does depend on alien heather which has created problems by crowding out indigenous vegetation. After the skylark number, Taranaki Falls, a narrow cascade from a blackened cliff, seemed almost inconsequential.

The following morning, I came upon a path into a dense beech woods verging on the narrow but noisy snow-melt waters of the Whapkapapaunui River. Perhaps good birding grounds. Without the narrow trail the mountain forest would have been passable only behind a bulldozer. In the past week, I'd learned one of the glories of that virescent land are tree trunks of immense girth, bizarre convolutions, and branched permutations that could take the aspect of gnarly old men, or rearing unicorns, or they might interlock limbs like Pyramus and Thisbe.

Even though New Zealanders use Euro-American names for certain of their native birds, the various species are usually markedly different and often unrelated. To have seen in America a goldfinch or a robin or magpie is not to have seen the New Zealand bird of the same name. While I was trying to sketch a massive and strangely trunked tree that looked something like a manticore, a small, green egg with feet began hopping smartly from branch to branch. Perhaps speaking of its footwork, it muttered, time and again, *Zip-zip, zip-zip.* Behold, a rifleman! All three inches of it in colors supposedly resembling the uniform of an early-British-era volunteer soldier. The measure

A rifleman, Acanthisitta Chloris

of my joy at finally spotting a rifleman was inverse to the size of the creature, something explainable, I think, only to the odd minds of dedicated birders.

*   *   *

As with other things there, the halves of the New Zealand boot show two topographies — one of fire, the other of ice. The North Island, the foot, is comparatively lower and rippled and ridged by volcanoes, whereas on the South Island, high mountains and glaciations determine things. At Wellington, I crossed from north to south through narrow and windy Cook Strait, a three-hour ferry ride, and arrived at the waterfront village of Picton and there

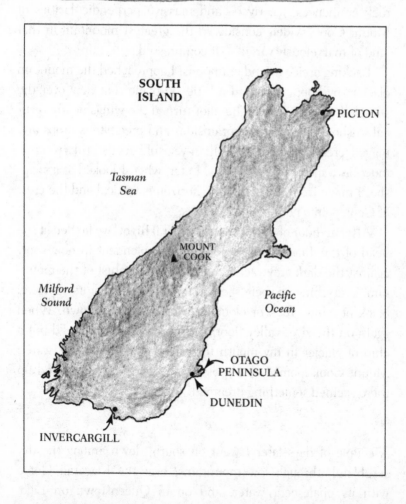

continued south down the east coastal road. Much of my course lay squeezed between the tourmaline sea and black mountains tipped in snow, creating a grandeur almost beyond the word *scenery*. After a while, I needed something to thin the richness, a helping of some palliation, this one a plate of boiled crayfish.

Raised on the edge of the Great Plains, I must take alpine scenery in moderation to avoid overdosing on the spectacular; I gained balance on the levels around Christchurch, a city lifted from early Victorian England. A day there prepared me for the rock eminences, ice rivers, and massive perpendicularities of Mount Cook, widely considered the greatest mountain in that land of marvelously varied — if compressed — terrain.

Lacking an ice ax and crampons, I approached the mountain glaciers by hopping aboard a little ski-plane that flew over the shingled Tasman River. The pilot turned the wings nearly vertical to show the steep mountainsides and precipitous drops and ragged crests of hundred-million-year-old rocks still rising as much as a meter every century. Later, when I looked at a snapshot I made from the plane, the horizon is vertical and the crest of Cook points not up, but sideways.

After an hour of occasional horizontal flight, we landed at the head of the Tasman Glacier blindingly splendent in new snow against the dark greywacke, mudstone, and schist of the mountain. Everything up there seemed to be one thing or its opposite: black or white, rock or cloud, wet or dry, up or down. When again on the river-valley floor, I looked back at where I'd put a chip of glacier in my mouth to taste thousand-year-old water: Mount Cook loomed so impossibly, to have walked around up there seemed something dreamed.

A couple of days later I went on south, down among the dry scrubland, through low mountains, over the Kawarau Gorge with its opalescent water, and on to Queenstown on Lake

Wakatipu, a long and slender zigzag apparently cut in by the sword of a geologic Zorro. The city, once a livestock shipping point, had come to depend on tourism, and its degree of pleasantness was contingent upon one's view of numerous people clad in thongs and floral-patterned shirts.

I was itching to board the famed lake-boat, the TSS *Earnslaw*, a seventy-five-year-old twin-decker that once carried more cattle and sheep than people, but to watch the jam-up at boarding, perhaps the change wasn't all that much. The coal-fired boilers threw a deep dinge across the lake to create a brief sunset sky, and the old vessel chugged out a course under a range of grooved but nearly barren mountains that caught shadows and held them like so much mist; it's the quality of light trapped in the eroded sides that gives the Remarkables their name: Over the next hour, the slopes changed from pink to orange to blue to gray to black, and the next morning the progression would reverse. A woman said, "I see why they call them the Impossibles."

Had the old boat still run all the way up the lake as it formerly did, we could have steamed to within about twenty air miles of Milford Sound on the Tasman Sea. The way by auto is 170 miles of lakeside road through hill country and then up along Lake Te Anau where the slow travel gives time to take in landforms deserving close observation. From the forest and alpine meadows, the road swung into the Earl Mountains before dropping down the steep slant of the Homer Tunnel which a claustrophobic may wish to undertake while blindfolded. The last miles twisted beneath treeless massings of high rock that in spring drop thousand-foot strands of snowmelt into a narrow, glaciated valley. Twice I stopped just to see the black walls: Their height, sheerness, and utter volume made it seem I was crouching.

Milford Sound—actually a fiord, since glaciers created it— is to New Zealand waters what Mount Cook is to the mountains—

renowned beyond all. Scenic flights were popular, but why look at water from above when a boat is available? I boarded the *Mitre Peak II* for a trip along the high cliffs lining the fiord all the way out to the Tasman Sea. The peak, standing five-thousand feet above the sound and extending a thousand beneath it, is one of the highest mountains in the world to rise directly from the ocean floor.

The slopes were in new leaf, and the granite cliffs, stained by residues of copper and iron to the color of roasted barley, were striated with upright water. At the biggest of the cataracts, Stirling Falls, the captain eased the bow of the stubby vessel into the long cascade turned to mists by the height of its drop. Of several people on the forward deck, one ran to cover, but the rest of us briefly left the sunshine to enter a more typical weather of watery air: During a single year at Milford Sound, twenty-eight feet of rain once fell.

That area, Fiordland, contains one of the oldest and most famous hiking routes in the world, the Milford Track, a thirty-three-mile hoof down alpine valleys, but its fame exacts a price: reservations and a requirement to move at a prescribed pace. For trampers of a more independent mind and idiosyncratic gait, other nearby tracks—the Hollyford, the Routeburn, the Dusky—suffer less from human overload but are as scenic and challenging. So I heard.

From the sea-indented mountains, I took a curving line, still southward, through grasslands of such importance to sheep farmers that in front of city hall in coastal Invercargill is a statue depicting a blade of grass. There I came at last to the bottom of the nation and the top of the upside-down boot.

The January crush of New Zealand vacationers was now bumper to bumper on the narrow roads (*highway* wasn't a word I used much there). Trying to escape, I made a run for the city of Dunedin. Although my birding had been of limited success, I yet had hopes of closing the trip with two things I considered the essence of the far, southern ocean: penguins and albatross. Opposite the city harbor, along a century-old lane atop a seawall built by Maori prisoners, far out on the Otago Peninsula, was one of the few albatross colonies in the world with a breeding ground on humanly inhabited land. Even among its kind, the royal albatross is one big bird: From the front of its bill to the tip of the tail, a royal can be the size of an eight-year-old girl, and its wingspan more than three meters. Because the nesting season was on, a small shed above the edge of a cliff provided a concealed vantage for watching the birds. Every so often one would raise its immense wings and go into a cumbrous and seemingly suicidal run toward the sea far below until, at the last moment, the dead air could hold it aloft, and then instantly its footed clumsiness became winged grace, and its white feathers slicked it quickly downwind and out of view.

On the other side of the peninsula, just above a fur-seal colony, I crept up behind a spread of yellow lupines above a beach where a half-dozen dark humps were pulling themselves out of the surf. They shook, waddled, stopped, shook, and waddled a little farther toward a tall dune against the sea cliffs. The sand was so steep and treacherous, the humps had to tack north, then south, then back again to gain their nests in the lupine at the top where they were at last close enough to become yellow-eyed penguins.

The yellow-eyed is the rarest penguin on Earth, and its survival is anything but assured. In all of New Zealand, I'd seen nothing that let me feel the antipodean

Yellow-eyed penguin

world and its imperiled creatures so much as that slow trudge of an improbably configured bird. The climb must have been tiring because every dozen or so steps the yellow-eyes rested, an act not usually apparent in birds that can take wing. When the penguins at last reached their nests, a fellow watcher said, "They made it!" For that day, one more time, indeed they had.

On the flight homeward the next morning, I got an aerial look at the penguin beach and an hour later a splendid view of snowy Mount Egmont rising through low clouds, yet what remains more indelibly now is not its marvelous eight-thousand-foot summit but a ninety-foot hillock of sand laced with footprints of yellow-eyed penguins.

A CRIMINAL
TO REMAIN
ANONYMOUS

I won't honor by giving his name the young man I speak of in this story, but I will say a judge found him mentally incompetent to stand trial. He was incarcerated in the Federal Medical Center at Rochester, Minnesota, and the last I heard he is still there.

On the Staked Plain

I'm writing this first draft of a sentence with a ballpoint pen given me three days ago by a geographer friend. Above his name and address is an imprinted proposition:

ALL LANDSCAPES SPEAK....

While the phrase is not mine, nearly all of my writing over the last three decades seeks to test and express his hypothesis — or is it a prescript? — behind that trio of words. At the least, many of my stories could employ his motto as a subtitle, since to me it is a perpetual subtext not just for some assemblage of words but for the assemblage that is my life. I believe as I do and I am who I am because of the perpetual murmur — and an occasional huzzah — from the land.

His ellipsis is part of the slogan, and from the emptiness of the unwritten words I hear the rest of the implied sentence as if from the Christmas carol "Silver Bells": *Are you listening?* And from that question comes a second, one of import: *And so?*

Americans believe in the spiritually redeeming efficacy of travel almost as if it were prayer. We are prone to try to modify our lives simply by just *going*, whether on a walk around the block or on a coast-to-coast trek. And why not? We're all descendants of travelers who reached these shores from the other hemisphere. Were stars not so splendidly cosmic a symbol, the blue union of our flag could well be composed of little footprints.

*   *   *

Not long ago, a Minnesotan took up a specific and peculiar itinerary. Motivated by philosophical questions not uncommon for his twenty-one years, this polite college student of graphic design set out to awaken Americans to issues he felt we are ignoring at our peril: pillaging our environments, suppressing human potential, failing to legalize marijuana. In one of his wandering manifestos he blithely wrote, "I'm dismissing a few individuals from reality, to change all of you for the better." Open to various ways of learning, he explored formal logical-discourse but the import of propositions of conjunction, negation, and disjunction apparently evaded him. He took up meditation, channeling, astral projection, and even gave a shot at communion with ghosts. But, in the end, his response to our heedlessness was to embrace a ready-made, moronic symbol to alert what he perceived as a gaggle of fools. Using an automobile like a pen, he planned to draw that image hugely across the very face of the country, and he employed that most American habit: He went *on the road*.

To strike out into the continent is not only a national obsession but a long and honored method of inquiry for us. We will use a highway as monks do holy texts: moving along yellow stripes on asphalt as if they are lines of scripture, and growing ever curious about where the journey will lead and who we will be when we finally fetch up somewhere.

The art student with the boyish Nordic face had played in a three-man grunge band called Apathy that recorded a CD titled "Sacks of People." If that name described his emotional state before lighting out for the territory, to use Huck Finn's phrase, his act of leaving home ground suggests engagement and a turning away from indifference. Like Huck, that All-American-boy traveler, the Minnesotan started out along the Mississippi. Using rural-free-delivery roads on each side of the river in Iowa and Illinois, with his automobile wheels he began drawing his chosen, revelatory image across the landscape. He stopped at predesignated places to leave in a mailbox a message, a kind of letter. Call it a Nailgram. Then he moved on a few hundred miles west into eastern Nebraska and took up a second gyration similarly marking out his design with more postboxes he'd selected. Charted onto a map, his route of letter drops created across the upper Midwest two large circles like hollow eyes.

Then he headed on to Colorado to begin driving a curving southeasterly route, and in it his master picture started to emerge across America: The student of design, now a deliverer of hazardous tidings, was coloring in his sketch with intellectually jumbled handbills accompanied by pipe bombs packed with hardware-store shrapnel. Putting a pen to the route of his map-sketch and connecting the mailboxes at last revealed a portrait: a gigantic, hollow-eyed smiley face drawn in victims' blood.

After three thousand miles, as he was initiating the smiley grin, something happened to him in the Texas Panhandle, a landscape that can work upon a traveler in ways deep, even if at first unperceived. It may intimidate, dominate, it may stupefy or awaken; its immensity of sky and sprawl of level ground all but force a wanderer to redefine the meaning of solitude and reevaluate the importance of connections and conjunctions, some of the very things the young Minnesotan tried to hawk but had found words insufficient. If only he could have come across this sentence of Pedro de Castañeda, contemporaneous chronicler of the 1541 Coronado expedition through western Texas: "I very much wish I possessed some knowledge of cosmography or geography so that I might render intelligible what I want to say." The student's urge to draw across a community of the damned a giant design to mock American foolhardiness changed, because he suddenly altered direction and abandoned his bomb art by turning west once again to follow a nascent longing to see the

Pacific Ocean, unaware he had been driving the whole time on the bottom of an ancient sea.

Why he divagated just there, I don't know because I've not talked with him, but I have traveled a staggering number of miles over the southern Great Plains. I do know he turned away from his gigantic smiley in an area of Texas so ostensibly and famously faceless that early Spanish wayfarers allegedly set up sticks to find their way back and forth over it, and from them comes its name today: El Llano Estacado, the Staked Plain, the largest level land in America.

I believe few visitors go into its long miles across a nearly boundless vacancy without sooner or later feeling the cosmos pressing down as if to call attention from the typical mundanities clogging a human life and thereby enable them to enter things greater and more lasting. A frequent response to the "Nothing's out there," to use the Llano's other name, often begins with a loathing of its monotony and an encroaching sense of disorientation and disjunction in a place once notorious for maddening mirages—not just of water holes but of entire towns. Yet for travelers who stay the course but yield to the landscape by accepting its restriction of trees and its apparent interminableness, if they get out from behind the steering wheel and walk into the Llano to hear it speak in its own tongue of wind and thunder and to see it look back at them through the slotted eye of a serpent, a clarity of mind can begin. That arid land has power to flush a brain clean of the fluff and fuzz from the feather bed of contemporary living. The grandly inescapable and wondrously level and forever distant horizon becomes a colorless and flattened rainbow promising not a pot of gold but something more immediately important—arrival: arrival somewhere, anywhere. The Staked Plain, especially now that the stakes are long gone (if they were indeed ever there), can be a wilderness composed of a nothingness that almost assures one of losing the way until the straggler searches within long enough to discover some internal reference point for establishing a line of emotional and intellectual stakes which create direction and prevent doubling back into absence. The goal is to turn terra incognita into a knowable land where a soul can find its bearings. Eventually, the roamer, if persistent, ends up *somewhere,* the destination no longer as important as simple disembarkation: Did the unsettling openness speak? And to what end?

Even the dullest of travelers out there may find, if nothing else, increased sociability. Fifty-thousand square-miles of the illimitable can make for loneliness, and at the end of a day on the Llano, a mere bowl of beans on a dusty, café table set with conversation can be a gift of considerable price. Once the wayfarer can sing—and comprehend—"O bury me not on the lone prair-ee," civilization comes to mean something invigoratingly different, because we begin truly to grasp it by having looked into its absence.

If only the young student of design had reached the Llano before he delivered the first of his eighteen explosive missives to some stranger who, hopeful only for a letter from the daughter in Montana or that check from the Florida sweepstakes, instead got a face full of tenpenny nails. I wish it because I believe in the power of such a grand topographic vastness to set us straight about the significance of the ordinary and seemingly monotonous land and one of its messages: Life, all life, can be at the same time less meaningful yet more worthy than we perceive.

Had the RFD nail-carrier traveled that great tableland before dropping off his fulminating messages, he might have found the beginnings of ways to connect himself to something larger than his own wishes and dogmas. Perhaps he could have clarified confusions as the Llano belittled them into their proper proportion in the cosmic scheme he tried to address with a two-thousand-mile-wide smiley face. I think he might even have encountered what Fabiola Cabeza de Baca, an early settler there, wrote about the Staked Plain:

It's a lonely land because of its immensity, but it lacks nothing for those who enjoy Nature in her full grandeur. The colors of the skies, of the hills, the rocks, the birds and the flowers, are soothing to the most troubled heart. It is loneliness without despair. The whole world seems to be there, full of promise and gladness.

I have no certainty, of course, that the young Minnesotan would have discovered these things, but I believe he might have because they have happened to me. In my half-century quest to memorize the face of America, I've come to value the communities of fellow travelers, even those who get no farther than over to the next hollow or across to the other side of the river.

A journey into the land is an opening to escape limitations of inadequate learning and go beyond bonds of prejudice and get past restrictions of ignorance. Such a trip is an invitation to listen to new voices—within and without—that will speak and inform. It's an opportunity to put a face on a country, a face composed of smiles, grins, scowls, of concerns, hopes, and dreams, all of them more useful on a human visage than on a yellow lapel-button or a road map.

ASSONANCE FROM THE UPPER MISSOURI

In the first decade of the twenty-first century, as American foreign policy in the Middle East became ever more destructive and costly to several nations, I thought I saw a kind of historical assonance in some diplomacy and negotiation practiced two-hundred years earlier by a wise President and a little expeditionary troop he sent into the upper Missouri River country, territory anything but hospitable.

(The encounter with the Tetons in this story appears more fully in River-Horse.)

The Pencil Makers

In June of 1995 I was traveling by rivers, lakes, and the Erie Canal from New York City to the Pacific Ocean west of Astoria, Oregon, on a voyage I would later describe in *River-Horse*. In ascending the Missouri River from its mouth above St. Louis to the headwaters close to the Continental Divide in Montana, my copilot and I were laboring our way twenty-five hundred miles up the Missouri against the springtime current. That portion happened to be the same route the expedition of Lewis and Clark—the Corps of Discovery—followed nearly two centuries earlier on their way to the great western sea. Over the lower stretches we traveled in a twenty-two-foot, flat-hulled vessel called a C-Dory that I named *Nikawa* (from two Osage words meaning "river" and "horse"). The long ascent was at times slowed to the point of tedium as the Missouri carried us back a portion of each mile we sought to gain.

One afternoon in central North Dakota we tried to dispel the onerous passage by pulling the boat up alongside a makeshift dock so we might disembark and walk about and eat a sandwich. Before we could, from a thick copse suddenly and quietly appeared five Indians: two men, a woman, and two children. Their earthen skin gleamed, and they were broadly built, with large, round heads like ollas. Different from so many Indians one meets today—even in the Far West—they clearly had not a jot of European ancestry. Physically, facially, they seemed to come from another time in spite of their denims and T-shirts.

We were on Teton land so I assumed they were about to accost us for trespassing. Holding cans of beer, the adults approached *Nikawa* slowly and asked in English where we had come from. At first they doubted such a small boat could make it from the Atlantic Ocean into the middle of the Great Plains, but curiosity overcame their suspicion. Of the few words I know in Osage, one is the name for the Missouri River — Ni-sho-dse — and I spoke it in the middle of a sentence otherwise in English in hopes context might help communication. Their name for the river was similar enough that the woman understood and laughed and nodded and gave the Teton pronunciation and waved toward the Missouri. It was as if I'd spoken a password, and with it they asked to step aboard.

The stern dipped deeply as all of them climbed over. The children bounced around the cabin, and the men peered at the depth finder, turned the wheel, tapped the compass, and the woman in entwined Teton and English asked for a ride. Our fuel was precariously low with miles of isolated country between us and the next gasoline, so I had to decline. To temper their disappointment I pulled out T-shirts imprinted with our boat emblem and name. The people were pleased and, to my surprise, promised for later what one of them wore: a shiny jacket lettered HUNKPAPA, their tribe, a division of the Teton Sioux. The Hunkpapas were such formidable fighters in resisting white encroachment, even in the middle of the nineteenth century, an Indian agent spoke of them as "now the most dreaded on the Missouri." Sitting Bull was a Hunkpapa.

I stood there, remembering Lewis and Clark: More forcefully than any other tribe, the Tetons threatened the passage of the Corps of Discovery in 1804. A council between the American captains and Teton chieftains began well enough, but soon the Indians grew dissatisfied with gifts proffered, finding them inconsequential recompense for the passage the Corps wanted, so the captains made an invitation. Clark wrote in his journal:

Envited those Cheifs on board to Show them our boat and
such Curiossities as was Strange to them. we gave them 1/4
a glass of whiskey which they appeared to be verry fond of.
Sucked the bottle after it was out & Soon began to be trou-
blesom. one [of] the 2d Cheif[s] assumeing Drunkness as a
Cloake for his rascally intentions.

Clark began the delicate, difficult, and dangerous task of getting the Tetons back onto the banks. Once again onshore, the
second chief deliberately staggered into Clark, made aggressive
gestures, and spoke deprecatingly of the presents and said the
expedition should not continue upriver. The captain drew his
sword, Lewis ordered the swivel guns on the keelboat readied,
the soldiers picked up their muskets, and the Indians drew
arrows from their quivers. Clark, through an inadequate interpreter, told the chiefs the expedition would indeed continue
onward and to understand the white explorers "were not squaws
but warriors," to which Chief Black Buffalo answered they too
were warriors and could easily pursue the expedition and pick
off the men "by degrees." Standing, staring, trying to face each
other down, the two sides calmed, and eventually Lewis resolved
the issue by inviting Black Buffalo and two others to reboard the
keelboat and travel on it five miles upriver to a council feast
the next morning. And so came a politic conclusion to a volatile
issue, one driven by economic concerns but at the moment more
a question of pride than right of passage through Indian land.

As my copilot and I talked with the Hunkpapas aboard the
Nikawa, I looked into the Teton faces and saw in our encounter
overtones of an episode from two centuries earlier, albeit conducted in better humor. While things over the last eight generations had changed by the time we arrived, still, the Lewis and
Clark Expedition seemed surprisingly immediate. In trying to

fulfill President Jefferson's directions of making a "friendly impression" on the native peoples and bringing them into a new political and economic relation with the United States, Lewis and Clark patently failed with the Tetons. Recalling Clark's later description of the tribe as "the vilest miscreants of the savage race [who] must ever remain the pirates of the Missouri," Jefferson—could he have been there with us—might have nodded appreciatively at seeing a couple of downstream people and the Tetons talking and trading and smiling aboard a little twentieth-century boat.

Not far from our meeting place with the Hunkpapas, Clark wrote his untypically severe and stringent "miscreants" comment when the expedition overwintered near the villages of the Knife River Mandan and Hidatsa, people who amicably and materially helped the Corps of Discovery survive the difficult Great Plains winter. The five palisaded earth-lodge settlements close to the log fort the Americans built were a grand nexus of commerce among the two resident tribes and the neighboring Crow, Cheyenne, Arapaho, Kiowa, and Assiniboin, as well as white traders; it was a place where the men of the expedition could witness and share the diversity of Indian life and culture existing across the northwest plains.

With each new stretch of their ascent up the Missouri, Lewis and Clark encountered a different tribe whose distinctive culture and disposition toward them required continually modified responses and approaches, a necessity the captains came to grasp and practice more wisely as they "proceeded on." For most of the upriver peoples, the soldier-explorers were not the first whites the Indians had met. For nearly three generations Europeans had been coming to trade with tribes, each having well formed if distinct notions about eastern strangers and their purposes, notions expressive of their ways of dealing with foreigners. For Lewis and Clark, it was up to them to discover means to overcome a negative or hostile response and to encourage warmer receptions. Given both the limited information they received before departure and their narrow understanding of the western Indian trading-network, the captains did not immediately fathom the welter of economic and political presumptions and expectations the various tribes held, a complexity furthered by differing tongues and by interpreters often struggling to translate among three languages—or sometimes four, if we count signing. And there was also the continual problem of conflicts among the tribes themselves. Just as the river presented new challenges with every riffle and snag-ridden bend, so did the native peoples.

The expedition, to be sure, was not one of simple exploration for the sake of scientific knowledge; whether we like it or not, the journey was also incursive and smacked of imperialism. After all, Jefferson and a majority of the Congress wanted to take complete and unchallenged possession of the huge territory just purchased from France and to open a commercial route to the Pacific. Among the various influences informing and shaping the goals of the Corps of Discovery were a chauvinism and presumption toward peoples whom whites wanted to remold into, as Clark wrote, "our Dutiful Children." Not surprisingly, such attitudes and expressions sometimes gave offense to proud and independent residents native to their land for at least twelve-thousand years. At Fort Mandan, British-Canadian trader Alexander Henry the Younger would later write that Hidatsa chiefs did not respond well to "the high-sounding language the American captains bestowed upon themselves and their nation, wishing to impress the Indians with an idea that [the Americans] were great warriors and a powerful people who, if exasperated, could crush all the nations of the earth." Such an attitude has been long in dying.

One assignment of the expedition was to help establish an economic and political hegemony under the "great father in Washington" by lessening the influence of Canadian traders and by making St. Louis the economic capital of the upper Missouri River country. As did Jefferson, Lewis and Clark believed political sovereignty and economic control would march west together, and it would be the Corps of Discovery to initiate those changes. On that, they were right.

And the Indians? Tribe after tribe saw the party as newcomer traders rather than explorers practicing rudimentary scientific inquiries to help "open" and hold the West for the young United States. What the indigenous people cared about, of course, wasn't ethnological inquiry—it was gifts and trade goods and the promise of increased barter. Although the Indians were curious about the strangers (especially Clark's black slave, York) and about their gadgets (Lewis's air rifle and spyglass, Clark's compass, and even writing paper), their greatest interest was an economic one: How could *they* obtain goods like those? Remove this primitive form of consumerism from the expedition and one can only imagine how differently—perhaps calamitously—the journey might have gone.

Despite the occasional fractious moments, the overall peaceful nature of those twenty-eight months of passage was much the result of immediate economic imperatives reasonably well comprehended by red and white alike with both sides seeking material benefits, a situation scarcely different from international diplomacy today. That a tribe or several in alliance did not wipe out the little American troop after one of its displays of pomp and mostly bluffing military muscle reveals the Indian desire for tangible goods. Indeed, as the affray with the Tetons shows, when gifts or the number of trade items failed Indian expectations, relationships became testy and occasionally dangerous.

The winter among the Mandan and Hidatsa villages gave the Corps a lengthy opportunity for closely observing two cultures to see how the people lived: their loves, quarrels, meals, beliefs, aspirations. During the nearly half-year the expedition laid over in North Dakota, the depth of the captains' understanding increased measurably. The whites attended ceremonies and feasts, practiced intimacies with the women, traveled with the bison hunters, watched births and deaths, learned what made a Mandan laugh, a Hidatsa distrustful. That winter the expedition at last had both enough time and an excellent location to examine and record ways of living they had grasped only haphazardly months before; they used those opportunities to reduce some eastern biases that earlier hindered the savvy necessary to fulfill their mission. A thousand miles into the voyage, the expedition journal keepers at last began to answer questions about Indian life Jefferson laid out in his 1803 instructions that effectively turned formally uneducated soldiers into part-time ethnographers whose learning would soon carry tremendous economic import. The president wrote Lewis: "The commerce which may be carried on with the people inhabiting the line you will pursue, renders a knolege of those people important." Among other questions, Jefferson specified inquiries into native traditions, foods, clothing, dwellings, diseases, remedies, and "peculiarities in laws, customs & dispositions."

The influential Philadelphia physician Benjamin Rush, an advisor to the Corps, gave Lewis an even more pointed—and peculiar—list:

> How long do they suckle the Children? At what time do they rise—their Baths? Is suicide common among them?— ever from love? How do they dispose of their dead?

That emphasis on research during the long winter on the plains helped educate Lewis and Clark and make them more effective in dealing with Indians for the remaining months of the trip. How much the new knowledge did to bring the tribes into mutually enriching commerce is problematic. Nevertheless, only two

Indians died at the hands of the Corps (Reuben Field stabbed one Blackfoot and Lewis shot another when a raiding party tried to steal guns and horses), an outcome as remarkable as the survival of the expedition itself (only Sergeant Charles Floyd died, brought down by an apparent appendicitis) and eventual safe return.

On the remainder of their westward trip, until reaching the Pacific, the explorers encountered tribes having little experience with white men so that relations and gaining safe passage through scarcely hospitable territory became trickier. Today, one can visualize failure or a disaster had that crucial education at Fort Mandan been missing. The captains' use of Indian instruction during the enforced layover at the Knife River villages benefited the expedition and later the country. (How many modern leaders truly value learning about a culture for mutual benefit rather than for domination?)

The nature of the North Dakota encampment was the key difference between the Corps of Discovery journey and those of many later expeditions having an intent too often solely commercial or imperial, with operations conducted by ill-prepared soldiers or avid entrepreneurs woefully short on comprehension of and sympathy for native ways. Understood as a military probe, the entrance of the Corps into the northwest quadrangle of the United States was the beginning of the numerous campaigns that would eventually bring down George Armstrong Custer and his cavalry in 1876 before finally terminating armed Indian resistance with the battle at Wounded Knee in South Dakota in 1890, eighty-four years after the two Blackfeet fell to Field and Lewis.

There is more logic than irony that I've written these words with my favorite first-draft implement, a cedar pencil made by the

Blackfeet of Montana. The logic is this: After Lewis, Clark, Jefferson, and Benjamin Rush, far too few people of forbearant intelligence directed the American entry into the West. Jefferson's grand hope, revealed in his instructions to Lewis, looks today around the globe sadly empty:

> Considering the interest which every nation has in extending & strengthening the authority of reason & justice among the people around them, it will be useful to acquire what knolege you can...as it may better enable those who may endeavor to civilize and instruct them, to adopt their measures to the existing notions & practices of those on whom they are to operate.

What Jefferson and the Corps began so promisingly soon collapsed almost utterly, an indictment of a nation claiming to believe in progress and to revere building upon humane wisdom and informed and compassionate behavior.

Common among the aboriginal peoples of America is the vision quest, typically a ritual trek into a natural remoteness where isolation and deprivation lead the sojourner to a new perception of existence extending into the cosmos itself and to an increased recognition of harmony to give the seeker an enlarged purpose. Lewis and Clark, on behalf of America, set off up the great Missouri on a kind of national, if unrecognized, vision quest which following generations have had the chance to continue as we search for identity, purpose, and the fair sharing of an abundant country. How far we yet have to go, I see in this stick of cedar in my hand, this product of the once powerful Blackfeet, today a nation of pencil makers.

BLACKFEET INDIAN PENCIL 2

WHY WE DO IT SO OFTEN (AND IN SO MANY WAYS)

For this story, the editor wanted something about why travel was significant to Americans: Why we do it so often and in so many ways. By chance, at the time I was on the road in the western Texas openness I find conducive to speculating on just about any question. Moving through those broad and sere reaches of landscape, I thought an answer might lie in the very rationale behind my books, a whyfor also useful to help evaluate the merits of the plethora of American road-books that had begun appearing about thirty years earlier. In short, I decided the editor's question was actually two: What's the purpose of the travel? And, does it effectively embrace the grand questions?

The Classic American Road Trip

I t's good to have a chance at last to put down the rumor that I've been advocating changing the design of Old Glory by turning the stars into spoked wheels and the stripes into yellow center lines. In spite of the appropriateness of wheels and highways to the rise of the United States—ignoring the issue of desecration—what would we do about the national anthem? "The Wheel-Spangled Banner"? Nonetheless, American history has more to do, at least at the subcelestial level, with wheels than stars. Ever since the early nineteenth century, while Americans might go forth by following a star, we have accomplished the travel more often with wheels than with feet, hooves, or hulls.

That we are the most mobile nation the planet has yet seen is the result of several things, especially all of us being descendants of immigrants from the Eastern Hemisphere. Further, we inhabit a landform where openness outreaches encumbering forests, a great interior is largely unvexed by mountains, a country where on the plains the transcontinental passage of the sun itself seems symbolically evident. To be sure, while we also travel longitudinally, preeminently, our routes, like our history, are ones of westering (or, in the case of the aboriginal peoples, significant eastering).

Even our tectonic plates, destinations unknown, are moving west. Sit in a lawn chair for an hour in Parsippany or Laramie and, when you get up, you and your chair—along with the Washington Monument, the Brooklyn Bridge, the Alleghenies, the Colorado River—all will have moved ever so infinitesimally toward the setting sun. The orbiting moon—its cartoonish face suggesting it too is a traveler—also appears to make a jaunt as if heading for the open spaces beyond the ninety-eighth meridian. I can almost believe that Americans, our bodies two-thirds water, are impelled by a lunar-asserted gravitational pull toward Pismo Beach or Tillamook Bay. To get up and go is in our blood genetically, cosmically.

I think there is no other nation in which movement—not simply change but *onward* movement, especially when linked to "progress," aka "growth"—is so practiced and revered. In our economic thinking, to speak of a "steady state" gets one branded a reactionary or a fool or unpatriotic despite the inescapable logic that infinite growth on a finite planet is, sooner or later, impossible and, worse, deadly.

The movement we as a people believe in and practice most often is linear rather than anything circular. We urge ourselves "onward and upward" and try to avoid "going in circles," never mind the whirling atoms in our bodies or in the great cosmic rotations and spiralings. Black Elk, the Lakota holy man of the last century, said, "Everything tries to be round," but perhaps he was out of step with American thought, and maybe I am too because I think in circles and cycles and circuits, rotations and revolvings and roundness. You can see that inclination right here as I circle my topic, the classic American road trip.

So, to bring things back around: We're a mobile nation because of where we are from, where we are, what we are, and what we hope to become. On the very backs of our hands, just under the skin, lie veins looking ever so much like little road maps, and as we age, those charts grow more pronounced as if to jog a memory of the journey we unceasingly undertake in our decision to continue to live. On my left hand, the bluish veins have matured to depict for me the crossing of U.S. Highway 40 (the old National Road) with the almost border-to-border U.S. 71, a crux where I was born, my hand now a continuing reminder

Arizona Highway 186, Cochise County

where I come from and, let me say, a *handy* contour map and psychic compass useful when entering unknown territory of mind or spirit. It's a memo of one of our oldest metaphors (or clichés): Life is a journey.

The American landscape, so providently formed for long-distance wandering that a dedicated motorist can between a midsummer sunrise and sunset cover the ground between, say, St. Louis and Denver, almost nine-hundred miles, an expanse roughly commensurate to a crossing of France and back again. If, by comparison with a European or Asian nation, our written history is more shallow, our landscape is at least equally deep, and that's one reason American ramblers so cherish space, penetrating it as Italian or English or Transylvanian wayfarers in their native land do time.

But in one of our recent linear movements that might be called the classic American road trip (appropriate acronym, CART), are we merely hyperkinetic or are we engaging in a more conscious search we could term hyper-excursive or meta-nomadic? Beyond ancestries and geographies, why do we take to the road whether we thumb a ride or ride in a forty-foot land-yacht? Why do we, for a spell, trade the security and comfort of a familiar *place* for the liberty offered by an unfamiliar *space,* a swap of domestic fixity for freedom of the open road? Even if we go as tourists, where *there* and *then* dominate the peregrination — rather than going like travelers, who each moment try to embrace the challenge of the *here* and *now* — don't we usually set out motivated by curiosity of one degree or another? (A tourist, of course, may grow into a deeper traveler just as a journeyman sawyer becomes a master wheelwright; and further, all travelers, even the most awakened, are at times forced into mere tourism.) When we go on a visit (related to the word *view*), what may we hope to see (related to *seek*)? And what happens within us when seeing develops into seeking that encourages further seeing? Is such questing not among the highest orders of human inquiry?

For the past three decades, travel — especially when it gets written down — often has at its center a defining solipsism: the self in search of itself in strange places promising to cast a different and edifying light on the quest even if perception often seems to reach only the traveler. In an era of self-absorption and self-gratification, where one period has become known as the Me Decade, such should be expected. On a stretch of open road, drivers can roll along with their window reflections of self laid over the landscape ahead so that one sees the territory *through* oneself, a kind of windshield therapy. And why not? It's probably as effective as couch counseling and certainly cheaper and more accessible, no appointment necessary. But stare into that reflectivated landscape long enough, and a catharsis can happen. On the road where no one knows your name or your history, the miles can efface personal identity and make a traveler ready for receptions instead of reflections and, when the going gets good, communion.

Yet for drivers who never see past their own glassy simulacra and on into the landscape beyond, into the otherness of existence, any road and any place is as good as another. But for a traveler who arrives somewhere not simply bodily but also emotionally, intellectually, and spiritually, and who then seeks out the *some-where* and a chance for escape from the isolation of selfhood and its concomitant alienation from otherness, *those* blessed travelers may find themselves landed not just in a different place on the map but in an enlarged elsewhere beyond their own earlier comprehensions. They will have reached an unknown shore and, in a sense, come into America for the first time, and it's then they can receive a temporary inheritance of territory due a temporal inhabitant. If exploratory travel is not about connection, then it's not worth the carbon expended to arrive, and if democracy isn't founded upon conjunctions, it's a driftwood temple built upon loose sand.

In a secular age—recent exudations of religious fundamentalism notwithstanding—the classic American road trip yet remains a timeless metaphor of passage through life, a chance to move from me to thee and from thee to us and on beyond to all. Going forth can be a form of religion-free prayer, an entreaty for reawakening, reanimating, rekindling, rebalancing, and reharmonizing a pilgrim. In America, our prayer wheels are pneumatic tires with vulcanized, nonskid treads.

BIPEDAL KALEIDOSCOPES

Perhaps because I began as a photojournalist, I write pictorially, or maybe the term should be kaleidoscopically: I gather pieces, try to add some reflectivity, then give them a shake to see what unpredictable pattern they fall into. Some structural connections may be minimal, with much reliance placed on a reader's wit and willingness to participate in making reconnections. After all, a human life itself proceeds kaleidoscopically: We accumulate memories often deliberately and always ineluctably, and over time see them form the pieces of who we are. Who remembers his life in wholeness or in its entirety? Shaped by fragments, we are bipedal kaleidoscopes of endlessly shifting arrangements more random than we may wish to admit.

Pictures from the West Country

GROCKLES IN BEER. I was a few miles from Beer — not the beverage but the English village in Devonshire. The day before a fellow solemnly advised me, "Beer's a good place for cider. The West Country, you see, there's where good cider be. A fine pint of perry too." I was potting along the lanes in a little rental auto at about ten-miles-an-hour. With six-foot-high hedgerows and even taller coppice fences on each side of the lane, I had only the narrow, winding byroad to look at and not a single sign to verify my course, a concern since for a good many miles there was no turning around. In my mind jingled a piece of English verse about a hedged lane:

> *When once you're caught in it,*
> *It holds you as a cage does a linnet.*

I had escaped the congestion of London to follow the coast road of southwestern England through the open country of Devon and Cornwall, but that morning, a closer look at my Super-Scale Ordinance Survey Atlas revealed there *was* no road along the indented coast of hundreds of smugglers' coverts. I was entangled, sometimes literally, because I had relied on an antique pocket-guidebook I esteemed for its lore and archaic turns of phrase as if it were a fellow traveler from another time.

Ahead were miles untold of narrow lanes — crooked and circuitous, deviating and devious — each giving off onto a slew of lesser ambages leading to unnamed places, none lying anywhere near my destination. In 1939 a top tune here went like this:

> There'll always be an England
> While there's a country lane.

Turn the reasoning around, and the lyrics could be prophecy. For anybody wanting to take time to get nowhere, the passage was ideal, but that day I was spending hours in a hunt for various routes (to name one, from Tolpuddle, across the River Piddle, into greater Puddletown), when what I wanted was the serrated coast. Had I come in the second century after Caesar's conquest, I could have used the marvelously straight Roman road, now a grassy strip I unnecessarily crossed four times en route to the very place it once directly led. The single lanes carried two-way traffic that forced drivers to edge their left side-mirrors into hedges while reaching out to pull back the right ones, usually executed somewhere between good humor and muttered vexation. To wend one's way toward and along the coast requires popping *into* and out of clipped whitethorn, so that scrapes on passenger-side fenders, like odometers, reveal one's mileage along living fences. My antiquated guide put it blithely: "There's no place like England for motoring." Excluding the road to Hell.

I must say, though, the byroads at least gave the *feel* of Olde England, and that was good because the hedgerows blocked any view of the land beyond. For an American, there's another merit to traveling those often veritable vegetative tunnels: Of necessity, moving slowly and unable to see how far you've gone or how far you haven't, a small island-nation spreads out as if a continent: Twenty miles of English lanes left me with a sense of an accomplishment commensurate to, say, driving across Montana.

Perhaps because of their notion that everything in America is gigantic, the English often asked whether I found things small in their country. Well, yes—roads, shops, lawns (and once upon

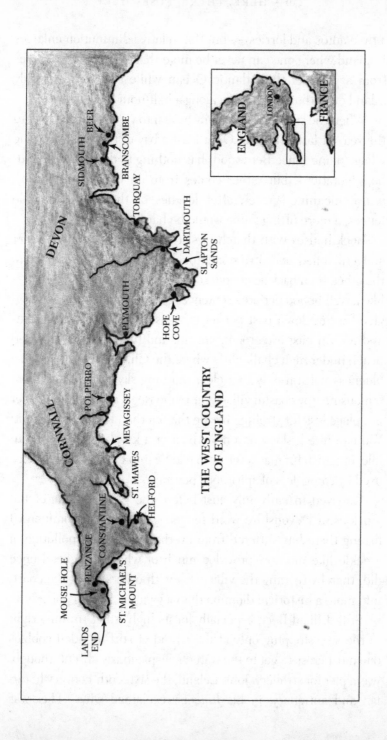

THE WEST COUNTRY
OF ENGLAND

DEVON

CORNWALL

BEER
SIDMOUTH
BRANSCOMBE
TORQUAY
DARTMOUTH
SLAPTON SANDS
PLYMOUTH
HOPE COVE
POLPERRO
MEVAGISSEY
ST. MAWES
HELFORD
CONSTANTINE
MOUSE HOLE
PENZANCE
ST. MICHAEL'S MOUNT
LANDS END

ENGLAND
LONDON
FRANCE

a time autos and lorries) — but that relative diminution enlarges England where one can never be more than about seventy miles from a piece of the Atlantic Ocean while still feeling snugly inland even though traveling along a half-hour from a coast.

When the sign for Beer finally hove into view, I turned toward the sea. At last! The sea! Or at least a bay of the Channel. The village name (once Berewood) has nothing to do with malt-and-hops potations, but rather comes from an Old English word, *bearu,* meaning "grove"; after leagues of thorn and bramble fences, a more fitting name would be hard to come up with.

Rock houses with thatch or slate roofs lined the high street and a rill rolled along in a stone trough on one side, then shifted to the other, then back again, not so much indecisive as digressive — like a well-honed periodic sentence. On foot I followed the straggle of water down past pocket gardens of hollyhocks and roses and ivy, on past a tearoom, an inn, and finally to the shingled beach under high chalk-cliffs where the Channel lay quietly in a blueness natural only to a clear morning sky. Unlike the more famous nearby coastal villages of Lyme Regis and Polperro, Beer is a place less for strolling beside the sea than for getting onto it: You can hire a sloop or a motorboat or a kayak to go out for an idle, or to fish for mackerel, or to paddle into Channel caves once used by smugglers of spirituous beverage.

I arrived in early July, just before the great coming of the grockles, a Devonshire word for tourists. Because commercial fishing there has suffered from overharvesting and pollution, a grockle like me now provided much of what a mackerel once did, thereby turning the village, as with others along the coast, into more a historical diorama than a genuine fishing port.

Still, I liked Beer, especially for its high street running right to the sea, stopping only at the strand of surf-rounded cobbles one must cross to get to the water; conspicuously absent, though, was a pier for strollers. John Leland, the sixteenth-century librarian and antiquary, in his *Itinerary* explained why: "Ther was begon a fair Pere for Socour of Shippeletes at this Berewood, but there cam such a Tempest a 3 yeres sins as never in mynd of men had before beene sene in that shore and tare the Pere in Peaces." When it comes to building a new Beer Pier, that storm has been a long discouragement.

I hoofed up to the Anchor Inn and sat by a sea-breezed window, and changed my plan from cider to a pint of bitter, a glass appropriate to the promontory outside called Beer Head. If Britons have yielded their empire, they have not lost capacity to produce a couple of things in uncommon excellence: actors and ale. Yet when I first began traveling here, in the mid-sixties, their great beers were disappearing fast because of the Americanization and conglomeration of their breweries. Then began a revolt called the Campaign for Real Ale—CAMRA—and its insistence on craft beers made with traditional methods using traditional ingredients and served in the traditional way in traditional public houses.

While industrialized, fizzed-up, watery semi-malt beverages might be passed off as beer in America (a nation that in the sixties yielded its own rich brewing heritage to corporate profits), CAMRA was not going to let that happen in England. Now, a quarter-century later, I could sit at the elbow-polished bar and drink a genuine ale containing but four ingredients—water, malted barley, hops, and yeast—hand-pumped from the cellar and brewed only a few miles distant. My pint gave a taste not of London or Birmingham but of Devon, a land of heathery moors and devilish whitehorn, both of which I imagined my tongue could detect.

BALLISTIC PRUNES. The next day, I had traveled only two miles farther down the lane, to Branscombe, a thatched-roof village scattered along the combe of the River Brans; the jumble of hills around it cut off any view of the sea, although I could hear it on the south wind. During a morning walk on one of my usual hunts for expressions of earlier lives, I went into the graveyard of the Norman church where an old inscription commemorates a farmer noted for wrestling prowess who died while shearing sheep:

> *Strong and at Labour*
> *suddenly he reels.*
> *Death came behind him*
> *and stroke up his heels.*

For lunch I went into the Mason's Arms (*arms* in its heraldic sense, not corporeal one), drawn by an inscription on the worn gantry sign: **NOW YE TOIL NOT**. It's only one traveler's opinion, but I think in rural England few meals surpass a pub lunch; that noon, mine was a fresh-from-the-Channel picked-crab sandwich and a glass of scrumpy, the latter a big-bodied if rough-edged cider the barman told me — only after I drained it: "She'll buzz through you like a ballistic prune."

As go the public houses in country England, so goes a journey there because a village pub is oftentimes the only place serving a meal, and it's predictably the most convivial spot for a wayfarer to find a conversation. But in the West Country, a traveler so inclined can also have a Devonshire or Cornish cream tea: a couple of buttery scones, a small pot of clotted cream, jam, and tea. A tearoom is an easier choice than just mainlining the cholesterol and getting it over with.

HYDRAULIC SALADS. I left behind the famously whitish cliffs along the Channel for the less lauded red bluffs around Sidmouth, the watering place neglected by virtually no nineteenth-century traveling pooh-bah, including William Makepeace Thackeray — author of *The Book of Snobs* — who in his following work, *Pendennis,* calls the place Baymouth. As a giver of wide berth to pooh-bahs, I was there only to enable informed comparison with neglected places noteworthy for ordinariness. Sidmouth lies in a wide valley of the River Sid where it enters the sea, but, unlike some Channel settlements, it doesn't attempt to protect itself by hiding in an estuary; instead, it confronts the Atlantic openly with a long esplanade for the display of poobahs ostensibly taking in the broad marine view. Likened to the Riviera, Sidmouth for years has been a spot for moneyed visitors, so much so that at the turn of the century novelist W. H. Hudson called it "parasitic" and boasted he stayed there only "a day or two." I didn't make it beyond a single evening. When in England I want England—even on the real Riviera I want England.

With morning light, I moved on due westward to get across the River Exe and avoid areas I'd traveled a few years earlier. Leaving the hedgy and trenched lanes, I found something remarkably like an actual highway, although given the British use of painted center-lines for passing, I wasn't always certain, but it did get me past the sprawl of Torquay and on to the narrow estuary of the River Dart. One of the ferries was down, creating a long queue of automobiles up the hill from the slip. By good luck, I got stopped in front of the Steam Packet Inn, and there fell into a conversation about river names with a fellow of more opinions than wit. He noted how Yanks preferred multisyllables. Take rivers: Mississippi, Chattahoochee, Atchafalaya. But the English, with greater purity, want single syllables: Dart, Sid, Brans, Taw, Nidd, Cock. I agreed by offering that had the English with their love of elision (Auchinleck comes out something like "Afleck") stayed longer in America, the Atchafalaya would today be the Chuff and the Chattahoochee the Chooch.

Then came a There'll-Always-Be-an-England conversation. The man was drinking lovage, a spirit made from an aromatic plant. "Helps regain your pecker," he said. "Of course, there's also shrub. Oh, and dandelion and burdock." He raised his lovage, pausing to ask, "Have you tried one of our country wines? The flavors are decidedly good—cowslip, parsnip, birch, gooseberry. I can't remember them all." I asked if he might be a botanist or perhaps a gardener, and he said, "No indeed, sir! An apothecary, retired." I explained I avoided beverages that might need weeding or pruning or those that could turn into a hydraulic salad.

The ferry opened again, the queue cleared, and I crossed to Dartmouth and its narrow streets twisting among aged buildings, a few having second floors leaning over the pavement like layer cakes, the top one slipping sideways and headed for the ground.

Only a year earlier in Dartmouth, I had a conversation with a man of considerable seniority, a slender disconsolate who appeared somehow broken—not in spirit but in a bodily way, like a toy soldier missing half its rifle and lower left leg. I remember his name: Chadwick Anvel. At my hello, he revived to ramble us into a conversation eventually leading to the D-Day ships that sailed from the Dartmouth harbor, a place I'd have thought too tiny to help launch the most massive sea and air invasion in history. Mister Anvel said, "We had to stretch out the fleet, you see, to disguise our intentions of invasion so Jerry couldn't be sure what was coming. Along the Channel, these old smuggling villages were good for keeping plans rather concealed, although Jerry bombed us anyway. You might know of the bombing he put on Plymouth." Pointing to the coastal villages on the map I had been studying, he said, "Scarcely a one, I daresay, that didn't get a hammering. But, to be sure, Hitler was no Caesar. The Führer was afraid to step ashore."

Mister Anvel became animated as he spoke of *the* War and the special bond it forged between America and Britain. When I first traveled in England, the Second World War frequently came up in conversation, often as a means of establishing shared ground. But of late, with people having sharp memories of that time thinning fast, pub topics became trickier: government failures, influxes of darker-skinned people, Eastern imperialisms,

American domination—all issues that can unleash unpredict-able directions leading to unpleasant encounters. It wasn't that a vanishing generation missed the war, but rather postbellum citizens often did miss being able to address a common past with an ally in a conversation calling for a pint of bitter to commemorate "the finest hour." When the fellow and I raised our glasses, I knew I'd shared one more thing I wouldn't ever see again.

DEVILS-ON-HORSEBACK. Dartmouth Castle lies near the mouth of the Dart estuary. Its earliest existing portion dates from 1388 when catapulting rocks at a seaborne enemy was the strongest response it could offer, but a century later weaponry had advanced—if that's the word—to large cannons termed *grete murderers* and to a huge chain that could be pulled across the river to block ships. Yet, as elsewhere, the mighty foe laying waste to the castle was not a Gallic or Teutonic incursion, but omnivorous Time, sometimes a creator of irony: Military engineers in 1940 built phony fourteenth-century castellations atop a World War II gun-platform to *camouflage* it.

Down at Slapton Sands, a few miles southwest, the war showed a more haunting aspect along a now-lovely beach where a fisherman had recently found a sunken U.S. tank that residents raised and hauled ashore to commemorate the almost one-thousand Americans who died when a German U-boat sneaked in close and opened fire during military exercises prior to D-Day.

Villagette, were it a word, would describe Hope, which sits near the southernmost piece of Devon, and there I found quarters in a room with a full view of the Channel. The small cove, quiet except for the sound of the sea pitching onto the rocks, had neither a promenade nor amusements other than those available to legs or brain: walking, talking, reading, playing cribbage. The harbor lay in repose, its special link to warfare long past living memory, but in a shop window hung a tea towel imprinted:

HOPE COVE

THE ONLY PLACE IN ENGLAND
WHERE AN ARMADA SAILOR CAME ASHORE.

It ought to be enlightening to observe the way later generations can trivialize and peddle the great wars of their ancestors by turning suffering into shillings and death into dollars. Surely, on the way was a tea towel or coffee mug showing a slaughterous Nazi U-boat or a Slapton Sands shattered tank.

How Hope could support two public houses one can understand only by remembering that an English country-pub is to an American bar what a living room is to a hotel lobby: a place where everybody knows your name, or soon will if you stand quietly near the taps. I ordered a supper of John Dory, a flatfish with a visage somewhere between grotesque and loathsome. The waitress gave reassurance it would taste "lovely—*if* you close your eyes." With each plate she served or picked up, she thanked me. Now, the English virtually never respond "You're welcome" to a proffered thanks, but they make up for it by saying "Thank you" all over the place. When I left the pub that evening, I nodded good night to a fellow entering, and he touched his hat and smiled. "Thank you."

I keep a list of descriptive terms for English dishes: bubble-and-squeak, chip butty, toad-in-the-hole, hubble bubble, parson's nose, spotted Dick. The next morning I added devils-on-horseback, a name as inexplicable as the ingredients: a rasher of bacon wrapped around a stewed prune (I trusted of the nonballistic variety). It failed to rise beyond its ingredients, neither better, worse, or in combination something unexpectedly different; it was good only as lore to toss into a slow conversation.

THE HAND THAT CUT THE PUDDING. I knew Plymouth from earlier visits, so I passed through to catch the ferry across

the River Tamar and enter Cornwall and towns along the way—
Freathy, Portwrinkle, Crafthole. I was headed for a place everyone advised I *simply must see,* even if the season was July.
Polperro is another reasonably genuine coastal village although
the lures now offered were not to mackerel but to the grockle,
hundreds of them—carloads, caravanloads, coachloads—all
parked well beyond the pale of local history, because Polperro
sits pinched into a combe opening to the Channel. Its streets,
while wider than alleys, were still sufficient to jam us together
like a school of mullet. The ancient domestic architecture was a
delight of stone and slate, but I became aware of behaving not so
much like a mullet as an emmet milling along in wavering lines,
bumping into other emmets blindly bent on some unseen goal.
Having learned by demonstration that in Cornish *emmet* means
"ant," I wedged my way out.

Mevagissey possessed what I was coming to accept as requisite Cornish quaintness, but it lacked the throng of Polperro. The
waters there, according to my antique guidebook, were formerly
"fishfull" enough to call the village Fishygissey. In a hardier era,
in 1601, John Carew returned home to Fishygissey after losing his
right hand at the siege of Ostend, and walked into his lodgings
and said to the hostess as he tossed his severed appendage onto
the dining table, "That's the hand that cut the pudding today."

The byroads toward the small harbor of St. Mawes opened
here and there onto cottages oozing droplets of fuchsia blossoms
and gardens shoving up pastel puffs of hydrangeas, and every so
often over the lane came a waft of honeysuckle. St. Mawes is on
the quiet side of a peninsula jutting into Falmouth Bay, a sweet
spot for a walk along the strand where I met a man who volun-
teered directions because he thought I looked lost, or so he said;
in truth he was after an audience. His stories contained more
words than its incidents could support, but I liked his ancient-
mariner turns of phrase and his unwillingness to let me proceed
without a passel of recitations. He enumerated the old vessels

here formerly fitted out—*victualized* was his word—prior to sailing into the open Atlantic; after the name of each ship he added, "And she, too, gone to grief." You mean *sunk*? "Aye, mate. Bound for Davy Jones, she were."

Henry the Eighth had St. Mawes castle built sturdily enough that some four-and-a-half centuries later its compact cloverleaf of squat, stone structures just above the fetch of the sea was nicely evident. A woman looking down on it from the lane above said to a nipper still too small for his name, "Oh, do come look, William! What a deliciously darling little castle!" With its carvings, inscriptions, and gargoyles, it is the most decorated of Henry's fortifications, one that expresses not the Renaissance but the Middle Ages of his predecessors. My guidebook: "There is something rather perverse in this deliberate archaism, especially where it hinders military efficiency."

THERE'S A QUEEN IN MY PINT. Headlands and estuaries break the line of the southern coast of Cornwall and enforce a wandering route whether on foot or behind a wheel. In its antiquarian, understated voice, the pocket guide advised that Cornish "byroads twist rather more than seems strictly necessary." At remote Constantine, a clustering of granite houses, I stopped in what I took for an ordinary groceryette to buy fixings for a seaside lunch. The back of the room was stacked full of hard spirits, some of them still boxed as if just hauled up from the beach by smugglers. There was, most notably, bottle after bottle of brandies and single-malt Scotches, including one costing nearly seven-hundred dollars; I started counting, lost track, and turned to a clerk, in fact the owner, Mister Rowe, to ask how many kinds were there. He calculated. "Today, a few more than two hundred." How could such a small shop carry an inventory outnumbering the village population? He motioned me toward a counter, pulled out a bottle of cognac, and poured us a tot, proof against the morning mist. "If you specialize in something," he said, "you can become known for it, and then people will seek you out." Build it and they will come? "This may be the second-largest selection of Scotches in England."

Leaving the coast for some miles, I ended up in Gweek, a name no more eccentric than many others in England: Nether Wallop, Clock Face, Bugthorpe, Fangfoss, Buttertubs, Nut End, Crank, and Lover come to mind. I crossed the River Hel from Mawgan where there is a funerary inscription waiting for a curious lector to decode its simple secret:

Shall   we   all   dye.
We   shall   dye   all.
All   dye   shall   we.
Dye   all   we   shall.

River of ominous name be damned, I followed it into Helford lying along a tidal stream below steeply wooded slopes allowing view of the place only in small segments so that, dreamlike, the village simultaneously appeared *and* vanished as I walked. Ivy-bestrung, thatched-roof cottages appeared to be taken not off an architect's drawing board but from an illustrated children's book, but the reality of the village was yachts and nouveau wealth.

The Shipwright's Arms was a seventeenth-century pub once noted for the dipping of shillings into beer to stick them to the skull-crackingly low ceiling. The practice recently had been out-lawed by the village council because, one fellow alleged, "From time to time a coin would come loose and drop into somebody's pint. You know, that could choke a bloke. So now, when a bob comes down, it goes into the lifeboat fund." But remaining across the yellowed ceiling were little round imprints of an inversed young Queen Elizabeth looking impassively down on the tipplers. "Twouldn't be proper, now, would it," he said, "to eat the queen."

The lane out of Helford took a southward course over the

scrub-grown Goonhilly Downs toward Lizard Point, the south-ernmost place in England, where a chaos of rocks lying offshore and obscuring fogs combine to create for mariners (said my pocket guide) "a deadly notoriety," adding, "human ingenuity could never invent a more speedy and sure means of destruction for ships than is offered by the Lizard promontory as designed by nature." But from high atop the headland on that morning, I watched a sea burnished with sun and polished by an innocuous wind. On the back of the Lizard, like warts, stood several little sheds selling snacks and gewgaws. In one higher than the others was a Mister Casley who for years had quarried dark-red, igne-ous serpentine mottled like reptile skin, which he turned on a lathe—as if the stone were wood—into a variety of lustrous juglets and small bowls that put a kindly face on the seamen's treacherous rocks.

St. Michael's Mount, a couple of hours westward, is one of the remarkable topographical features in England: a high and truncated, granitic cone surrounded by sea and surmounted by a castle–church–country seat all built into each other. If you're familiar with the more famous—and somewhat grander—for-tified cathedral high atop Le Mont Saint-Michel in Normandy, you have an idea of this cross-Channel English counterpart. In fact, monks from Saint-Michel founded the Benedictine priory here in the twelfth century, although subsequent events made the history on the north shore one of soldiers instead of the holy fathers who departed long ago.

Just as at Saint-Michel, travelers can wait for low tide to walk a stone causeway across the shallow flats to the whilom harbor villagette at the base of the islet, and from there make a steep climb to the castellated buildings on top. The high and inspiring if precipitous views from the windows cause some visitors to keep a half-step back from the sills and bend cautiously at the waist for a peek down at the boisterous waves having a good whack at the dark boulders.

VINEGAR AGAINST THE PLAGUE. Penzance no longer—if it ever actually did—conjures up the romance of Gilbert and Sullivan's pirates, but a couple of miles on along the coast is Mousehole (pronounced *Mow*-zull), the name coming from a lost Cornish word apparently having nothing to do with mice or holes. Pinched and bent streets, narrow rock-stairs, everything seemed to hang above the compressed haven, and in front of the stone houses, old boats served as planters. Gulls sat atop chimney pots to dispatch cries beginning at one end of the village and moving across the slates and tiles like breaking surf.

Outside one doorway was a thick stone, a couple of feet square, its center scooped into a shallow declivity. I asked the shopkeeper what it was. "We dug it up when we were refurbishing," he said. "We've been told it's a plague stone that used to sit at the edge of the village. During the Black Death, this basin held vinegar so outsiders could drop in their coins to disinfect them. What they needed, of course, wasn't vinegar but rat traps."

A DRAUGHT OF ADAM'S ALE. Grimness from another era lay at the end of the southwest coast, at the western promontory where England stops—or begins: the Land's End, a place arousing English sentiment and curiosity beyond a foreigner's comprehension, and an honored lure for grockles. I don't believe more than one in a hundred Americans could name with precision the most western—or eastern, southern, or northern—point in the contiguous States, yet any alert English child knows and reveres this narrow cape, maybe because on maps it's so clearly pointing into the Atlantic like the toe of an elfin boot. (Adults might discern a phallus engaging the seminal sea.)

The Land's End, to my eye, was a modest piece of the remarkable Cornish coast, a stony protruding shoulder (to change the anatomical allusions) that gives way to several seabound rocks of shapes odd enough to have earned names: the Armed Knight,

Irish Lady, Kettle Bottom, Shark's Fin, and one only the English would come up with: Dr. Syntax's Head (after the three early nineteenth-century poetic parodies of travel books—the first being *Dr. Syntax in Search of the Picturesque,* created by William Combe and Thomas Rowlandson). Those peculiar stony outliers are the western end—or beginning—of English ground. Next stop, North America.

Wilkie Collins, author of the classic mysteries *The Moonstone* and *The Woman in White,* speaks of the importance of the Land's End to the English in his 1851 book of travels, *Rambles Beyond Railways.* If you will tolerate its length, let me set it down:

> Something like what Jerusalem was to the pilgrim in the Holy Land, The Land's End is—comparing great things with small—to the tourist in Cornwall. It is the Ultima Thule where his progress stops—the shrine towards which his face has been set, from the first day when he started on his travels—the main vent, through which all pent-up enthusiasm accumulated along the line of route is to burst its way out, in one long flow of admiration and delight.
>
> The Land's End! There is something in the very words that stirs us all. It was the name that struck us most, and was best remembered by us as children, when we learnt our geography. It fills the minds of imaginative people with visions of barrenness and solitude, with dreams of some lonely promontory far away by itself out in the sea—the sort of place where the last man in England would be most likely to be found waiting for death, at the end of the world! It suggests even to the most prosaically constituted people, ideas of tremendous storms, of flakes of foam flying over the land before the wind, of billows in convulsion, of rocks shaken to the centre, of caves where smugglers waited in ambush, of wrecks and hurricanes, desolation, danger, and death. It awakens curiosity in the most careless—once hear of it and

you long to see it—tell your friends that you have travelled in Cornwall, and ten thousand chances to one, the first question they ask is: "Have you been to The Land's End?"

My earlier memory was of an open and generally level hedged-in pasture under the salt wind, a place still recognizable from his description. But now before me was an amusement park, a plastic England of yore: the Mariner's Chest Arcade, Shipwreck Play Area, Legendary Labyrinth, the Smellorium ("Can you tell the difference between whisky, rum, and even gunpowder?"). Were Collins to describe things today, he might use words like *hokum, humbuggery, fakery, fabricated, dissimulated, concocted, a counterfeit jiggery-pokery,* and those are the very qualities grockles come for. After ten millennia of Celtic-Anglo possession, John Bull had allowed foreigners to own the hokums and reshape the Land's End, a name become an apocalyptic, ecological double-entendre.

The sea wind followed me up the road a half-mile to the long-standing First & Last Inn, its walls dating from at least the four-teenth century when it was lodgings for men building the propinquous St. Sennen, "the first and last church in England." In front of the inn, now a pub, lay a field of barley. Never in my searches for the perfect alehouse had I come upon the principal ingredient growing so close to the end of a tap.

The amusement park, said the publican, had so increased his business that he extended the walls of the structure to enclose a long-unused well which he judged—from its distinctive square sides—to be the work of Phoenicians trading in Cornwall long before the arrival of the Roman legions in 55 B.C. Knowing that ancient Cornish wells were often shrines, he didn't fill it in nor conceal it with flagstones to match the surrounding floor; instead, one evening he drew up a bucket of living water and set it atop the bar to dip up brimming pints of Adam's ale, draughts of continuity, quaffs from the ages. He installed a small light within the shaft and placed over it a plate of clear glass so that a grockle fleeing the Smellorium could now peer down into the quiet darkness to have opportunity to recognize that stationary objects—if genuine—can be vehicles as suitable for the conveyance of a traveler's imagination as any atop wheels.

I went down to the coastal path to get closer to the end of England to try to see it in its ancient aspect and hear its mayhem of surges shattering onto the black rocks that now seemed in sufferance before their inevitable resolution into the sea, nature blessedly blind to legendary last labyrinths and smelloriums. I heard only the invincible thump and plunge of the cold Atlantic that will always be the end of things here until *the* end.

Chronology of Publication

In Acknowledgment

At Little, Brown and Company: Tracy Roe, Kay Banning, Peggy Freudenthal, Liese Mayer, Brandon Coward, Melissa Mathlin, Geoffrey Shandler, Michael Pietsch.

Along the way: Edgar Ailor III, Kelly Archer, Steven Archer, M. K. Blakely, Clive Chisholm, C.L.D.W. Hutt, L. J. Keown, O. J. Litzinger, Michael Mansur, David Pulliam, Cathy Salter, Kit Salter, David Trogdon, Lois Wallace, Richard Wallace, and magazine editors *cum multis aliis*.

Index of Places

Note: *Italic* page numbers refer to illustrations.

About the Author

WILLIAM LEAST HEAT-MOON, the pen name of William Trogdon, is of English, Irish, and Osage ancestry. He lives in Missouri, on an old tobacco farm he's returning to forest.

His first book, *Blue Highways,* is a narrative of a 13,000-mile trip around America on back roads. His second work, *PrairyErth,* is a tour on foot into a small corner of the great tallgrass prairie in eastern Kansas. *River-Horse* is an account of his four-month, sea-to-sea voyage across the United States on its rivers, lakes, and canals. His three books of travel have never been out of print. Heat-Moon is also the author of *Columbus in the Americas,* a compendium of the explorer's adventures in the New World.